STORMING THE CASTLE

ALSO BY JILL DOWNIE

A Passionate Pen: The Life and Times of Faith Fenton

Storming the Castle

THE WORLD OF DORA AND THE DUCHESS

Jill Downie

KEY PORTER BOOKS

For Stan 'n Beth Vince

Canadian Cataloguing in Publication Data

Downie, Jill
Storming the castle: the world of Dora and the Duchess

Includes index.

ISBN 1-55013-999-1

1. Devonshire, Evelyn Cavendish, Duchess of. 2. Lee, Dorothea Mary. 3. Great Britain –
Social life and customs – 20th century. 4. Nobility – Great Britain – Biography. 5.
Domestics – Great Britain – Biography. I. Title.

DA574.B48D68 1998   941.083'092'2   C98-931395-6

The Canada Council | Le Conseil des Arts
for the arts | du Canada
since 1957 | depuis 1957

The publisher gratefully acknowledges the support of the Canada Council
for the Arts and the Ontario Arts Council for its publishing program.

Key Porter Books Limited
70 The Esplanade
Toronto, Ontario
Canada M5E 1R2

www.keyporter.com

Design: Peter Maher
Electronic formatting: Heidy Lawrance Associates

Printed and bound in Canada

98 99 00 01 6 5 4 3 2 1

Contents

Acknowledgements

No writer has ever been more fortunate in her researcher than I have. My husband, Ian, spent countless hours on this project, making dozens upon dozens of enquiries, ploughing through newspapers and directories, filling in the spaces, putting flesh on the bones so that the stories of Evie and Dora could be told. His photographic skills were indispensable in reproducing postcards and menus, and in improving the quality of old and faded snapshots. Together we worked at Chatsworth, reading the hundreds of pages of the Ninth Duke's diaries, sharing the discoveries in the Ninth Duchess's correspondence and notebooks. This wonderful journey was all the more satisfying because it was taken together.

In Canada, my sincere thanks go to the staffs of the Ontario Archives, the Robarts Research Library of the University of Toronto, the Mills Memorial Library of McMaster University, Hamilton, the Metro Toronto Reference Library and especially Gordon Glasheen, who always went that extra mile, and Marianne McLean, Robert Fisher and Robert Mackintosh of the National Archives in Ottawa. Special thanks go to Diane Jamieson and the staff of Burlington Central Library who gave invaluable help, Claire Peart and Glen Suyama at the Halton District Board of Education, and Stéphane Thibodeau at the City of Ottawa Archives. I am grateful to Jo-Anne Colby, system co-ordinator with the Canadian Pacific Archives, who responded promptly to my enquiries with much useful information on the viceregal train. Sincere thanks to Patricia McRae, archivist at Rideau Hall, and to Nancy Anctil, head of visitor services at Rideau Hall, who gave Ian and myself a private guided tour of the governor-general's residence, and a great deal of help with regards to the structure and furnishings of that ever-changing building.

In Germany, my grateful thanks go to Edith Geis, of the Stadtmuseum/Stadtarchiv, Bad Schwalbach, who ploughed through numerous variations and combinations of the name "Cavendish," until she found Evie and Victor. Thank you also to Hilda Michel for her help in translating and composing the German correspondence.

In Great Britain, my grateful thanks go to Sue Garland, archivist with the Guinness Brewing Company, who responded to my request for a photograph of Walter Guinness by providing one swiftly—and free of charge. I am also indebted to Sir Francis Newman and his mother, Mrs. Andrew Crawshaw, who helped with the identification of photographs in Dora's collection, and gave further insights into the Newman family. Ian and I spent a fascinating morning with Susan Scott, archivist for the Savoy Group who, at short notice, gave up precious hours of her time to show us round that beautiful, newly refurbished hotel, sorted slides for us, and provided as well a photocopy of *The Observer* article on the Savoy scandal.

Rather late on in this project I had the good fortune to contact Dr. Kate Fielden, the curator at Bowood House, the Bowood Estates, Wiltshire. Knowing that I had a looming deadline, she did a superb job of putting together a package of illuminating extracts from Evie's letters—none of which were in order or catalogued, all of which had to be handwritten. It was Dr. Fielden who confirmed for me what I had been told—that Victor had gone to India, or had met his future wife in India—but which, up to then, I could not prove. I owe an extraordinary debt of gratitude to her, and to the Earl of Shelburne, Evie's great-nephew. Lord Shelburne responded to my initial enquiry, and then generously gave permission for the letters to be used in the book, allowing Evie's voice to be heard and thus immeasurably enriching the story.

Susan Scott at the Savoy archives defined the professional

staff at Chatsworth by saying that "they take the gold star." Stellar indeed they are. Their expertise, generosity and commitment to "The House" extends to those who are fortunate enough to work in the archives in that extraordinary place. Peter Day, the keeper of collections, corresponded with me initially, informing me of what material would be available, arranging the times we could do the research and setting up interviews. Over the course of the two weeks we were there, Charles Noble, the assistant keeper of collections, Tom Askey, archivist, and Ian Fraser-Martin, silver steward, gave up hours of their time to us, helping in every possible way with advice, information, anecdotes. It is not just their expertise we shall remember; it is the pleasure of their company. An additional thank you to Ian Fraser-Martin for the beautiful work on the photographs chosen for the book, and to Charles Noble for keeping in touch with additional information after we had left Chatsworth.

We did not have to storm this particular castle; we were literally welcomed in the front door by Andrew, the Eleventh Duke of Devonshire. For about an hour he talked with us, not only about his grandmother, but about Canada, international politics, war and family, with warmth, wit and generosity of spirit. It would have been impossible to do justice to the Ninth Duchess without the generous access we were given to her private correspondence. I am very grateful to Deborah, Duchess of Devonshire, who allowed me to see the Ninth Duchess's notebooks on Chatsworth.

I owe another debt of gratitude to Peter Day for telling me in one of his letters about Stanley G. Vince and his remarkable mother, Dora Lee. For Ian and myself, meeting Stan and Beth Vince has been an unexpected bonus and delight. Thank you also to Dora's granddaughter, Brenda Vince, for lending the Prince of Wales' brooch—which she was left by her grandmother—to be admired, and to be photographed for the book. The hospitality of Stan and Beth, the generosity with which

Stan responded to this total stranger asking to be admitted to his mother's life, memories and belongings has been extraordinary, and I only hope that I have done justice to this wonderful woman.

Finally, thank you to my agent and dear friend, Frances Hanna, who first set my feet on this biographical path; to Bill Hanna, for not only introducing me to Martin Gilbert's *First World War*, but giving me the book; and to my editor at Key Porter Books, Barbara Berson, who turned the final stages of this project into a wonderful collaborative experience.

The rich man in his castle, the poor man at his gate,
God made them, high and lowly, and order'd their estate.
FROM THE HYMN, *ALL THINGS BRIGHT AND BEAUTIFUL.*
MRS. C.F. ALEXANDER (1818–1895)

A Hatbox of Memories

It's the same the whole world over,
It's the poor wot gets the blame,
It's the rich wot gets the pleasure,
Ain't it all a blooming shame.

ANON. FROM A 1914–1918 WAR SONG, WITH
VICTORIAN MUSIC HALL ROOTS

Full-blown cabbage roses line both the hatbox and the steamer trunk, the green of their fabric leaves and the crimson of their woven petals faded with time. The hatbox is hefty—more of a hat trunk. It is a foot and a half in height and width, as solidly constructed as the matching trunk, which bears the labels "CPR," "Cunard," and "Not wanted on voyage." Open the lids of both and the memories fly out, memories of voyages taken, journeys made, the story of a life.

Or, more accurately, clues to a life. But this project did not start with the hatbox and the steamer trunk, which are the property of a woman who belonged to the British servant class. It began with princesses, duchesses, countesses and marchionesses—more precisely, the women who came to Canada as wives of the governors-general. Without exception they were, of course, members of the British ruling class.

As I investigated the possibility of writing about the Rideau wives, I began looking at the handful who left letters, papers, diaries. Many of these women lived so deep in the shadows of their illustrious husbands that no one has seen fit to keep any of the papers that recorded their own thoughts and feelings on the events of their lives. In one case, the daughter destroyed the mother's diaries and some of the letters that—from clues gleaned from some that have survived—might have thrown an interesting light on the role of viceregal spouse. It would have been much easier to write about the governors-general. But where are the wives?

In the course of trying to answer that question, I wrote to the present Duke of Devonshire at Chatsworth and received a reply from the keeper of collections, Peter Day. He confirmed that there were indeed papers and letters of Evelyn, the Ninth Duchess, whose father and husband had both held the post of governor-general. His letter concluded: "Earlier this year a Mr. Stanley G. Vince wrote to me about his mother Mrs. Dorothea Mary Lee, who served the 9th Duke and Duchess as head cook while they were in Canada."

That was how I discovered Dora—Dora who had been a star in her own world, who had broken down barriers and entered what had always been considered a man's realm: the kingdom of *haute cuisine*.

Dora was more than a cook; she was an artist. She could whip up sauces fit for kings and princes, spin sugar into culinary edifices that turned dinners into dreams. Millionaires, a beer baron, an American dollar-princess, a countess and a dyed-in-the-wool duchess used her skills to impress the rich, the influential, the easily bored and the difficult to please. Yet, apart from telling her children that she had trained with Escoffier and worked for the Guinness family and the Duchess of Devonshire in Canada, she kept most of her story to herself—and, fortunately, in her Edwardian hatbox and steamer trunk.

She may not have told her three boys much about her life before she married their father, but they remember her cooking. They always had a meat and fish course—it was something they took for granted; she would quiz the butcher in Barrie, Ontario, about how long he hung his meat, and demand certain cuts that baffled the poor man; she poured a touch of port into the melon for dessert, even for the children; she talked nostalgically of "sparkling Moselle"; she only wanted salmon from the Restigouche and the Gaspé, like the salmon the Duke of Devonshire caught on his fishing holidays. She made puff pastry from scratch, rolling and folding and resting it, to cover pies savoury and sweet with its melting perfection. But once she was married, she never cooked professionally again, and even one of her closest women friends did not know till after her death that Dora had trained with Escoffier and worked for dukes and millionaires.

Sadly, even in Canada, for most people being a chef meant being a cook, and that meant being "in service"—particularly if you were a woman.

Tracing Dora's story began by looking at the contents of box and trunk at the home of her eldest son, Stanley Vince, in London, Ontario: there were her chef's hats, white and starched—her *bonnets*—the badge of her profession, worn so rarely by a woman, and her aprons, some still marked where she had wiped her hands on them. Alongside them was a long black skirt and some lustrous black ostrich feathers, a little leather-bound almanac and, tucked away in a pocket, a miniature hand-stitched notebook—so tiny it is a miracle it has survived the years. There were also photographs, testimonials and some letters. But most of the room was taken up by the postcards—hundreds of them, albums-full, years of laughter and sorrow, a record of endurance and achievement by Dora, and dozens of young girls like her, struggling their way through that punishing downstairs world.

There is something about that collection, doggedly kept together as Dora made her way up the ladder and around the various houses that would be her home for a year or two before she moved on, that suggests the owner of that life wanted those who came afterwards to know her achievement, however silent she may have been during her lifetime. The silence is deafening; it is a story that cries out to be told.

Silence can also be misleading. When I set out to write this book, the picture I had in my mind of Evelyn Devonshire was of a remote and haughty woman with few, if any, tender feelings, a cliché of an aristocrat. The picture is not entirely inaccurate but, like most one-sided pictures, what it conceals is more interesting than what appears on the surface. Her husband's diaries and, above all, Evie's letters, reveal a more complex and emotional woman than the distant duchess who stares back at us, shyly, in the days of her youth, and coldly, in tiara and pearls, in the official photographs taken year after year.

Evie would almost certainly not thank me for revealing her humanity. That façade had been carefully constructed to preserve both her and the institutions she served throughout her life as duchess and mistress of the queen's robes. Destiny had made her a duchess, and she took on the mantle with reluctance at first, but with increasing dedication. She may not have wanted some of the duties that came with the territory, but there was one magnificent edifice that symbolized *par excellence* the power and privilege of her position, and she devoted herself to it with all the passion of her hidden emotional nature: Chatsworth.

THE DUCHESS OF DEVONSHIRE'S TEA. *Extract from a letter to Jackson's (of Picadilly) from the Duchess of Devonshire: "I consent to the registration of the words 'Duchess of Devonshire's Tea' as a trade mark for tea."* Thus reads the legend on a tea caddy obtained during a visit to Chatsworth in Derbyshire, the home of the Devonshire family since 1694. It was purchased at the gift shop, which is the final stop on the Chatsworth tour. There were plenty of items to choose from: jams, biscuits, pot-pourri, sweaters, china, books on the estate, some written and signed by the Eleventh Duchess herself.

The Derbyshire estate, first created in 1549 by the redoubtable Bess of Hardwick and her second husband, Sir William Cavendish, has changed constantly through the centuries. It has been a prison for an unhappy queen, Mary Queen of Scots; it has survived civil war by being occupied by both sides (the family motto is *Safety with Caution*); it was gloriously rebuilt in the seventeenth century by the First Duke, who gained his title by helping William of Orange ascend the throne of England; its park was remodelled in the eighteenth century by Capability Brown.

By the turn of the century, well over 90 per cent of the land in Britain was held by the aristocracy. In a population of around thirty-two million, about fifteen hundred families not only sat on top of the heap, but owned most of it. Members of those fifteen hundred families administered an empire with a population of about four hundred million that covered one quarter of the globe.

Among that ruling class none had a more distinguished history, and few had a greater fortune, than the Devonshire family. True, the fortune fluctuated depending on land values and the income from investment in the new wealth of the Industrial Revolution but, all in all, the owners of Chatsworth, Bolton Abbey, Hardwick Hall, Chiswick House, Devonshire House and Lismore Castle in Ireland, were at the very narrow top of a very exclusive layer of the pyramid of British society.

Maintaining control of an empire or, for that matter, a stately home like Chatsworth, was no easy task. The fifteen hundred families who promenaded in parks and ballrooms, relaxed in music rooms and orangeries, roamed over veldts, ruled over jungles, and plundered diamond and gold mines, needed the help of a vast army of supporters with a complex hierarchical system of its own: the servant class.

Dora and Evie, the two women who are the subject of this book, were both born in the second half of the nineteenth century, but so far apart in the British class structure that "parallel lives" seems peculiarly inappropriate to describe the space they occupied in time. Yet the events that shaped the world they lived in give their lives an inescapable parallelism, for both women were profoundly affected by two major phenomena of that turn-of-the-century world: the rise of the women's movement—suffragism—and the First World War.

In 1894, two years after Evie was married and Dora was born, women took their place on district and parish councils in Great Britain, but it would take another ten years for the public to take much notice of women's struggle to serve their community in the broader world beyond the local level, and to be given the right to vote. British historian R.H. Gretton, writing on the brink of the First World War, describes the "extraordinary baffling situation" brought about by women suddenly behaving as centuries of conditioning had taught them *not* to behave: marching in the streets, padlocking themselves to railings, interrupting politicians at by-elections to such an extent that "no cabinet minister could open his mouth anywhere without interruptions."

The actions of what had at first seemed a lunatic few now began to affect the way thousands of women viewed their place in society. For some, it was a threat, for the status quo suited them very well; for others, it was a challenge and a glimpse of new possibilities. Not surprisingly, the scullery maid had the most to gain from this struggle, the duchess, the least. Yet even for Evelyn, the women's movement changed the way she viewed her world, her class, and her expectations for her daughters.

Still, it is likely that none of this would really have affected the duchess in any meaningful way if the upheaval among her sex had not coincided with a far more cataclysmic upheaval: the Great War. The war fought by the women's movement may have had more impact on the scullery maid's life, but the 1914–1918 war destroyed for ever the golden certitudes of the rich man in his castle and, by extension, those of his duchess.

The face of Europe changed as kingdoms fell, and in Britain the aristocracy was decimated by the death of so many sons and heirs. In her book *Unquiet Souls*, Angela Lambert writes, "Not since the Wars of the Roses had the English aristocracy suffered such losses as those which they endured during the Great War." That "lost generation" of young men changed the lives of those who survived, and the lives of the women they left behind them.

The duchess and the scullery maid were also linked by a cultural upheaval in society's familiar pattern: an epicurean revolution. From behind the closed doors of their homes in the purdah of Victorian England, the women of the Edwardian Age walked out in public and opened their mouths—to decorate, to table talk, and to satisfy their appetites. Most of those women were from the upper echelons of society, and their emergence in public had more to do with their status as trophies than their political or intellectual relevance in that arena, but they were now sharing the same space as their male consorts: the dining-rooms of the great new luxury hotels. They became seen, if not heard. And when Lillie Langtry and Alice Keppel dined in public with the heir to the throne, other women began to emerge from the parlour.

All this meant that it was no longer acceptable to provide indifferent food to those who now dined at the Savoy or the Carlton. The cuisine provided by the cooks of the great houses became as important as the quality of the grouse provided by the gamekeepers on the moors, and the door belowstairs opened—slowly, and with much creaking and protesting—to the woman chef.

Sitting backstage, as it were, at Chatsworth, beyond the great doors that lead into the Painted Hall, looking at the Ninth Duchess's correspondence, the two worlds of Dora and Evie were ever present. When the great door into the Painted Hall opens and closes, and you find yourself on one side or the other, there is an extraordinary feeling of being in the transformation scene of an elaborate pantomime: rags to riches with one wave of a magic wand. Outside the room in which archivists and researchers work is the flagstoned corridor along which the servants came from the kitchens to serve that other world of Axminster carpets and gilded stucco ceilings, carvings by Grinling Gibbons and cut-velvet curtains, tortoiseshell-inlaid Boulle cabinets and coffers of Coromandel lacquer. The room in which all the archival records and materials are kept was once the servants' own dining-hall.

Briefly, once, the worlds of the scullery maid and the duchess met at Chatsworth, when I found a picture of Dora at the centre of her Rideau Hall staff, and Evelyn Devonshire at the centre of her Rideau Hall household in the same box. For Evelyn's life is also held in boxes now, just like Dora's, at Chatsworth and at Bowood House in Wiltshire, the home of the Lansdowne family.

With the discovery of that hatbox and steamer trunk of memories, what started as a book about women born to wealth and privilege turned into a story about two women from very different sections of society's pyramid: a duchess and a scullery maid. The individual lives of Dora Lee and Evie Devonshire trace the passing of an age in the crucible of a war that would change Canada and Western society for ever.

PART ONE

Scullery Maid

High and
Lowly

*The scullery-maids crept out of their attic bedsteads in the murky
chill of five or six in the morning to clean the kitchen ranges and get
them lighted ... They were little more than children—thirteen or
fourteen years old—and after a late supper party they were
often kept at the sink, washing-up till one in the morning.*
ADELINE HARTCUP, *BELOW STAIRS
IN THE GREAT COUNTRY HOUSES*

The crowd gathered about the fashionable Gothic church
of St. Margaret's in Westminster long before two-thirty,
the hour fixed for the wedding of Lady Evelyn Emily Mary
Petty Fitzmaurice, eldest daughter of Lord Lansdowne, Viceroy
of India, to Mr. Victor Christian William Cavendish, heir pre-
sumptive of the Eighth Duke of Devonshire. There were many
high-society weddings at St. Margaret's, but the nobility-
watchers in London knew that the show on this Saturday,
July 30, 1892, would be particularly worth waiting for.

In a flurry of flunkeys and a clattering of hooves the carriages
began to arrive, and seasoned observers on the crowded pave-
ments identified the occupants to the casual gawper and the
uninitiated: the Duke and Duchess of Abercorn (the bride's
grandparents), the Duke of Devonshire, Lord Frederick
Hamilton (the bride's brother), the Dowager Marchioness of
Lansdowne, the Dowager Duchess of Abercorn. There were earls
and countesses, dowagers and marchionesses, and countless
ladies—among them the ladies Cecil and the ladies Churchill.

Accompanied by his best man—his brother, Mr. Richard Cavendish—the bridegroom arrived just before two o'clock, looking like a mildly worried bloodhound. This had nothing to do with wedding-day jitters, but was Victor Cavendish's habitual expression, concealing an intelligent and astute mind and —to judge by the diaries he doggedly maintained most of his adult life—a lack of imagination that gave him a serviceably straightforward and undecorated approach to a wide range of experiences.

The hurrahs of the crowd gave way to oohs and ahs as the eight bridesmaids descended from their coaches in a froth of snowy frills and fichus, the white feathers and pink roses in their broad-brimmed Gainsborough hats stirring in the light July breeze. The experts among the observers would have remarked on the number—more than ten bridesmaids would have been considered vulgar by some—and pointed out the diamond snake brooches worn by each young lady: the Cavendish family crest, a present from the bridegroom. Motherly sighs and manly chuckles would have greeted little Master Harry Streatfield in his page's costume of white velvet, his diamond snake worn as a scarf-pin.

Promptly at half-past two a great cheer went up as the bride arrived, to be greeted on the steps of the church by the clergy and choir. At the high altar waited the Bishop of London, who also happened to be the bridegroom's uncle. The summer sun glinted off the bride's pearl and diamond necklace—a gift from her father—three diamond star brooches given to her by her mother-in-law-to-be, and a superb diamond bracelet presented to her by the Viceregal Staff in India. The dressmakers and ladies' maids in the crowd commented on the rich satin duchesse of her gown with its trimming of exquisite Brussels point lace.

The seasoned nobility-watchers on the pavement would have noted Evelyn's aristocratic features: aquiline nose, chiselled lips, the long, slender line of her body. Maybe a wit in the crowd would have remarked on the union of the fine-bred greyhound and the pure-bred bloodhound, to be shushed by those around him who watched in awe and wonder. Their reactions may have been tinged with envy but, in spite of some on their Hyde Park soapboxes advocating a British Republic, the angry roar of class warfare was not yet heard in the land. It is unlikely that many in the "large crowd" referred to by *The Times* on Monday, August 1, 1892, questioned the relative lot in life of those outside on the pavement and those sitting in the pews of St. Margaret's, as the eldest daughter of India's viceroy walked up the aisle on the arm of her brother, the Earl of Kerry, while the choristers sang "The voice that breathed o'er Eden." Viceregal duties had kept Lord Lansdowne in India.

Evelyn's journey up the aisle of St. Margaret's begins in Simla in 1890. High above the beautiful hill-town in northern India towers the Vice-Regal Lodge, built in an uncompromisingly English Renaissance style of architecture. Its limestone and sandstone walls look over snow-covered ranges to the north, and a magnificent expanse of plain to the south, through which winds the river Sutlej. The English stately home leitmotif is continued inside, where the teak and walnut woodwork in the fifty-foot-high gallery and the state dining-room was carved by workers sent out from Messrs. Maple and Company in Britain. Even the carpets were sent out to Simla, causing Lord Lansdowne to wonder in a letter to his mother, "Why have they got them from Maple's when such lovely ones are made here?"

In the terrace gardens below the lodge a gardener, specially hired for the purpose, shoos away one of the hordes of monkeys who damage the tropical plants and English roses in which Lord Lansdowne and his daughter, Evie, take such delight. No respecters of the British Raj, these incorrigible intruders serve as reminders of the alien and untamed territory beyond the domain of Mr. Parsons, the English gardener of Simla.

But Evie is not gardening, that Simla season of 1890, or riding in her accomplished side-saddle style above the lush valleys of the hill-town. Although records show that the Lansdownes were in Simla between April and October that year, Evie will miss much of the Simla season. She is preparing to go back to England, to stay at Montagu House in London with her aunt Tiny, the Duchess of Buccleuch, who is her mother's older sister. This is no trip on an idle whim, for Evie is returning to be presented at court to Queen Victoria—the queen will declare her "a charming girl"—and, most important of all, to look for a husband.

Evie is the Lansdownes' jewel. She is beautiful, she is accomplished, her blood lines are impeccable. She has turned the heads of many of the bachelors of that Raj society, and one, Willie Peel, a career soldier, has lost his head over her. He bombards her with letters, which will follow her to England, even though he himself cannot. Mad with love, and mad also with the fevers brought on by heat, malaria and perhaps drink, he is an Englishman destroyed, as so many were, by that tropical jewel in Victoria's crown—quite as much as by unrequited love.

Evie's contacts with the world have been rigidly controlled by her mother, who does not believe in friendships even between girls, if they are not siblings. But there is no need for Lady Lansdowne to worry about Evie, for all contacts will be sanctioned and approved by her aunt. She will attend the right balls, visit the right country houses, be seen riding elegantly and skilfully in Rotten Row. All Evie has to do is to attract the right attention from the right prospect.

And that is exactly what she does. In 1890 she leaves the balls, tennis-parties and gymkhanas of Simla and, at some point along the carefully mapped route, she meets Mr. Victor Cavendish, the heir to the Devonshire dukedom. She returns to India, but is back in England for the season of 1891–1892. By July of 1892, she has achieved the goal expected of her and has married a suitable husband.

Perhaps Evie met Victor when she was strolling in the garden of Devonshire House, and he was on one of his frequent visits to his uncle. The London properties of the Lansdownes and the Cavendishes were divided only by a narrow passage. Perhaps she met him in India, for Victor was there in 1890. A photograph shows him wearing a large topi and standing in front of a tiger that, apparent from Victor's position in the picture, he shot. There are two other white men with him and they are surrounded by native bearers. In another photograph Victor is with a group that includes Lord and Lady Lansdowne and their son, Lord Kerry—but not Evelyn. It is also possible that Victor was pursuing other quarry when he came to India— an elusive, dark-haired beauty who would not give him an answer, and whom he had met first in England.

On August 25, 1890, Lord Lansdowne writes to his mother:

> … You have heard I suppose that Evie has had a little affair with Victor Cavendish, she had known him 6 weeks and I am not surprised that she has not given him encouragement. I should have liked the connection, I believe the boy is a good creature, though very plain. He is moreover very young. I should like her to find a really nice husband, who would make her happy and contented through life.

Lord Lansdowne's use of the phrase "a little affair" simply means that Victor has paid court to his daughter, and she has responded somewhat kindly—but not said yes to engagement or marriage. This letter, and *The Times'* court circular for July 2, 1890, suggest that Evie and Victor met before his trip to India. The guest list for a dinner-party given by the Duke and Duchess of Buccleuch on July 1 includes both Lady Evelyn Fitzmaurice and Mr. Victor Cavendish.

It is possible that other prospects were held up for inspection by her aunt in England, and it looks from this letter as though Evie is resisting Victor's suit, as well as her father's apparent endorsement of it. But it was Victor whom she thought about, when she returned to India. As she said to someone in the family, "I can't get Victor's ugly old face out of my mind."

Naïve, perhaps, to think their destinies lay in their own hands, and that chance played any part whatsoever in the marriage of Victor and Evie. The "ugly old face" was undoubtedly given an aura of glamour by one of the oldest titles in Britain. The Buccleuch family were not only related to the Lansdownes, but had financial as well as class ties to the Devonshires. The dukes of Devonshire and Buccleuch were prime movers in the development of the Furness Railway that connected the iron mines of Lindal and the slate quarries of Kirkby to Barrow-in-Furness in Lancashire. The ancient home of the monks of Furness Abbey, in the Vale of Nightshade, had become a centre of dark, satanic, and prosperous, mills.

By the time Evie met Victor, Barrow had iron and steel works, a corn mill, and a jute and flax factory that mainly used female labour. Ship-building took on a new importance after the construction of two new docks—christened the Devonshire and Buccleuch docks and built with the financial backing of the directors of the Furness Railway. Class revolution there may not have been in England's green and pleasant land, but the dukes of Devonshire and Buccleuch had made sure they were part of that other revolution that changed the face of much of England before the century turned.

By May 29, 1892, Lord Lansdowne writes from Simla to his mother:

> I hope you are as pleased as I am. I have always felt that if Victor still cared for Evie, and if Evie really liked him, she could not make a better match ... You know that I like the family—and I am sure they will be friendly and easy to get on with—I should have hated a marriage which connected Evie with a second rate or rowdy set. And so would you.

So, whatever her hesitations may have been, at two-thirty, on July 30, 1892, Evie walks down the aisle towards her waiting bridegroom in a glimmer of satin duchesse and a cloud of Brussels lace. She has made an advantageous match, and her parents will have been well-pleased. All that remains of the task that is her purpose in life is to produce an heir for the Devonshire dukedom.

Would Evelyn ever give much thought again, in later years, to the bougainvillaeas and frangipanis of Malabar Point in Bombay, to the train journey through the splendour of the Ghats? Did she ever dream about the Taj Mahal by moonlight, as she had seen it when she was on the brink of womanhood and marriage? Did she treasure the memory of the time spent with her father every afternoon between four-thirty and six-thirty on horseback, riding in the pure, pine-scented Simla air past thickets of ilex and tree rhododendrons, gazing at the snow-capped mountains across precipices on each side of the road that, according to her father, "would make you shiver"?

Had it changed her in any way that her mother could speak Hindustani, and that Lady Lansdowne's servants would weep when she left India? How had that privileged colonial childhood affected the young woman who walked down the aisle of St. Margaret's on the arm of the heir to 186,000 acres of England to the strains of Mendelssohn's "Wedding March," as the church bells rang out what *The Times* called "a merry peal," and she danced with her new husband to the strains of Herr Wurms's White Vienna Band?

Afterwards, the bridal pair left for Bowood Park to begin their honeymoon and their life together. Evelyn wore "pale blue radzimir, trimmed with white embroidered lisse, with large revers of white moiré antique, and … a large black hat." The seasoned watchers on the pavement outside St. Margaret's and Hampden House, the town home of the Duke and Duchess of Abercorn where the reception was held, would doubtless have agreed that anyone who was anyone in Great Britain had been there.

There were, however, some notable exceptions. Queen Victoria had been living a reclusive life since the death of her husband, Prince Albert, in 1861 but, although she had not attended the wedding, she had given Evie an Indian shawl and Victor a bronze statuette of herself. Her son, Edward, Prince of Wales, was also not at the wedding. In fact, the only member of the Marlborough House Set who attended was the Eighth Duke of Devonshire—who could hardly have absented himself from the wedding of his nephew and heir.

The Eighth Duke, who rejoiced in the nickname "Harty-Tarty," was the quintessential member of that coterie of rich, titled and beautiful people who had gathered themselves around the portly figure of "Tum-Tum," the heir to the throne. As a young man, the then Marquis of Hartington had even shared the same mistress as the prince, the notorious and stunning "Skittles," a high-class prostitute from the slums of Merseyside. This in itself was not particularly unusual or disturbing, but so enamoured was Harty-Tarty that he had even considered marrying her, to the horror of his straitlaced father.

His other great and lengthy love affair was with Louise, Duchess of Manchester, who was already married. Here, class was no barrier, so the Eighth Duke married her later on in life, when he was fifty-nine, after the death of her husband. There were no children, and thus it was that his brother's child, Victor Cavendish, became heir to the dukedom.

Marginalized by his mother's refusal to allow him any part in the affairs of state—he did not get even a glimpse into the red cabinet boxes until he was over fifty—Edward, the heir to the throne, substituted a life of pleasure for the life of duty he was denied. Easily bored and with a short attention span, it took a wider circle than the fifteen hundred families of the British upper-class to keep the prince amused, so bankers, industrialists, foreigners and Jews found themselves admitted to the Marlborough House Set. From the racecourses and grouse-moors of Britain to the watering-places of Marienbad and Baden-Baden, the prince rollicked his way through the society seasons as he waited out forty years of adulthood before he became king, asking only to be entertained and fed large quantities of food, surrounded by, above all, pretty and pleasing women.

Tum-Tum loved the company of women. They were amusing and decorative; they flattered his ego, damaged by his mother's contempt for his abilities and even for his physical appearance—she considered him chinless and bandy-legged. After ten years of marriage Alexandra was rumoured to have banned him from her bedroom, so he satisfied his sexual appetite elsewhere—although it was also rumoured that his prowess in the bedroom was less than stellar. Stories of the bedroom ban may have come from the servants' quarters, may also have been pillow talk passed on by the legion of ladies whose discretion about their royal lover was not as all-inclusive as he might have wished.

His prowess at the table, however, was legendary. In an age and class that ate huge quantities of food, Edward was considered a trencherman. Even after a breakfast of poached eggs, bacon, haddock, devilled kidneys, kedgeree and woodcock—not to mention the cold table of pressed beef, ham and tongue, plus pheasant, grouse and partridge—he could eat a heavy lunch that usually included his favourite lobster salad. On special occasions, such as the Ascot race meeting, lunch might have fourteen courses.

The evening meal was gargantuan. On the eve of his last trip to Biarritz, in old age and failing health, Tum-Tum consumed turtle soup, salmon steak, grilled chicken, saddle of mutton, snipe stuffed with foie gras, asparagus, fruit, a rich iced dessert, followed by a savoury to top it all off. "Tell me what you eat, and I shall tell you what you are," declared Brillat-Savarin. One wonders what the great gourmet would have made of the great glutton.

Women and food were the Prince of Wales's chief delights, but there was one dilemma. Women were supposed to dine only in the privacy of their homes, maintaining an other-worldly illusion of fairy creatures who neither toiled nor spun—nor ate. Even in their own homes ladies could not ask for anything at the table, but had to trust to the attentiveness of the gentlemen present. Benjamin Disraeli had gone so far as to declare, "If a woman eats, she may destroy the spell, and if she will not eat, she destroys our dinner." Small wonder the women of Victorian England consumed massive quantities of sandwiches and other portable delicacies in the privacy of their bedrooms.

With Edward, this was about to change. Just as money now opened the doors to palaces and the royal circle, so women began to gain entrée into public places. Victoria's son wanted to laugh across the tables of *Le Faisan Doré* in Cannes, or the Hotel Weimar in Marienbad at Lady de Grey and Lillie Langtry and Daisy, Countess of Warwick, while he surfeited himself on oysters, caviar and quail. Like the *cocottes* and *demimondaines* of Paris, Vienna and London, the "professional beauties" of the Marlborough House Set moved their appetites out of their bedrooms and into the dining-rooms of that golden Edwardian world.

On May 14, 1892, a domestic servant called Annie Lee gave birth to a daughter in Tiverton, Devon. Annie Pitts had married Samuel Lee, a wheelwright, in the Wesleyan Chapel on the corner of St. Peter and Bridge streets on March 9, only two months before her child was born. They were both twenty-one years old. Whether Annie had concealed her pregnancy for as long as she could, or whether it had taken considerable arm-twisting to get Samuel Lee to the altar, is not known. In the only photograph that survives of Annie, one can see what attracted Samuel Lee: large, soft eyes, full lips and a curvaceous figure. Her father, a tanner, and Samuel's father, a carpenter, were present at the wedding, as was Annie's mother, Rosa.

When she held her little girl for the first time, Annie may well have seen the resemblance to herself, and in photograph after photograph her daughter will appear with her mother's round features and full figure. But the eyes that meet the world are bolder and more challenging than her mother's—even in a photograph of that little girl when she was two or three years old. Time and experience will make her more worldly-wise, but Annie Lee's daughter was born confronting life head-on. Annie called her Dorothea—a splendid name, worthy of a lady of leisure. Dorothea Mary Lee.

There were no crowds for Annie's wedding—no pealing of bells, few gifts, perhaps a modest wedding meal when they returned to her parents' home from the Wesleyan Chapel in Tiverton, Devon. That society wedding celebrated in St. Margaret's Church, Westminster, on July 30, 1892, two months after the birth of Annie's daughter, was as far removed from the wedding of the domestic servant and the wheelwright as the classes into which those bridal couples were born. Yet the twin passions of the heir to the throne would have a more profound effect on the life of Dorothea Mary Lee, who would always be known as Dora, than on the young couple who walked down the aisle in July 1892 to the merry peal of St. Margaret's bells.

PEASE PUDDING

Pease pudding hot, pease pudding cold
Pease pudding in a pot, nine days old.
Old English nursery rhyme

To each pound of dried peas allow 1 oz. dripping and 1 egg. Bring the peas to a boil in a large pan of water and cook slowly until tender. Rub through a sieve. Beat with the dripping and egg and season well. Put in a greased basin and steam for one hour. It is advisable to soak the dried peas first.

PETITS POIS FRAIS À LA FRANÇAISE

The chapter of green peas is still continuing, the impatience to eat them, the pleasures of having eaten them, and the anticipated joy of eating them again ... it is a fashion, a craze.

Madame de Maintenon

1 firm head of lettuce
3 cups fresh shelled
   green peas
12 small peeled white
   onions
half cup water
half teaspoon sugar

6 parsley sprigs, tied
   together
6 tablespoons butter, cut
   into half-inch pieces
half teaspoon salt
2 tablespoons soft butter

Remove any wilted lettuce leaves, trim the stem and rinse. Cut the lettuce into four to six wedges and tie each wedge with string to keep in shape while cooking. Bring the peas, lettuce wedges, onions, parsley, 6 tablespoons butter, water, salt and sugar to a boil over moderate heat. Toss lightly, then cover the pan and cook 30 minutes, stirring from time to time, until the peas are tender and the water almost cooked away. Remove the parsley and cut the string off the lettuce wedges. Gently stir in remaining butter and season to taste. Serve in small bowls and eat with a spoon.

~ ℰ ~

Two

Poor Little Devils

The lot of the negress in the Equatorial Forest is not, perhaps,
a very happy one, but is it so much worse than that of many
a pretty orphan girl in our Christian capital?
GENERAL WILLIAM BOOTH, 1890

N
o one in Devon lives more than twenty-five miles from the sea, and from that glorious southwest coastline sprang a race of seafarers and explorers. But the Devon of Dorothea Mary Lee was quite different. Well before the Industrial Revolution Tiverton had a solid industrial as well as an agricultural economy, as the early cloth-makers set up shop alongside the rivers and streams of the county. In 1815, John Heathcote moved his lace-making business to Tiverton away from the north of England and the perils of revolutionaries and machine-smashing Luddites, establishing one of the largest machine-lace factories in the country.

Dora's father, Samuel Lee, was a wheelwright—a profession essential to both the industrial and the agricultural community in those pre-automobile days. Business must have been steady, but it is possible that it was economic reality rather than reluctance that kept Samuel from walking up the aisle with Annie Pitts. Annie would have lost her job as a servant as soon as her employer found out about her pregnancy, and her family would not have been happy about taking back another two mouths to feed. Samuel first had to find somewhere for them to live, and Annie probably worked as long as she could before either the pregnancy was discovered or she gave up her position. In country communities it was not considered as shocking or unacceptable, as it would have in nineteenth-century middle- or upper-class society, for the marriage to have been consummated before the ceremony.

The roots of the Lee and Pitts families went deep into that West Country soil. Their Neolithic farming ancestors had tilled the earth and buried their dead in communal chambered tombs on their fields, raising huge granite slabs above them to mark their resting-place. They worshipped their gods in religious ceremonies among the menhirs and stone circles that still dot the landscape of Devon and Cornwall. Later ancestors built their homes in the valleys and protected their towns with hilltop forts and castles, long before the arrival of the Roman armies. For centuries, Dora's ancestors had lived within the narrow compass of the land around the River Exe.

Samuel and Annie did not have very long together. By 1895 Dora had a sister, Beatrice Rosa, and by 1896 Samuel Lee was a widower and the two little girls were without a mother. Annie died at her mother's home in Tiverton of tuberculosis, with her mother, Sarah, by her side. She was twenty-five years old and had been ill for quite some time. Possibly the birth of her second child had weakened her already feeble health.

Annie left Dora what may well have been her only precious possession—the silver horseshoe brooch she is wearing in her studio portrait—and Dora would one day give it to her eldest son to wear on his uniform when he left to fight for his country. It would bring greater good fortune to her daughter and grandson than it had to Annie Lee herself.

For the next five years Dora and Beatrice lived with their grandmother while their father plied his trade—indeed, it is possible the family had always been under their grandparents' roof, for that is where Dora was born. With her mother gone, Dora must have picked up extra responsibilities very early in her life, looking after her younger sister and helping out her ageing grandmother. Samuel Lee seems to have moved to the neighbouring county of Somerset at some point, because Axbridge is the town of residence shown on the marriage certificate when he married for the second time in 1901. He chose as his second wife a thirty-one-year-old called Mary Western, who came from Yorkshire in the north of England. Possibly her family had moved away from industrial trouble in the north, to find work in the cloth-making factories of Devonshire.

Samuel's bride was a year younger than him, but she was still old for a spinster in the nineteenth century. Doubtless the prospect of taking on a widower with two small children of nine and six years old was, in consequence, more attractive to Mary Western than it would have been to younger girls. Clearly she was meant to be a second mother for his daughters, because Samuel re-established the family unit when he remarried. But with the arrival of Mary, and the birth of her half-brother, Charlie, Dora's life changed for ever.

"I know nothing of her and she knew nothing of me," Dora would say in later life of her stepmother. Dora, who said remarkably little about her early life, gave her children to understand that they didn't get along. Nevertheless, she was fond of her half-brother and he of her, and they would keep in touch long after Dora had left Devon.

It must have been difficult on both sides. Mary arrived in a household where her new mother-in-law and her granddaughters were emotionally linked by the death of her new husband's first wife. Dora found her mother supplanted by a woman who even spoke with an unfamiliar accent quite unlike the soft, rounded sounds of Devon speech. It is also likely that Mary did not have the level of education of Annie and her children, since her father had signed his name with an "X" as a witness on the marriage certificate, and gave his occupation as "labourer." Both Samuel and his father were skilled tradesmen with their own businesses.

Looking at Dora's bold and challenging gaze, one cannot imagine she gave Mary an easy time, nor that she took kindly to being given orders, treated harshly—or simply ignored. Over the next four years there must have been some battles royal before Dora was sent away from Tiverton. At the end of 1905, possibly just before Christmas, thirteen-year-old Dora was put into service as a scullery maid in the small market-town of Charminster, just outside Dorchester, in the nearby county of Dorset.

In all fairness, it should be said that this was not just the cruel act of a wicked stepmother, but common practice at the time. Although the age of thirteen was about as young as these little girls became scullery maids, by the early 1880s one in three of all girls between the ages of fifteen and twenty was in domestic service, and most of them came from the country, like Dora. In fact, it is likely that the Lee family found her the position, because her grandfather had business connections in the town. Dora's first place of employment was at "The Ferns," on Mill Lane, the home of a Mrs. Clarke. One of the earliest postcards—part of the extensive collection that Dora built up and took with her wherever she was living and working for the rest of her life—is addressed to Dora "c/o Mrs. Carlyle," who was probably the housekeeper.

The Ferns is a pretty stone house built flush to the road on a steeply rising hill. It has an elegant pillared entrance and extensive gardens behind the house that must have required the attentions of a gardener and possibly a gardener's boy. It is a smart, solid dwelling, but certainly not a stately home. Mr. Clarke may have been a prosperous local merchant, or had a business in Dorchester. Apart from the housekeeper, Mrs. Carlyle—who may also have been the cook—it is likely that Mrs. Clarke had a parlour-maid. Dora, as scullery maid, would have been the lowliest member of that servant class.

In a country with one of the more complex class systems in the Western world it is hardly surprising that the servant class had a hierarchy of its own. Mrs. Carlyle, the house-keeper, would have been at the top of the tree, with the cook (if there was one) following close on her heels. She in turn would be followed by the parlour-maid, unless the household boasted a lady's maid—whose closeness to the mistress of the house would give her precedence. Nurses were in a separate category, which caused all kinds of demarcation problems, and occasionally they had nursery maids under them.

There were no demarcation problems for the scullery maid, who was, without question, at everyone's beck and call, and given the longest hours and the dirtiest tasks. Dora was up by five o'clock every day, and—particularly in a middle-sized household like The Ferns—to her may have fallen the task of cleaning out the grates and lighting the fires. There would have been fires in the drawing-room, dining-room, study and all the bedrooms, and that would have required shifting about three tons of coal a week in the winter. If there was a coal-fired range in the kitchen, it would have been cleaned and lit by six a.m. and black-leaded every morning. In many households the servants had to put together their own cleaning materials, making up blacking from a substance confusingly called "ivory black," to which was added treacle, beer and sulphuric acid. Furniture polish was a mixture of linseed oil, methylated spirits, turpentine and white wax. If Mrs. Clarke had not yet installed electricity, there would have been dozens of oil-lamps to be cleaned, trimmed and filled.

The elegant front entrance of The Ferns would have to be cleaned before breakfast every day—the brass door handles, keyhole, letter-box, bell-pull and knocker rubbed to a gleaming shine, the doorstep swept and scrubbed. Dora's hands, in and out of water all the time, washing vegetables, washing dishes, scrubbing the tiled floor of the kitchen and the stone-flagged passages in the basement, would have been chapped and bleeding, particularly in the winter.

"Poor little devils, washing up and scrubbing away at dozens of pots and pans, saucepans and plates, up to their elbows in suds and grease, their hands red raw with the soda which was the only form of detergent in those days," was the recollection of one of the Astor family's butlers. "I've seen them crying with exhaustion, pain, the degradation too, I shouldn't wonder. Well, let's hope they got their reward in heaven."

Dora may have said her prayers and sobbed herself to sleep the first night she found herself in her attic bedroom, but she was not prepared to wait for heavenly rewards. Very early on in her Charminster life, Mrs. Clarke's scullery maid plotted an escape route. She did not intend to break the rules, or dig any tunnels, metaphorically speaking, beneath those hierarchical foundations. Dora looked up that downstairs ladder and decided to climb it rung by rung. But there was one thing about which she had to make up her mind: whether to move from the basement to the upper floors and serve as parlour-maid, lady's maid, and then housekeeper, or whether she should stay belowstairs in the kitchen and take a different route altogether.

The life of Evelyn Fitzmaurice, the daughter of an aristocrat, also changed profoundly when she was thirteen years old, but she was destined for a very different fate. To the thirteen-year-old scullery maid it must have seemed as if the walls were closing in around her, removing her from family, friends and freedom. For the aristocrat's daughter, on the other hand, the walls were not breached when she was thirteen, but they expanded, just a little, to broaden the conventional horizons of her class.

Noblesse oblige. Duty was the price paid by the privileged: duty to their great estates, duty to their tenantry, servants and the lower classes, duty to their country. Rich in possessions and impeccably blue-blooded though he was, Evelyn's father, the

Marquess of Lansdowne, had inherited a debt of £300,000 on his father's death. "Poverty," as David Cannadine points out in *The Decline and Fall of the British Aristocracy*, "was the great spur to proconsular office." There was no net income from the Bowood estate and the rent-rolls on his Irish properties had drawn the ire of the Land League, so when Prime Minister Gladstone offered him the Governor-Generalship of Canada in 1883, he reluctantly accepted. Many of the early governors-general came from the ranks of the Anglo-Irish aristocracy, including the first governor-general to live in Ottawa, Lord Monck. By the 1880s, as Cannadine says, "the growth and con-solidation of the formal empire led to the creation of new and attractive plumage positions, which were most appropriately filled by men of high status and illustrious lineage."

It was a heavy price for the home-loving Lord Lansdowne. He had more than one home to love, but he was particularly attached to Bowood, his English home in Wiltshire, and Dereen, his Irish home in County Kerry. Southern Ireland at the time was described by one of the Lansdownes' friends as "the only English-speaking country where there is no 'middle class,' one of its greatest charms." For Lady Lansdowne there was a little cottage at the mouth of the Shannon where she could get away from it all—*à la* Marie Antoinette playing shepherdess at *le petit Trianon*.

In a letter to his mother the marquess wrote: "Even to me the announcement comes as some sort of a shock ... The time, be it longer or shorter, is a long one to look forward to, and my heart fails at times when I think of it, but the years will pass by, and when they are gone, I believe we shall all of us admit that it would have been wrong to refuse." Thus, thirteen-year-old Evelyn Fitzmaurice found herself uprooted and in Canada in 1883 with her father, the reluctant governor-general.

The various scions of noble and aristocratic families who served in Canada in the viceregal role were not only represen-tatives of the Crown; they were also agents of the imperial government. Under the Colonial Laws Validity Act of 1865, a colonial legislature was inferior to the British Parliament, and this would not change for another sixty-six years—long after Canada became a dominion. When Confederation was formed in 1867, John A. Macdonald had wanted the new country to be called the Canadian Kingdom, but that was too extreme for the Colonial Office back in London. In 1883 Evelyn Fitzmaurice arrived in Britain's oldest self-governing possession, a country larger than the whole of Europe, whose every legal move was controlled from London and countersigned by her father in the name of an ageing queen.

Evelyn, of course, would never have questioned any of this, and it is doubtful she gave it much thought. But there is evidence that her years in Canada gave her some freedom from the shackles of tradition and convention that bound girls of her age and class in the mother country. She was thirteen years old when she arrived, and eighteen when she left—five of the most important years in any life. From the moment they landed in Quebec in October 1883, a change came over even her restrained and undemonstrative father. When speaking in French, which he spoke well, his manner changed from "the strictest gubernatorial style, without gesture or motion," and—to the surprise of even those who knew him well—he delivered his speech with Gallic gestures and oratorical fervour. Members of the House of Lords would have had difficulty recognizing their former staid colleague—the "genius of the French language had taken possession of him," according to one surprised observer.

His residence in the Citadel in Quebec, however, was furnished like an English country house, reassuringly filled with family pictures, furnishings and china that had made the three-thousand-mile trip with the marquess. The viceregal summer retreat, New Dereen, stood on the banks of the Cascapedia River in New Brunswick, where Lord Lansdowne could fish for salmon in one of the greatest sports-fishing rivers in the world.

Rideau Hall was acquired as the official viceregal dwelling in Ottawa during Lord Monck's term of office, and had been altered and embellished by its various occupants. The original building was described by the Reform leader, George Brown, as "a miserable little house ... the grounds those of an ambitious country squire." Lord Dufferin added a large ballroom complete with stage, and a full-size tennis-court that could be converted into a supper-room by the ingenious lowering of a red-and-white canopy from the roof and a carpet spread over the floor. It was here, in Canada's capital, that Evelyn was introduced to the delights of a Canadian winter.

The dry, furnace-heated air of Rideau Hall that played havoc with the exquisite marquetry of the Lansdownes' French inlaid furniture and cracked the surface of the Romneys and Gainsboroughs was an endless source of amusement to the Lansdowne children. They soon discovered the joys of shuffling across the carpet, creeping up on some unsuspecting member of the family, touching them—preferably on the ear, a sensitive spot—and giving them a shock. They found out how to light the gas by charging up the static electricity in their bodies and putting their fingers to the gas-burners. If they rubbed the gold bindings of their pretty books—a fur cap worked best, apparently—the gilt began to sparkle and flash with light like a miniature fireworks display.

But it was the winter world outside the walls of Rideau Hall that brought the most pleasure. The viceregal residence had two open-air skating rinks, two toboggan slides and its own covered curling-rink, where Lord Lansdowne was introduced to what the locals called "the roaring game." His brother-in-law described the Canadian game as "a sort of billiards on ice," because it was possible to play with far greater accuracy in a constantly flooded covered rink than outdoors as they had played it in Scotland. For special occasions, such as inter-city matches, the ice was stencilled with roses, thistles and maple leaves. The governor-general became quite an aficionado, heading the Rideau Hall team that democratically included one of the footmen, elevated above his station by his curling talents.

Skating was Evelyn's joy, and she was out on one of the skating-rinks every day. Every week, Ottawa society turned up for the skating parties at Rideau Hall, to dance to the music of a military band housed in an ice-palace built specially for them. The slim, elegant figure of Lord Lansdowne's eldest daughter drew many admiring comments as she glided across the ice and danced the quadrilles and lancers so popular with Ottawa society at the time. When they were not skating at Rideau Hall, they were down at the Ottawa Skating Club for the weekly club dance, to waltz beneath brilliant arc-lights and a bunting-bedecked ceiling, amid garlands of artificial flowers and foliage.

The Lansdowne children had their own ice-house, built for them by their uncle, Lord Frederick Hamilton, complete with its own furniture and pictures. The girls made red twill curtains for the ice-windows and a frill for the mantelpiece, and the little house stood for over three months. They invented snacks and treats for their guests—"Jerusalem the Golden" was a big favourite: put milk and honey outside to freeze, then break it up into chips, serve, and enjoy.

For Lord Lansdowne's "Arctic Cremornes"—the two great skating and tobogganing parties held every winter—the rinks were festooned with fairy-lights and Japanese lanterns. Bonfires and arc-lamps blazed against the darkness and lit the snow like diamonds. Men and women wore blanket-suits in the colour of their various skating or curling clubs—the Rideau Hall colours were white with purple stockings and cap, and a red sash. Supper was served in the curling rink on tables set with silver branched candelabra and fine plate, attended by footmen and staff in fur coats and caps. The French chef at Rideau Hall had to be careful what he prepared—frozen meringues became "uneatable cricket-balls," according to the children's uncle.

The Lansdownes were in Montreal for the Winter Carnival in 1887 and the great fancy-dress skating *fête* at the Victoria Rink, where they made a spectacular entrance in costume, skating a series of elaborate figures down the ice, followed by Evelyn, her sister and brothers. On the great toboggan slide of Mount Royal, with its sixty-foot drop, the Lansdowne boys took their toboggan—christened the Ottawa River Express, and complete with bells and lanterns—up to sixty miles an hour, standing erect as they flashed past amazed onlookers and possibly apprehensive parents.

On snowshoe treks through the winter woods at night, Evelyn and her sister could emulate their brothers' toboggan-ing prowess—running ahead of groaning adults who clutched their aching calf-muscles, vaulting ditches and fences with their snowshoes still strapped to their feet. Like their uncle, the Lansdowne children likely always remembered a Canadian winter as bathed in sunshine, its chill, fresh air like wine against their faces.

Life in Canada was not all music, lights and carnival, cer-tainly not for the governor-general. There had been the pos-sibility of his Irish problems following him to Canada—authorities were on the lookout for Fenian attacks when he arrived—but this had not materialized. Many of the social functions were lengthy and boring and took up much of his time: there were all those interminable "Drawing Rooms"—an "awful ceremony," he called them. But when provincial and federal representatives had travelled as much as two thousand miles to be in Ottawa to attend, one's duty must be done.

One of the functions of the governor-general's office was the power to exercise the prerogative of mercy. It was during Lord Lansdowne's term of office that there occurred what he described in a letter to his mother as "a disagreeable little out-break." The disagreeable little outbreak was the Riel Rebellion in 1885, for which Louis Riel was sentenced to hang. The decision to carry out the sentence was taken by the Cabinet, in spite of pressure from the French-Canadian members, and Lord Lansdowne chose not to oppose the execution.

Given Lansdowne's authoritarian attitudes and his reactionary views on the upholding of the status quo in Ireland (even by the standards of many of his own class), his choice in the Riel matter is not in the least surprising. In his letter to Queen Victoria he said, "There is undoubtedly some feeling, a survival of old race antipathies, among the French-Canadians in favour of Riel, but Lord Lansdowne does not consider that it is universal or very deep-seated."

A century later it is patently safe to say that those old race antipathies have proved to be very deep-seated indeed.

The "genius of the country" suited the Lansdownes so well that it would be with genuine regret that the marquess left five years later in 1888 for his new appointment as viceroy of India. Again, reluctantly, he accepted—"instead of living in a corner of a house in England, perpetually worried by financial trouble," as he told his mother. Later on in the same letter he added, "Evie would I suppose go with us." By December 1888 Evelyn and her family were in India. So sudden was the transition that Lansdowne would say in the "cool pure air" of Simla, "... there are moments when I fancy I am back in Ottawa again."

By 1905, the year that Dora was put into service, thirty-three-year-old Evelyn Cavendish had been married thirteen years, but she was not yet a duchess. She and Victor Cavendish lived at Holker Hall, Cartmel, amidst 20,000 acres of glorious countryside between Windermere in the Lake District and Morecambe Bay in Lancashire. But—duchess or no duchess —her arrival there in 1892 had all the pomp and splendour of a more primitive, feudal age. Men from the estate greeted the newly-weds at the station, unhitched the horses from the carriage bearing their master and mistress, and dragged it up the flower-strewn road to the hall. Twenty-five years later, from his hospital bed in another country half a world and half a war away, the wounded son of an old coachman on the estate would remind the Ninth Duke of Devonshire of that day at Holker Hall.

The servant hierarchy of great estates like Holker Hall, Bowood or Chatsworth was far more intricate than that of Dora's household, The Ferns. For centuries the "downstairs" at Chatsworth, the country seat of the dukes of Devonshire, was not belowstairs at all but alongside the great halls and state rooms of the mansion. At the beginning of the nineteenth century, when the Sixth Duke came into his inheritance, even distinguished visitors had to go past stables, hen-coops, wash-house, scullery and kitchens before reaching the front door. Once inside they still had to navigate the staff quarters, including the back stairs and the cook's bedroom, before reaching the Great Hall. Before the extensive alterations that were undertaken by the Sixth Duke and his architect, Wyatville, most of the ground floor, in fact, was occupied by the servants.

There was never any confusion, however, about the demarcation lines between those servants. The house steward, housekeeper, wine butler, under-butler, groom of the chambers, valet, head housemaid and lady's maid were known as the Upper Ten —whether there were ten of them or not, and there were usually considerably more. The Lower Five embraced all other categories, and the two groups even ate separately. Visiting nobility brought their own staff, and the staff dinner mimicked that of their masters, with the steward leading the way into the upper servants' dining-room (always known, for some reason, as "Pug's Parlour") in full evening dress, with the highest ranking visiting servant—usually the lady's maid—on his arm.

Strangest of all was the custom of calling each upper servant by the name of the master or mistress—thus, the Chatsworth manservant and lady's maid would have been called "Devonshire" when visiting other great houses. In some houses there were even certain names that were given to the various positions—the first footman would be called John, the second James, and so on—to avoid the problem of having to remember new names when there were staff changes. This custom was still in existence at Chatsworth in the 1920s. The loss of personal identity does not seem to have been as significant as the hierarchical importance of the name itself—John, presumably, being a step up from James.

The footmen and the coachmen were almost a class unto themselves, chosen for their decorative qualities—"calves before character," as the saying went. A *Punch* cartoon of 1854 shows a footman saying to his employer, "Ham I engaged for work, or ham I engaged for ornament?" As postillions they rode the crested carriages of their titled masters in the magnificent liveries of their household. They adorned state banquets, a footman behind every chair—not that there weren't certain drawbacks to having a footman behind one's chair at dinner, particularly if the diner was bald. Lord Lansdowne once complained of a heavy-breathing footman who "me jete des courants d'air sur la tête" (who's blowing draughts onto my head). The tallest footmen commanded the highest wages; one of the Chatsworth footmen who was hired in 1928 nearly lost the job because he was only five feet nine inches and was replacing someone who was six feet two inches tall.

Well beyond the end of the nineteenth century and the wearing of powdered wigs and embroidered coats by their noble masters, these magnificent men, costumed as if for a fancy-dress ball, embellished their owners' homes like the paintings by Verrio and Laguerre on the ceiling, the Canova statuary in the Orangeries.

Like the liveried servants, the cook was in a class on his own. Although he belonged in the Upper Ten, he was a craftsman —to some an artist, an aristocrat of that netherworld. Most of the great families preferred to have a chef, and usually the woman cook acted as supporting cast for the star performer who was, preferably, French—although Italian confectioners were favoured. Most important of all, the cook was paid more than other servants and had other servants to perform the more menial tasks for him.

The servants moved with their masters between their town and country homes. Devonshire House in London provided park-like gardens and tennis-courts in the heart of London for younger guests, and it was a splendid place from which to watch royal and ceremonial processions. Untouched by change inside, it retained the air of a bygone age with its tarnished gilding and faded damask walls that still bore the stains made by the wigs of powdered footmen who had used them as head-rests. Hour after interminable hour their yawns echoed down the miles of dimly lit corridors, up the marble and alabaster staircase and past the Titians, Tintorettos and Rubens, as they waited to serve their masters.

Stuck in the basement of The Ferns in a small village she may have been, but Dora found she was part of a huge network of servants who kept in touch with each other the length and breadth of the British Isles. From the time she arrived in Charminster the postcards began to arrive from other young maidservants like herself, and Dora would keep most of the friends and the postcards they sent her for the rest of her professional life and beyond. In fact, she must have announced her intention of building up a postcard collection. The earliest reference is on a card dated January 12, 1907, that reads, "Just one more to swell the number. Look for me in church on Sunday. Best ever from Kate Woolfries." There is a card dated March 12, 1907, with a sepia-tinted photograph of four people riding donkeys on the beach; the sender has written on the picture, "puzzle find me." The message on the card reads:

> Dear D. I am sorry I have not written to you before but you see
> I have not forgotten you. This is one for your collection but I'm

afraid it is a very poor one. Puzzle to find out who it is. I am amongst them. It was taken down at Weston on the water shute and the donkeys. I am writing especially to know if you will come and spend Easter with us. Don't say no but come. Mother wishes to be remembered to your father & mother & Charlie. Tell Charlie we have not forgotten him yet. I expect he is a big boy now & goes to school. Write soon & let me know about Easter & have not any more to say now. With love from F. Burnell. Our address is still the same. F.B. Trying to dry this & happen to scorch it so please excuse it. F.B.

The hurried writer is probably fourteen-year-old Florrie, who will stay in touch with her girlhood friend over the years. It is clear from this postcard that the two knew each other before going into service, and this looks likely in the case of at least one other correspondent, who also appears to know Dora's family. While on holiday in Blackpool in May 1907, Lila Hawkins writes to Dora:

> My dear Dora: I hope you are still in the land of the living. I am still working at Greens. I will write you a letter soon. You must write to me and tell me all the news. Give my best love to your Ma and Pa and Charlie. Write soon as I am longing to hear how you all are. I do miss you so much even now. From your everloving friend, Lila.

Florrie, Lily, Lila, Kate, Laura, Lucy, Ada, Eliza, Libby, Nell, Alice, Ruth, Muriel, Elsie, Ethel, Kitty, Annie, Peggy: a postcard parade of maidservants will contribute to Dora's collection their messages of encouragement, affection, shared jokes and sorrows, information passed on from one to another. By the time Dora puts away her collection there will be well over three hundred cards, besides the many that were not stuck into albums. Some of them will be from family, some from boyfriends, some not sent to her at all, but given to her simply as new and interesting acquisitions. However, the bulk of her collection is from all those young women like herself who found themselves belowstairs as teenagers.

Clearly the messages from Florrie, or Ada, or Alice, would have to be circumspect and carefully worded, for they would certainly be read by the housekeeper before being passed on— in fact, many of them are addressed to the housekeeper's attention—but it is impressive how much they manage to convey without the writer running the risk of being shown the door. What is also impressive is how well those young servants could write, in spite of an education that came to an end in their early teens; indeed, the fact that the postcard was a speedy and "instant" form of communication gives the messages an unstudied immediacy and refreshing spontaneity.

Somewhere around the summer of 1907, fifteen-year-old Dora Lee took her courage in her hands, and used one of those belowstairs contacts to get herself a position in London, at 6 Queen's Gate Place, the home of a wealthy elderly widow, Mrs. Lewin.

It is unclear if she secured the position before she left, but there is a postcard dated July 7, 1907, addressed to Dora in the care of a Mrs. Fudge in Dorchester—Peggy Fudge was one of her postcard friends—that asks her to "please call at Mrs. Rulls" and contains a word that could be "hiring." Most of the message is illegible. Whatever the reality, it looks as if Dora set out on her journey about as unprepared as Dick Whittington, travelling-bag in hand, to see for herself if the streets of London were paved with gold.

Even in the palmy days of the Edwardian era, there was a

problem training and then keeping good servants; housekeepers and employers shamelessly wooed promising candidates
from rival owners. Fifteen-year-old Dora showed her talents
early, for her departure was quite sudden, taking even her
friends by surprise and leaving Mrs. Clarke without a scullery
maid. "A," possibly Alice, writes from Charminster on
September 27, 1907:

> Dear Dora: Sorry to hear that you feel so lonely. You will soon
> know plenty of people there. How do you like your new job,
> just getting used to it ... Poor C., because you're gone, is still
> looking for a girl.

And in November of the same year Lila writes:

> Dear Dora: Thanks for P.C. Sorry I have not written before.
> Surprised to hear you are in London ... I am still at Mr. Greens.
> I can hardly realise that shy little Dora Lee is actually staying
> in smokey LONDON. Love from Lil. I will write a letter soon.
> XXXXX

In spite of her courage, shy little Dora Lee was all alone
and homesick that summer in the city, without her local
friends around her. Even her sister, "Beat," seems to have
been taken unawares, and mislaid, or not known, Dora's new
address. In an undated card that seems to have been either
hand-delivered, or posted in an envelope, she writes, "What
on earth has happened to you dear ... now my dear do please
buck up and let us know how you are as we all get so worried about you." By October Beatrice is writing, "... glad to
hear you like your place." In that short space of time, Dora
Lee had found her feet.

How did she do it? Did she, perhaps, go to London for a
summer holiday and simply stay there, or answer an adver-
tisement in the local paper? Was Mrs. Lewin a friend of the
Clarke family, who visited and lured away Mrs. Clarke's hard-
working and talented scullery maid? Most employers required

written testimonials of some kind, and a girl had to be given a "character" by a previous employer, so this part of Dora's story is a mystery.

What is not a mystery, however, is what motivated her. For the capital city in which she found herself that summer of 1907 had changed profoundly since 1890, as the century turned. When "shy little Dora Lee" arrived in London and made her way to 6 Queen's Gate Place, the social pattern of her employers' lives had been transformed by a remarkable Irish, French and Swiss triumvirate: Richard D'Oyly Carte, Auguste Escoffier and César Ritz.

CUISSES DE NYMPHES À L'AURORE
(Nymphs' Thighs at Dawn)

This dish was the culinary highlight of a party held by the Prince of Wales at the Savoy. It was not until after it was served that Escoffier identified the main ingredient, concealed within a coating of rosy-tinted sauce—frogs' legs—thus becoming known as the man who taught the English to eat frogs. As he himself said:

For various reasons I thought it best, in the past, to substitute the mythological name 'nymphs' for the more vulgar term 'frogs' on menus, and the former has been universally adopted, more particularly in reference to the following 'chaud-froid à l'aurore.'

The voluptuous connotations of the name will not have gone unappreciated by the members of the Marlborough House Set.

Poach the frogs' legs in an excellent white-wine *court-bouillon*. When cooled, trim them properly, dry them thoroughly in a piece of fine linen, and steep them, one after the other, in a *chaud-froid* sauce of fish with paprika, the tint of which should be golden. This done, arrange the treated legs on a layer of champagne jelly, which should have set beforehand on the bottom of a square, silver dish or crystal bowl.

Now lay some chervil *pluches* and tarragon leaves between the legs in imitation of water-grasses, and cover the whole with champagne jelly to counterfeit the effect of water.

Send the dish to the table, set in a block of ice, fashioned as fancy may suggest.

THREE

An Epidemic of Smartness

In London ... the political and social worlds were intimately linked.
Power was still in the hands of the great families and "political hostesses"
made and unmade ministries in the course of a weekend ... César Ritz
founded the first of his great hotels in London because, as he said,
"I realized that there were a great many people ready to spend huge
amounts for the best ..."
PHILIPPE JULIAN, *LA BELLE EPOQUE*

Certainly in European eyes, the British had always been considered poor cooks. In a country that produced some of the choicest basic ingredients in the world, something disastrous happened in that magic process involving the hot breath of the oven or the slow simmer of the hotplate. This phenomenon was shared by rich and poor alike.

At the beginning of the nineteenth century there was a brief flourishing of that most continental of art forms, *haute cuisine*, when Talleyrand's ex-chef, Antonin Carême, arrived in Britain to cook for an earlier Prince of Wales, "Prinny," in his extraordinary extravaganza, the Royal Pavilion in Brighton. He brought in an immense new *batterie de cuisine* of five hundred and fifty copper utensils, huge Doulton stoneware barrels, hotplates, hot closets. Having overhauled the kitchens, Carême set about overhauling British attitudes. Carême's *pieces montées*, elaborate set-pieces, had been done before by royal chefs, but Carême always used complementary flavours, *garni à la régence*, as it was called—sole with shrimp, sweetbreads with foie gras or truffles—rather than an indiscriminate hotchpotch of seafood, turkey or ham. Most extraordinary of all were his architectural constructs in pastry and cake, particularly of the Royal Pavilion. Appearance was as crucial as taste, and all dishes offered to guests were set out together in immense still-life displays—*service à la française*.

There were two major drawbacks to these still-life displays: the food got cold and you were only supposed to eat the dish closest to you. Thus, if your neighbouring dish was larks in individual patty-cases of oven-toasted bread lined with creamed chicken livers, and you really fancied stuffed partridges in aspic, you would be out of luck. Not surprisingly, therefore, *service à la française* was eventually replaced by *service à la russe*, in which dishes were served in sequence by footmen and servants. The Russian nobility were more concerned with hot food than appearances and were well supplied with servants on their feudal estates. The new method made the liveried footmen even more vital, since there was usually one behind each aristocratic chair.

Forty-course meals were set before the Prince Regent, with their choice of eight soups, eight fish dishes, followed by eight meat dishes, which were then followed by fifteen entrées—a final total of one hundred and sixteen dishes. The after-ball buffets featured elaborate constructions in the shape of cascades, fountains, pavilions and palaces. Clearly, simplicity was not the name of the game. It is only in the light of such excess that the credo of his culinary successor makes any sense.

Faîtes simple. "Keep it simple" was the lifelong motto of the blacksmith's son, whose childhood ambition was to be a sculptor. Auguste had not inherited the muscular build of his blacksmith father—who was also the village locksmith, toolmaker, schoolmaster and mayor of the Provençal village of Villeneuve-Loubet, where Escoffier was born in 1846—so his father placed him with his brother François, who ran the

Restaurant Français on the Quai Masséna in Nice. Auguste found himself an apprentice cook at the age of thirteen, the same age that Dora Lee found herself put out to service as a scullery maid.

In a kitchen of the period the work was particularly hard for someone who was small, and Escoffier had to wear specially built-up shoes so that he could reach the great iron stoves. It was a world of blood, sweat and grease, fourteen-hour days, hard physical labour, obscenities, fights and drunkenness, where the apprentice was a virtual slave for the three years of his apprenticeship. It was a life usually spent below ground in areas kept unventilated so the food should stay hot, while the cooks breathed in the foul air of the coke-ovens and the charcoal-burning stoves. A medical report at the turn of the century shows that there were more occupational diseases among cooks than among miners. The great Carême himself died at forty-nine.

It was during those apprenticeship years in Nice, when wealthy tourists from England, Russia and elsewhere in France began to take up residence from September until April, that Escoffier learned to cater to the international set who would become his clientele. From the Russian chef at *Le Français* he acquired the recipes and the skills that would assure him a faithful following of Russian clients throughout his career—and a preference for *service à la russe*. To perfect his knowledge of the *pâtissier*'s art he worked with one of the best *pâtissiers* in Nice, Monsieur Autheman, whose *pâtisserie* was almost next door to *Le Français*. When he acquired his professional certificate in 1863, he was made *chef de cuisine* of the Hotel Bellevue at the age of eighteen, responsible for the buying, cooking and administration of the kitchen with a brigade of kitchen staff numbering anywhere from twenty to a hundred men.

Escoffier may not have taken after his father physically—at the age of eighteen he was only just over five feet tall—but he had inherited the intelligence of the schoolmaster, the business acumen of the man who ran three of the most profitable businesses in a nineteenth-century French village, and the political and diplomatic savvy of the mayor. And from those early contacts with the rich and powerful he learned how to succeed in an uncivilized business: he became a gentleman. Impeccably dressed, courteous, soft-spoken, before he left his teens Escoffier created the persona that would give him success with those new denizens of the dining-room: the gentler sex.

"Gentler sex" is a bit of a misnomer for the first women in Escoffier's professional life, but fits the girl who gave him his initial breakthrough. He prepared a couple of simple dishes for a sick young girl staying at the hotel, who was turned off by the rich food provided in the dining-room: a chicken breast *chaud-froid*, and a chilled, perfectly poached pear, decorated with a violet he had picked himself. The invalid's father happened to be a Monsieur Bardoux who owned a fashionable restaurant in Paris: *Le Petit Moulin Rouge*. He offered the young chef a job as assistant *rôtisseur*, and in 1865 Escoffier found himself in Paris.

You can become a cook, said Brillat-Savarin, but you have to be born a *rôtisseur*. Standing before the huge spits loaded with poultry, game and roasts of every kind, Escoffier would have to regulate their speed, adjust the distance from the heat, baste, judge the different quality of the wood and relate it to the thickness and texture of the meat. It was hot, hard labour, but forty years later, in his own *Guide Culinaire*, Escoffier was still denouncing the oven-roasting of meat in favour of the natural heat of the open spit.

Two years later he moved from the heat of the spits to the cool of the larder. He was made *chef garde-manger*, in charge of the great storage cupboards that housed the raw ingredients from all the restaurant's suppliers and prepared them for cooking. By 1868, he was *chef saucier* of *Le Petit Moulin Rouge*.

Carême described sauces as the hallmark of classic French

grande cuisine, and the *sauciers* were the aristocrats of the kitchen. They made all the basic stocks; they were in charge of the *bain marie*, the hot water kept simmering around all the *veloutés* and *fumets*, the elements from which all sauces derived. They were also the artists and decorators, the ones who prepared the *garnitures* for all the dishes. Sauces would be one of the hallmarks of a dish by Escoffier, and many were named for the women who would make him famous: "My best dishes," he said, "were created for ladies."

Not that there were many "ladies" at *Le Petit Moulin Rouge* in the 1860s. Paris was just entering the heyday of the *grandes horizontales*, spectacular women as famous as any star in the theatre, as much a part of the social structure as the aristocracy or the civil service, as essential to many in the upper echelons of that social structure, *le gratin*, as their racehorses, their packs of hounds—or a good meal.

Just off the Champs-Elysées, *Le Petit Moulin Rouge* stood in its own grounds, with a discreet side entrance. The main dining-rooms were on the ground floor, and on the floor above were the *cabinets particuliers*, the private rooms where the cocottes and *demi-mondaines* entertained their lovers. The Prince of Wales was a regular, there was a large contingent of Russian princes, nobles and army officers, and there was even an artists' table.

The women who came to *Le Petit Moulin Rouge* were as outstandingly successful at what they did for a living as was Escoffier. He watched them order strawberries out of season at a price that made even their wealthy lovers blench, or command the creation of special dishes as an expression of their power over the men who paid the bill. For the luscious and ruthless Cora Pearl, born Emma Crouch in Ireland, but one of the most sucessful *demi-mondaines* of the early years of the *Belle Epoque*, Escoffier created *Noisettes d'Agneau Cora* and *Pigeonneaux Cocottes*. The implications of the latter will not have been lost on Cora, who was adept at the art of "pigeon-plucking." *Le Petit Moulin Rouge* may not have been a house of ill repute exactly, but it was while cooking for women of dubious virtue that Escoffier first saw the potential when women were accepted in public dining-rooms and restaurants.

When Napoleon III declared war on Prussia in April 1870, the French army elite did not lose sight of its priorities. A senior staff officer was sent post-haste to *Le Petit Moulin Rouge* and hired Escoffier, who had already done his military service. During siege conditions at Metz, in northern France, he built up a secret farmyard of chickens, rabbits, ducks and turkeys, and the General Staff enjoyed splendid meals for a while, until their chef had to resort to doing wonders with horsemeat, and making watered-down *sauce Béchamel* from goat's milk. "Horsemeat is delicious," he would say wryly later in life, "when one is in the right circumstances to appreciate it."

By October 1870 he was a prisoner of war in Mainz after the surrender of Metz to the Prussians, but was swiftly seconded by an equally discerning enemy elite to the *Kursaal* restaurant in the fashionable spa of Wiesbaden, which was just outside the city.

In 1871, when the peace treaty was signed, Escoffier was back in Paris, where he met the great Sarah Bernhardt, who became a lifelong friend—because, so Escoffier said, of a *timbale* of sweetbreads and fresh pasta, served with a purée of foie gras and decorated with truffles. Sarah loved the way Escoffier cooked scrambled eggs for her, although he would never tell her what the subtle flavour was—a clove of garlic whisked through the eggs on the tip of a fork and removed. Sarah couldn't abide garlic, so she said—too many close encounters on stage, perhaps, with garlic-laden leading men.

For Sarah, who loved strawberries, he created two desserts: *Soufflé Sarah Bernhardt* was a *mélange* of vanilla-flavoured custard baked with macaroons soaked in Curaçao, covered in strawberry purée and *crème Chantilly*, and served with whole

Curaçao-soaked strawberries; for *Fraises Sarah Bernhardt* Escoffier topped a pineapple mousse with a Curaçao mousse, surrounded by strawberries dipped in orange-flavoured liqueur and macaroons.

The gifted and the gorgeous, the famous and the infamous, the women of Escoffier's world flocked to *Le Petit Moulin Rouge* in the summer, and in the autumn they dined at his own restaurant on the rue d'Antibes in Cannes, *Le Faisan Doré*. For the Empress Eugénie there was *Riz à l'Impératrice*, and peaches with wild strawberries sprinkled with kirsch and maraschino, then covered with a *sabayon* made with champagne. For the Empress Elizabeth he alternated vanilla soufflé with pralined violets and macaroons enmeshed in a net of spun sugar.

He and his wife, Delphine Daffis, daughter of a Paris publisher, divided their time between the south of France and Paris, where Escoffier became director of Chevet's in the Palais Royal. Chevet's not only catered to embassies, palaces and government ministries, it laid on complete travelling shows: movable feasts were dispatched abroad to Germany or England complete with cutlery, tableware and waiters—an undertaking that took planning of military precision. In 1884, after leaving Chevet's, he opened a new casino restaurant in Boulogne-sur-Mer.

Meanwhile, in Monte Carlo, the general manager of the Grand Hotel was in a quandary, having lost his brilliant chef, Jean Giroix, to a rival, the Hotel de Paris. But only a few miles away was a superbly gifted young chef called Auguste Escoffier, creating a sensation among the food-writers and epicures who covered the opening of the new casino restaurant. César Ritz contacted Escoffier and offered him the post, which he accepted.

From his first major breakthrough as restaurant manager of the Grand Hotel in Nice at the age of twenty-three, César Ritz had been involved with a dizzying number of the *de luxe* hotels of the 1870s and 1880s: the Rigi-Kulm in Switzerland, the Grand Hotel in Locarno, the Hotel Victoria in San Remo, the Grand National Hotel in Lucerne, among others. His name was associated with hotels in Menton, Trouville, Cannes, Baden-Baden, Frankfurt-am-Mein, Salsomaggiore—anywhere in Europe favoured by the wealthy and the nobility. Driven by a superabundance of nervous energy, Ritz moved across the face of Europe with the single-minded speed and efficiency of one who had organized his life around an encyclopaedic knowledge of railway timetables, and a set of suitcases packed and labelled for virtually every possible destination.

Like Escoffier's, Ritz's father had been mayor of his village; like Escoffier, he had survived a war with style and backed his way into a career he had largely created for himself. When the powerhouse troubleshooter, creative consultant and visionary hired the chef of the casino at Boulogne-sur-Mer in October 1894, it was a match made in heaven. On the surface they had a great deal in common. They even looked somewhat alike, with their gentlemanly air, neatly trimmed whiskers and their understated and elegant dress. But the secret of their hugely successful eighteen-year partnership was the blend of two perfectionists with two distinct personalities: one a disciplined and highly organized individual, the other a demanding, driven dynamo, whose name has passed into the vernacular and become synonymous with everything in life that is—quite simply—of the very best.

Constructed in 1882 when Monaco was beginning its glamorous career as one of the great gambling resorts in the world, the Grand Hotel boasted two hundred and fifty rooms, hydraulic elevators and electric light. But the *pièce de résistance* was the restaurant, *Salle Mauresque*. Guests were greeted by a magnificent Ethiopian doorman in livery, and finished their meal with Turkish coffee served by a turbaned African in blue-and-gold robes.

Although it seems glaringly obvious today, at the time even a certain level of cleanliness in top-class hostelries was considered a novelty, as was the drawing power of a hotel with a superb restaurant. But Ritz gave the customer what he wanted before the customer knew it himself. Of course his international clientele would want electricity as soon as it was available, and telephones, plenty of cupboard space and private bathrooms—even if their own mansions had only one bathroom that could be permanently tied up by the visiting monarch, as was the case at Chatsworth.

Discretion was the order of the day, and to Ritz fell the unpleasant task of dealing with the body and the brouhaha when some unlucky gambler blew his brains out in his hotel bedroom. Only Ritz could have calmed the abandoned mistress of the playboy Duc d'Orléans when she started breaking furniture, or persuaded the Prince of Wales to take another suite when his particular favourite was occupied by an upstart American millionaire, who saw no reason to move for royalty.

By 1885 its reputation was such that the Prince of Wales came to stay at the Grand Hotel in February, followed in swift succession by a constellation of European princes, Grand Dukes and international stars. The first hotel in the new partnership was the Ritz Hotel in Paris, and it would set the tone for everything that followed.

Le tout Paris came to the opening, that rainy June day in 1898 on the Place Vendôme. In the kitchens Escoffier surprised the reporters who covered the event by his refusal to use modern technology to cook his great dishes. Still insisting on what he called natural heat, the only gas he used was the *feu éternel* under his copper marmite of beef stock, and the only pans he used were copper, iron and earthenware. Not an aluminum or enamel saucepan in sight. Those same reporters marvelled at the wine cellars, built so that the clattering of carriages and horses in the great square outside could not penetrate and disturb the expensive sleep of 4000 bottles of wine, or the 180,000 kept in the reserve cellar close by.

In London, the flamboyant Irish entrepreneur Richard D'Oyly Carte read about the Rothschilds, the Vanderbilts, and the Marlborough set arriving at the Paris Ritz in the Place Vendôme, and set about acquiring the services of the two men who had created it. He had just launched his own luxury hotel in London: the Savoy.

Richard D'Oyly Carte was a man after César Ritz's heart, the kind of showman who would build a whole new theatre to put on the operettas of the hit composer and librettist of the day: Sir Arthur Sullivan and W.S. Gilbert. By 1889 D'Oyly Carte had completed the Savoy Hotel between the Embankment and the Strand.

The Savoy Hotel was revolutionary in many ways: the first steel-framed building in London, the first to use concrete, it had its own generator for electricity and its own artesian well in the basement. D'Oyly Carte, like Ritz, believed in offering more than a bathroom for every hundred or more guests, prompting the builder of the seventy bathrooms to ask if the guests were amphibious.

D'Oyly Carte had seen elevators in top-class American hotels, and he used them at the Savoy. Panelled in Japanese red lacquer, these "ascending rooms" built by the American Elevator Company had a practical application besides the elimination of stair-climbing: D'Oyly Carte could charge as much for his upstairs rooms as for those on the first floor. As it said in his sales brochure: "Those [suites] nearest the sky are just as spacious and lofty as those on the ground floor." The penthouse suite was born with those "ascending rooms."

But all was not well in D'Oyly Carte's beautiful terracotta Renaissance palace, in spite of the William Morris wallpapers, the palm trees, the satsuma pottery and the scarlet-and-gold coffered ceiling in the restaurant. The senior management had no commercial experience, and running a restaurant was a very different matter from working in even the best private establishments. Public interest sagged—and so did the shares in the hotel. D'Oyly Carte was not a man for half measures; he fired all the managerial staff.

Some say it was Lillie Langtry who urged D'Oyly Carte to bring César Ritz to London—Lillie understood the vital importance of ambience, and she knew just how wonderfully that indirect lighting of the Paris Ritz flattered her titian hair and incandescent skin. When Ritz agreed to come, it was on condition he bring Escoffier along with him to organize the kitchens. Ritz knew that the key to success was the restaurant. The international set, like the army, now marched on its stomach from watering-place to seaside resort to capital city.

Auguste Escoffier and César Ritz arrived on a Victorian Sunday in April 1890 to find the kitchen and storerooms in a shambles, every pot and pan and supply destroyed, down to the last package of salt. The spurned employees had taken a final revenge. To add insult to injury, the shaken and justifiably insecure Savoy directors expected the master chef to cook them a sample meal, just to see if he passed muster—which, presumably, he did.

Escoffier was forty-four years old, he spoke not a word of English—and never would—and he had left one of the most glamorous capital cities and gorgeous coastlines in the world for a city of fog, rain and shuttered Sundays. No dining out on the Lord's Day, no music, no entertainment. Faced with the chaos in front of him, even the imperturbable Auguste must have wondered what he had done. In fact, he was on the verge of his greatest successes.

Ritz used his political and aristocratic contacts to get the law changed to allow restaurants to stay open on Sundays, and to extend the evening hours so that opera- and theatre-goers could entertain each other and the stars they had seen on stage. Sunday dinners at the Savoy became *the* thing, just like *les Dimanches* at the Paris Ritz—not only could you eat out on a Sunday, but you could enjoy your *filets de sole Véronique* to the sound of a Strauss waltz, conducted by the composer himself. By 1906, many of Escoffier's creations were legend, because the people for whom he created them were legends.

Through the stately homes and the country estates and humbler establishments like The Ferns, word spread of the man who had turned being merely a cook into being a monarch in his own realm. Young girls belowstairs read about the "professional beauties" and the divas and the playboy princes in the tabloids of the day, such as *Tit-Bits*, which had found a market eager for such stories since beginning in 1880. So, there stood fifteen-year-old Dora Lee, bag in hand, peering down the steps into the "area" below, plucking up courage to go down them and knock on the servants' entrance. There was one thing about being at the bottom of the heap, she must have reckoned: if she was going to be up to her elbows in dishwater, it might as well be in a scullery in smoky London. If she was going to be on her hands and knees scrubbing doorsteps, how much better to be doing it in Mayfair than Charminster.

The aristocratic area of London known as Mayfair was centred around Green Park and Piccadilly, close to St. James and Westminster. By the beginning of the twentieth century, members of the wealthy classes had begun to move westward towards Hyde Park, Kensington Gardens and Knightsbridge, and it was here that Mr. and Mrs. Lewin had taken up residence at 6 Queen's Gate Place. Mr. Lewin, who died in 1876, had been a barrister-at-law at Lincoln's Inn, and one of the conveyancing counsels to the Court of Chancery.

The "area," as it was called, was actually what saved many of London's servant quarters from being the windowless dungeons of the European servant class. Although the rooms were darker and the ceilings often lower than in the ground and upper floors, at least there was a chance to see the sky and the sun, when it broke through the rain and the fog—which it did more often since the passing of the Smoke Nuisance Act in 1853. The bell and the knocker on the door shone just as brightly as those on the master's and mistress's door, because they too could be seen from the road, and the little space in front of the entrance was scrubbed clean.

When Mrs. Lewin's housekeeper opened the door that day she was probably relieved at what she saw. Here was no under-fed waif who would have difficulty lugging buckets of coal or standing for hours on end, as was often the case with young servants coming from impoverished backgrounds. Young Dora was proud of her twenty-inch waist—she would still boast about it years later to her family, saying "took a lot of lacing, but twenty-inches it was"—but she was well-built, and of medium height for a woman of the period. The word "shy" on the postcard suggests that she had learned when to lower that direct gaze of hers to suit the situation, and she was well-spoken, with a sound, basic education.

As a child, Dora had been mostly in the care of her grand-mother. It would have come naturally to her to take to a much older woman, and among Dora's possessions is a little scrap of evidence that suggests she took to Mrs. Lewin, and that Mrs. Lewin—who was childless—took to her. To the end of her life Dora held on to a tiny notebook she made for her-self while she was at Queen's Gate Place. It consists of thir-teen pieces of paper cut to fit the cardboard cover, folded over, and hand-stitched in place. The largest is only three inches long and two and a half inches wide.

There are very few entries in this miniature notebook, as if the effort of maintaining a diary of any kind, while being a scullery maid, was just impossible. But what she did have time to write becomes all the more important, however trivial it may be. There are twelve dated entries, starting in February 1908 and ending on March 9, 1909. Three of the entries note a marriage and two note deaths, probably of fellow servants.

Two entries are about the removal of teeth, three in all. Someone at Queen's Gate Place was taking care of Dora, who was clearly suffering from terrible toothache when she came there.

And someone, almost certainly Mrs. Lewin, was taking care of her spiritual as well as her bodily needs. With the little notebook is an Anglican Confirmation Certificate, stating that Dorothea Mary Lee was confirmed by the Bishop of Kensington on July 1, 1907, at St. Paul's, Onslow Square. Being confirmed was a major undertaking at the time, involving learning the extensive catechism by heart and lengthy classes with the local clergyman. There is a sympathetic postcard from Lily:

> My dear Dora: You will I know by now think I have clean forgotten you but I have not. Many thanks for your PC that you sent. I hope this will find you quite well as it leaves me not at all bright with teeth ache and a nasty cold the weather down here is so changeable. I am longing to see your face. Dear the time will soon fly now. I expect you will be glad when your confirmation is over like I was. Good bye my dear, take care of yourself. From yr Loving and Everlasting Friend Lily.

It is most likely that Dora had been raised in the Nonconformist church—her parents were married in the Wesleyan Chapel—but she would have been expected to assume the religion of her employers. Even religion was not free of class connotations, as the Nonconformist churches were associated with the working classes and movements for social change that the establishment, not unnaturally, found threatening. Mrs. Lewin gave Dora a prayer-book to mark the occasion, "Prayers for Private Use," inscribed, "To Dora Lee, from Mrs. Lewin."

Dora, it seems, had arrived in a protective environment. In some respects London society had changed only little since the mid–nineteenth century, when the medical journal, *The Lancet*, estimated that one house in sixty in the city was a brothel, and one woman in sixteen was a prostitute. A servant could still be summarily dismissed and turned out the door into the street, and for a young girl far from home there were many dangers, not only from the predators in the streets outside, but from those under her employer's roof.

In addition to such mundane notations, there is an entirely different group of entries in the notebook. They are undated, but most likely were written in Dora's first months at Queen's Gate Place in 1907. When Dora went to her attic bed that night, in a room she undoubtedly shared with at least one other girl, she may have been very homesick, but she probably already knew she had landed on her feet. Those first five miniature pages are covered with the names of dishes, and are in French—sometimes correctly spelled, sometimes phonetically—with translations. It would seem that when Mrs. Lewin's housekeeper introduced the new scullery maid to the staff, among them was a French chef, or a French-trained chef.

The elaborate hierarchy of the servant class would have made it difficult for a fifteen-year-old scullery maid to approach such a godlike figure. Getting on in that Byzantine world meant knowing how to play the game, and smart little Dora would have known better than to have done so directly. So, while she scrubbed vegetables and floors, she kept her tiny notebook hidden in the pocket of her skirt with a scrap of pencil and, when no one was looking, scribbled down what she heard, or copied the names of dishes from the menus.

Some are correctly spelled: *omelette aux rognons*, for example, alongside which Dora has written the translation, "omelette with kidney." Or, *consommé paysanne*, which she describes briefly as "soup cheese." *Langue de bouef* [*sic*] is jotted down as "tongue bullocks." The list continues with *tarte aux pommes*, "tarte with apples"; *faisan à la broche*, "pheasant roast"; *côtelettes d'agneau grillés*, "cutlets lamb grilled." The reader is given a good idea of how Mrs. Lewin ate and entertained her guests: fine food with a continental touch and French names, but nothing too esoteric.

There are two other entries, and they are phonetic: "We madame—yes madame," and "Suker [Dora's approximation of the French *sucre*]—sugar." What is interesting about these two notes is that they suggest that Dora is not only following the chef around in the kitchen, but she is listening to his exchanges with Mrs. Lewin, or actually waiting at table. Two further entries in the notebook suggest that the Queen's Gate Place scullery maid has become invaluable to Mrs. Lewin.

About six months after her arrival, Dora notes: "Wages rose 6 Queen's Gate Place—Dec 2nd 1908—£14." The other entry reads: "New black dress Dec 12th 1908. 19/6." For a girl who had earned less than £14 that year, it is a colossal sum of money, and one of the postcards makes it clear that it did not come from Dora's regular wages, but was a special gratuity for services rendered. On December 24 "Louie" writes to Dora:

Dear Dora: Just to wish you the same old thing and a merry Xmas. Haven't had time to write before. What are you going to do with that twenty bob? Kindly remember the poor, we are up to our eyes in work, got them all at home so you can guess. F.S. sends his love and heaps from me. Louie. XXX

"Bob" is, of course, slang for a shilling, and Dora had gone out and blown all but sixpence of her windfall on a beautiful new black dress. It is highly unlikely such a large sum of money came out of the housekeeper's pocket, however well-disposed she was to Dora. One possibility is the chef, but the most likely source is a grateful Mrs. Lewin. A strong, intelligent and motivated young girl could become absolutely invaluable belowstairs, but it is certainly surprising that it was the lowly scullery maid who was recognized in such a munificent way.

Among the possessions Dora kept all her life is a skirt that looks as if it were part of two original pieces—many "dresses" of the period were constructed as separate skirts and shirt-waists. The material is a very fine-quality black silk chiffon, draped, and hand-stitched into the waist is a label from Swan and Edgar, a large and prestigious store on Regent Street West in London that served "the quality." The label bears the lion and unicorn crest of an emporium patronized by royalty, with the crown on top and the royal motto, "God and my right." The waist has been extended later on to accommodate a more mature Dora, but the original is small, to fit that twenty-inch waist of which she was so proud.

Perhaps before Christmas, when the Mayfair set returned from the beaches of Biarritz and the gambling casinos of Nice and Monte Carlo, Mrs. Lewin had arranged a big dinner-party at 6 Queen's Gate Place. The French chef had had lengthy consultations on the menu, and all the staff were put on alert, polishing silver and every inch of the elaborately decorated and cumbrous furniture that had replaced the elegant lines of Regency and Georgian decor in most homes. At some point in the preparations, a crisis arose. Perhaps one of the parlour-maids gave in her notice, or maybe it was the kitchen maid, who was one step up in the pecking order from Dora.

From the amount of money that fifteen-year-old scullery maid was given, the chances are the crisis was major, so it is possible there was a problem involving the chef. Dora later spoke of the hot tempers of French chefs. They threw things, she said, and you had to be quick on your feet. "Good thing I didn't understand what they were saying," she would add. Whether he walked out, or whether he needed Dora as an assistant—which is the most likely scenario—it is likely that

Dora's role was as a cook, rather than as an extra parlour-maid to wait at table.

Even that would have been a considerable jump for a scullery maid, but one thing is quite clear about Dora. She had a gift. Escoffier's greatness lay not only in his invention of new dishes and new techniques, but in his ability to know when to add an extra touch of salt, or a *soupçon* more meat glaze. It was said by an admirer he could cook a thistle and it would be palatable. Years later, Dora's daughter-in-law, Beth Vince, would say that Dora could make boiled water taste good. It is possible the chef had had an opportunity to see that the scullery maid could cook, and—even if only out of self-interest —had helped her to develop her talent.

The postcards contain another clue as to Dora's new status at Queen's Gate Place. Around September 1907 a couple of them, from the Charminster area, are addressed to "Mrs." Lee, and do not come care of Mrs. Lewin. "Mrs." was the courtesy title given at the period to cooks and housekeepers, whether they were married or not. It would seem that young Dora had made a meteoric rise in the servant hierarchy, but

it is more likely that her new success in the culinary field gave her bragging rights to the title, certainly as far as her family and her friends back in Dorset were concerned. There is a card from Lily addressed to 6 Queen's Gate Place that suggests Dora had indeed been showing off, just a little:

My dear Dora: Very many thanks for your welcome letter. I was so delighted to hear from you my Dear. Hope this will find you quite well as it leaves me jolly at present. I have often thought and talked about you since you have been

back. You must please excuse PC instead of a letter. I will write
a letter next time. Hope you will send a view of your house,
just to let me see what sort of a Palace you live in.

The postmark on the card is obliterated, but clearly Dora
has been back home on holiday, talking about Mrs. Lewin's
"palace." And on October 14, 1907, "A" writes that she "should
like to be up in the city very much. I suppose you find life
different to Charminster yet I expect you are quite tired of it
by now."

For the little girl who was turned out at thirteen to be a
skivvy, what a thrill it must have been to show them just how
far and how fast she had risen—even if she *was* stretching the
truth a little! The address also suggests that Dora's relationship with Mrs. Lewin was such that the old lady would not
have reprimanded her for such *lèse-majesté*.

So, on December 2, 1908, a grateful and relieved Mrs.
Lewin gave her scullery maid twenty bob, and on December
12, Dora walked into Swan and Edgar's on Regent Street West
and bought herself a splendid dress. It is a touching and
delightful picture: fifteen-year-old Dorothea Mary Lee in her
best everyday dress and hat, walking past the carriages drawn
up outside, many of them with heraldic crests on their doors.
Along with the carriages by now would have been an occa-
sional motorcar—Mr. Victor Cavendish had seen a nice
Mercedes at the Motor Show at Olympia in 1905, and not
long after had his own Mercedes and a Rolls-Royce. Brush-
ing past the ladies with their ladies' maids, Dora made her way
to the dress salon, there to select her own gown.

One can imagine the looks she would have encountered
from the shop assistants and the staff, who would have unerr-
ingly placed her as a servant—and one can guess how those
looks would have been returned by those bold, unafraid eyes.
Her money was as good as anybody's and, when she pulled
out those twenty shillings, she must have felt a thrill at the

shop assistant's undoubted surprise at this young servant girl's unexpected wealth.

For all her nerve, it doesn't look as if Dora stayed to try on her lovely dress. Maybe she did not have enough money left over to pay Swan and Edgar's prices for alterations, which would certainly have been more than sixpence. There is a postcard dated December 19, 1908, that reads: "Dear Dora: I received your letter this morning, am glad your dress goes alright. The skirt does up at the 'back.' Love to all from Ethel."

Dora had carried her dress back to Queen's Gate Place in triumph, tried it on and found it needed some alterations. So she took it to her friend Ethel who worked in Streatham, which is just south of the Greater London area.

The new black dress was a sound investment. It would be perfect for the occasions when Dora had to look particularly well-turned-out in her professional capacity, and it was grand enough for her to wear at the servants' balls and celebrations that would become part of her downstairs life. There would be even larger gratuities from even more exalted figures in her future, but this marked her first major breakthrough. That black skirt, kept through every move in her life, long after the top had worn out and the skirt itself was a shadow of its former glory, would remain the symbol of her early success for Dora Lee.

If the brief entries in the tiny notebook mark significant events in those first London years, then the entries on January 19 and January 20, 1909, say something about the importance of Mrs. Lewin in Dora's life. The first reads: "Mrs. Lewin died 19th Jan. 1909, buried 23rd, age 81 years." The second is even briefer: "Came to Portman Square 20 Jan. 1909."

As soon as the woman who had befriended her needed her no more, Dora was on the move again, and so swift is her departure, it is clear that the little scullery maid left nothing to chance. Dora had learned the hard way, at the age of thirteen, never to trust her security and happiness to others. From now on, she would take control of her own destiny, just as much as it was in her power to do so. She made her plans during Mrs. Lewin's final illness and stayed until the day of her benefactor's death, going back to attend the funeral. As she stood in a London cemetery on a cold, grey, January day, she must have wept for the kindly Mrs. Lewin, and for herself, just a little. She was now truly on her own, little Dora Lee in smoky London, without even a surrogate mother to watch over her.

Among the belongings that Dora kept on her travels is a small leather-bound almanac that is something of a puzzle. It was printed by R. and A. Suttaby of Stationer's Court, London, and it contains a selection of poems by Tennyson and others at the front, some fine-quality coloured illustrations of various British beauty spots, spaces for account records and a daybook or diary section. It is called "Marshall's Elegant Pocket Souvenir for 1856." With its fine leather binding and snap closure, the superior quality of the paper and printing, it is indeed the kind of notebook owned by a lady.

The puzzle, of course, is the date, for 1856 is well before even Dora's mother and father were born. But it is likely that this was a special gift from Mrs. Lewin to the little scullery maid who had worked so hard for her in her final days—something that had been a special gift to the old woman, and which she had never brought herself to use. Dora herself did not start making entries in her smart notebook until a few years later, as if she had treasured this elegant *memento mori* for a while before daring to sully its elegant pages.

In March 1908, while Dora was with Mrs. Lewin at 6 Queen's Gate Place, "Harty-Tarty" died in Cannes, after a lengthy struggle with heart disease, and a succinct, philosophical death speech: "Well, the game's over and I'm not sorry." So the Cavendishes became the Devonshires and Evelyn became a duchess, which was, of course, how it was supposed to happen. This is what the Abercorns and the Lansdownes and the Buccleuchs had planned, all those years ago, when Evie came home from Simla. And though both husband and wife knew this was their destiny, it is not surprising that the new duke regretted the end of his Commons parliamentary career.

From 1891, Victor Cavendish had held his family's seat in West Derbyshire as a Liberal Unionist member of parliament in the House of Commons, and it was as much a pleasure to him as it was an inherited duty and responsibility. In 1903 he was appointed financial secretary to the Treasury, which required spending large periods of time in London. From now on, the political tone of the duke's diaries changes.

On Tuesday, May 5, 1908, the new duke recorded returning his uncle's Order of the Garter to the king and taking his seat in the place he called "that Mausoleum": the House of Lords. Sometimes he does not even bother to say what happened while he was there, thus creating some of the more amusing transitions in his accounts of the day. Not one for hyperbole as a diarist, Victor always moves effortlessly from the momentous to the trivial, as in: "Got my hair and corns cut. House of Lords."

The writer of Uncle Cav's obituary in *The Onlooker* declared, "In these democratic days when restlessness and instability are not confined to one class of the community, it is as well, perhaps, that British society is leavened by the sobering influence of a few great historic houses like that of the Cavendishes as a safeguard against the prevailing epidemic of smartness."

Evelyn was not attracted to that prevailing epidemic; the fast life of Duchess Louise and the Eighth Duke, whom the family called "Uncle Cav," held no charms for her. She had no desire to winter on the Nile, or to dine in Monte Carlo with "La Favorita," Alice Keppel, one of Edward's favourite ladies, or to entertain the dubious likes of Lillie Langtry. From the time she married Victor Cavendish, Evelyn had carved out for herself a very different role from that of the eccentric and raffish Louise.

What is surprising is that Evie appears to have resisted the change into duchess in the symbolic and ceremonial sense of the role. On the death of the dowager duchess two years after her husband, Evie was expected to take on the post of Mistress of the Robes to Queen Mary. It was considered a foregone conclusion; her aunt Tiny Buccleuch had previously been Mistress of the Robes, and her mother was a Woman of the Bedchamber. Loftier than being a mere lady-in-waiting or Lady of the Bedchamber, it was a ceremonial position that carried great cachet, and was the female equivalent of the Lord Chamberlain. Usually there were two Ladies of the Bedchamber and four ladies-in-waiting, who attended the queen on her more important public functions, but were not expected to reside in the palace. As an official member of the queen's entourage, Evelyn would be expected to be present at all court ceremonies, "the Sovereigns' Courts," such as the numerous presentations at court of the season's debutantes.

"Coming out" was a lengthy ritualistic affair, in which young, unmarried girls of the upper classes made their official entrée into society, and it played a crucial role in the marriage market. As many as eight hundred girls might be presented to the king and queen in one evening, and the honour was extended to girls from the dominions, who might not have titles, but whose families were sufficiently elevated by reason of birth, business or political connections. Evelyn Fitzmaurice herself had "come out" in 1890, and found a husband.

Evie Devonshire, however, resisted. To persuade her, they brought out the heavy artillery in the shape of Earl Carrington, whose splendid title was "Joint Hereditary Lord Great Chamberlain," in which capacity he had been appointed for the reign of George V. Victor's diary reads: "Carrington ... [has]

been to see Evie & strongly urged her to take the Mistress of the Robes. V. tiresome but cannot be helped."

So Evie capitulated. The old life at Holker Hall was over. Now there would be even less time with her growing family— less time to learn to roller-skate with them in the gardens of Devonshire House, less time for the Christmas play, less time for the new baby she was expecting. While she accompanied Queen Mary to the courts of Europe to witness the marriage of the kaiser's daughter, it was Victor who played charades and hide-and-seek with the children, Victor who had to make up new categories for the favourite family card game of Quartettes —a version of Happy Families using the names of kings, queens, generals and so on. The German governess caused problems by choosing German military commanders nobody had ever heard of.

It was Victor who had to deal with the crisis when Maria the nursemaid had hysterics, or when one of the parlour-maids ran away. It was Victor who had to cope when scarlet fever broke out at Eddy's school, and his delighted son and heir returned home with no clothes and only a jar of Devonshire clotted cream in his bag. It was Victor who had to decide what to do when a footman showed Eddy and his cousin Francis how to make gunpowder: he decided not to worry. Whether it was explosives or economics, Victor's refusal to worry about any such matters would be a source of anxiety for Evie in the years to come.

The first task for the Ninth Duke and Duchess was to pay the death duties on Uncle Cav's estate. In 1894, the Liberal Chancellor of the Exchequer, Sir William Harcourt, had introduced the measure that was seen by the great landowners as a body blow against their privileged position: a tax on all estates worth over £5000, rising to 8 per cent of an inheritance over £10,000. At the time the Conservatives, including Uncle Cav, had vociferously opposed it, but ensuing Tory governments had failed to repeal the law. In a 1910 entry in his diary the Duke noted, "Afraid the Inland Revenue are going to be very exacting and slow over the death duties." Instead of borrowing or paying off the amount gradually, the new duke's solution was both draconian and practical.

First, Victor sold off one of the ducal homes, Chiswick House. It was virtually unused and in urgent need of renovation, and the new owners, the local council, promptly turned it into what contemporary accounts describe as a lunatic asylum. Victor's next move was to send off twenty-five Caxtons and a number of Shakespeare folios and quartos to Sothebys, who disposed of them to the Huntingdon Library in California for £750,000. The actual transaction was far more prolonged than his swift decision would suggest, for it is only in 1913 that he notes in his diary, "... Barlow got a firm offer on the Caxtons and the Plays. Seems quite satisfactory, but of course I do not know the value. Wired to accept." Clearly, he was hoping to keep the sale of his belongings private, for he notes with irritation in 1914 that word had got around about the sale of those precious books to America. "We suppose it was given away at the New York Custom House," he writes.

Finances were not the only problem at Chatsworth, which was still, literally, in the Dark Ages. There was no electricity and, more seriously, no mains drainage. While these were installed, the Cavendish family spent a candle- and oil-lamp-lit autumn and winter of 1908 in Hardwick Hall, which is seventeen miles from Chatsworth. One of the most magnificent Elizabethan mansions in England of its time, it was built by the same formidable powerhouse of a woman who created Chatsworth: Bess, Countess of Shrewsbury. Married four times to increasingly rich and powerful men, Bess of Hardwick created the three great dukedoms of the Cavendish family by her second marriage to Sir William Cavendish, the only marriage to produce children. She survived the hazards of court intrigue and bitter family disputes to die at Hardwick at the age of eighty-one, still in full possession of her faculties. Dominating the hill on which it stands, the great house with its huge windows is crowned by Bess's initials, E.S., standing taller than a man above the four storeys on each side of the central façade, proclaiming her power, wealth and unshakeable belief in herself.

Living in the colonies tended to make Britons leery about the water supply, but there is little doubt that Evelyn's future obsession about drains—a depressing subject her granddaughter-in-law, the present duchess, says it was difficult to get her off once she was started—dates from this time. And no wonder, for Evelyn was expecting her seventh child. She had already given birth to six children: two sons—Edward and Charles—and four daughters—Maud, Blanche, Dorothy and Rachel. Evelyn celebrated her thirty-ninth birthday on August 27, and her labour started soon after. On August 30 her last child, Anne, was born just before nine in the morning. Whatever the problems may have been, it must have been the cause of immense satisfaction to the Ninth Duchess when she gave birth to her daughter Anne at Chatsworth—the first ducal offspring born in the great house since Georgiana's daughter in the eighteenth century.

POULARDE DEVONSHIRE

Escoffier made a distinction between dishes named *à la*, or "in the manner of," and dishes directly attributed—as in this case, to "Harty-Tarty." The latter were creations dedicated to the person named.

Bone the breast of a choice pullet, season it, and stuff it with chicken forcemeat, blended with cream and half its weight in finely minced sausage meat.

In the middle of the bird set a salted and cooked calf's tongue, with the thin end towards the pullet's tail. Sew up the breast with string, allowing for the swelling of the stuffing while cooking. Truss, cover with larding bacon, then poach until done.

The breast is sliced prior to serving, so that there is a combination of the three ingredients: chicken, stuffing and tongue. It is then replaced between the legs and the wings and served as if whole. Coat with *sauce Allemande*, finely chopped tongue, and a border of *timbales* made from a purée of fresh peas, each nestled in the base of an artichoke.

Sauce Allemande is one of the classic compound white sauces—that is, a specific range of ingredients added to the basic white *velouté*. It consists of egg yolks mixed with a light veal or chicken stock, which is then whisked into the *velouté* and boiled down over low heat until it coats the spoon. Butter is added prior to straining the sauce through cheesecloth, and it can be kept in a *bain-marie* (double boiler) until needed, with the surface buttered to prevent a skin forming. Sometimes a pinch of nutmeg or a squeeze of lemon is added.

PART TWO

Kitchen Maid

Tut Tut, Dora

Bigger fleas have little fleas upon their backs to bite 'em,
Little fleas have lesser fleas, and so ad infinitum.
AFTER JONATHAN SWIFT, ON POETRY, 1733

The postcard trail that follows Dora to 27 Portman Square —an area to the north of Mayfair and Hyde Park—also leads in the same year to Red Rice House in Andover, Hampshire—a county that lies between Dorset and Surrey in the south of England. It is a clear indication that Dora was hired as a kitchen maid, since scullery maids rarely made the transition between the town and country properties of the wealthy, like many of the other servants. The postcards move, like Dora, between Portman Square and Red Rice House, Andover, during 1909 because they are the town and country houses of Ernest Haliburton Cunard, and Dora is their new kitchen maid.

By the time Dora joins the household, Ernest Cunard has been married only six years to an American widow, Florence, but he and his wife have established themselves as active members of the social scene. Ernest Cunard was well-connected in the city, serving as director of the Cunard Steam Ship Company, the Great Western Railway Company, the Peninsula and Oriental Steam Navigation Company, the London County and Westminster Bank, the Royal Exchange Assurance Corporation, and the British India Steam Company.

The Cunards' new kitchen maid is someone of value

downstairs, because she has been hired with the direct involvement of their French chef. Among the memorabilia in Dora's hatbox is a wire sent post-haste from Red Rice House, Andover, in January 1909 and headed, "Telegrams, Red Rice, Anna Valley." It reads, "Dear Dora, Your character is quite satisfactory and shall expect you on Saturday. Yours sincerely." The signature appears to be "M. Leronicu," (the "M." in this case possibly standing for "Monsieur") but is not entirely clear. It is highly unlikely that the housekeeper would have been of a nationality other than British. The only "foreigners" in the household would have been the chef or the lady's maid, who might have been French—and certainly the lady's maid would not have been involved with the hiring of the kitchen maid.

For the kitchen maid to be directly appointed by the Cunards' French chef suggests that Dora's culinary skills are already becoming known, either because of the chef with whom she had worked at Queen's Gate Place, or by that house's reputation for fine cuisine. Perhaps she had an interview at Portman Square and impressed Monsieur Leronicu with her knowledge of French nomenclature—with smart Dora throwing in the odd "Oui, monsieur." And perhaps she got that interview because Mrs. Lewin knew the Cunards, and wanted her little protégée to be assured of a good "place" when she was gone. It would explain the speed of Dora's move.

With her more peripatetic lifestyle, from now on the postcard network becomes even more vital to Dora and her friends. Most of the houses in which Dora worked would by now have had telephones, but servants would certainly not have had access to them for personal calls. About the only person who would have picked up a telephone when it rang would have been the butler, and possibly the housekeeper. But, such was the efficiency of the British postal system at the time, that this was not much of a handicap. For the price of the card and a halfpenny stamp, the girls in London could arrange to pop on the omnibus or the tuppenny tube, which had opened in 1902, and see each other. The postmark is legible on most of the cards in Dora's collection, and there is clear evidence of rendezvous made and changed within the course of a twelve-hour day. One of the cards, posted at one p.m., reads:

> Dear Dora: don't come to see me tonight as I can't enjoy your visit as I hear we have a lunch and dinner party. I do get wild however, any other night you can spare very soon, am looking forward to having a good old talk.

The main problem for the correspondents would have been privacy and, besides writing letters, they overcame this in a number of ways. An entry in Dora's handmade notebook says, "Will first letter 9th March 1909." Someone called Will, purporting to be her nephew and addressing her as "Auntie," mailed Dora a card from Henley-on-Thames at 12:15 a.m. on June 29, 1908. It reads: "Dear Auntie. Will come over to see you tomorrow night. Fondest love, Will."

There is no family record of a nephew called Will, nor is it likely that Dora would have taken the trouble to jot down the arrival of a first letter from a relative, however special, in that precious notebook. Even less likely is the idea of a small boy sneaking out to post a letter to his favourite aunt in the middle of the night! Eighteen-year-old Dora had an admirer, and "followers" were grounds for instant dismissal for even the most talented of kitchen maids.

An obvious method of concealment was to use a kind of "shorthand" between themselves about events and opinions that the two correspondents alone would understand, and the cards are full of such subterfuge. Lily Riglar was brilliant at packing a pile of gossipy information into a small space; here she is, writing from Charminster to sixteen-year-old Dora at Queen's Gate Place:

> Dearest Dora: thanks for your PC, so glad to hear you arrived safe and sound, but do miss your company so. B and me have laughed a good many times over the Ducks bones and mutton wings and what about no 1 London … what about last Sunday. Is this like the Dell in Hyde Park, it is very much like Wanchard Lane that we went through that Friday together, I did enjoy myself. Well now I must say goodbye my dear. With fondest love from your everloving Friend Lily. XXXXX

The Dell in Hyde Park is the picture on the card, and the reference to food and "no 1 London" may well have been a joke they shared at the expense of Dora's employer. "B" is probably Dora's sister, Beatrice.

On February 25, 1908, Lily writes one of her chatty missives from Charminster, in which everything is perfectly clear except for a small portion of one sentence:

> Dearest Dora: Many thanks for your letter, it really cheered me up to hear how you was getting on. I thought I would just send a card to let you know I was still about. I cannot find time to write a letter till we have moved. They are having such a lot done to the house that it will take a fortnight before we shall be in. I think I shall really like it better than this one. I will write you a long letter then and tell you how I like it. I hope this will find you well as I am at present. Don't you say a word about flirting Dora I will tell you [end of sentence illegible]. With love from your dearest friend Lily Riglar.

How Dora managed to read Lily's concealed message is not clear, but it would appear they had devised some way of passing information. While at 6 Queen's Gate Place Dora herself put together an arcane message, apparently to her fictitious nephew. Then she seems to have got cold feet, never mailed it, but kept it in her collection. It reads:

> Dear: Well how are you getting on all this long time. It is ages since I saw you. I hear you wear a khaki coat now. I hope you will get fatter now, not be thin as the last photo I saw of you. From Dora. You liked to be called uncle.

There are a couple of other cards from the period that mention "Territorial," and it looks as if Dora's current beau in a khaki coat is a man in uniform. On one card, with the printed caption, "My Time Is Fully Occupied at Present," the message reads: "How's this for a flirt. I never thought it of you. Much love, Territorial."

In fact, most of the cryptic messages are to do with that forbidden subject, romance:

> Dear D. Many thanks for the P.C. What about that long letter of your (naughty naughty) How are things progressing (alright I hope) How would tea at the Pap suit? Not bad eh. Yours, Sardine.

One card is addressed jokingly to M.H. Hath(?) c/o the Borough Asylum in Canterbury, Kent, from L.P., and is completely in code—even if it is quite easy to break: "Noa Leta aywa nceoa gainas mau ollyja ladga" (On the way once again am jolly glad).

Perhaps the most puzzling is a postcard sent to Dora during the First World War when she was twenty-four years old,

ONLY A FADED ROSE (2).

Only a faded rose, only a few brown leaves,
Only a tear that, falling, tells of a heart that grieves.
Only a faded rose, only two lives apart,
Only a dream of what might have been, only a broken heart.

particularly when the message is taken in conjunction with the picture on the card. The unsigned message is written perfectly clearly, but makes no sense at all, apart from the final salutation: "I suppose you do any of this sort of work as they are doind [*sic*] on the other side that up you in the mine years ago so good bye XX." Possibly the jilted lover was not a great communicator, but the standard of penmanship suggests someone who could have written quite sensibly, if he had wanted.

Quite early on in Dora's downstairs life in London, the cards bear witness to her popularity with the opposite sex. There was the pseudonephew, Will, and at Red Rice House there was a smitten servant, John, who seems to have handed over his card from Louie to seventeen-year-old Dora for her collection.

DO YOU REALLY LOVE ME? Tut Tut Dora.

The picture on the card is a comic photograph of a man in top hat and tails sitting on a bench under a tree with another man, dressed as a woman, and the caption reads, "Do you really love me?" Alongside the words someone has hand-written, "Tut Tut Dora." The message is brief: "Well John have you had the answer. I am landed in dear old Norfolk. Louie."

But for a young, attractive female servant, the dangers did not only lie in being caught in a relationship with another servant; they lay with unscrupulous and unprincipled male

84

members of that upstairs world. The time might have passed when a master could treat a pretty maidservant as his to do what he liked with, but an innocent and inexperienced young girl could still be led astray. Three years before Dora came to Portman Square, there was a scandal involving another branch of the Cunard family—Sir Bache Cunard, third baronet and a cousin of Dora's employer —and a guest at his London home.

Edward Horner, the son and heir of Sir John Horner of Mells and the despair of his parents for his gambling and drunken debaucheries, lured his host's pretty parlour-maid to an upstairs room after a luncheon party and seduced her. "Seduced" is the verb used in most accounts, but since Horner was six foot four and of a powerful muscular build, the more accurate word is probably "raped." The fate of the young parlour-maid is not known, but the reaction of fourteen-year-old Diana Manners, daughter of the Duke of Rutland, is on record. She thought it was "eighteenth century and *droit de seigneur* and rather nice." However ignorant and protected from reality that fourteen-year-old might have been, the blind unfeelingness of her observation is quite stunning.

Dora, with her bold eyes and lush figure so admired by Edwardians could have been a prime target, but she was less at risk because of the path she had chosen. Most of her contacts with the upstairs world would have been through the cook or housekeeper, and when she was called upon to discuss a menu or arrangements for the shooting-party picnics, she would have met with the lady of the house. However, she would have had to be discreet about any liaisons.

In spite of the to-ing and fro-ing between bedrooms during the average country-house weekend—about which the servants would have known a great deal—the upper classes felt they had a finer grasp of morality than their servants could ever hope to achieve. That double standard was unashamedly enforced. When Lord Curzon discovered that one of his housemaids had spent the night with one of his footmen—presumably he had been informed by the house-keeper or butler—he instantly dismissed her: "I put the little slut out into the street at a moment's notice," he wrote to his wife. Later in life, Curzon's mistress would be Elinor Glyn, the successful author of popular romances that were considered scandalous in their day. But the streets of London were full of girls like Curzon's housemaid.

Mrs. Beeton, in her *Book of Household Management*, advised the lady of the house to keep a watchful eye on the acquaintances and habits of her servants, adding, "The moral responsibility for evil rests largely on the employer ...," thus suggesting that those poor benighted souls belowstairs had no innate sense of good and evil. When Dora chose to stay belowstairs and not to climb the servant ladder by becoming a parlour-maid, or that most privileged of servants, a lady's maid, she freed herself to some extent from the eagle eye of the lady of the house.

Paradoxically, of course, servants were meant to be invisible. For many upstairs servants, that simply meant that their employers were so unaware of their presence that conversations and even scandals went on in their presence as if they were inanimate objects. Indeed in some households, their presence, however necessary, was intolerable, and the maids had to get all the work done early in the morning, so that the family and their guests would not have to see them. During the Tenth Duke of Bedford's time at Woburn Abbey, the family seat, a sighting by the duke of a maid meant instant dismissal. More palatable was the solution arrived at by the Ninth Duke of Portland in the mid–nineteenth century, during the winter months: if he came across a housemaid at Welbeck Abbey, he ordered her to go outside out of his way, and skate on the rink in the grounds. Such a solution must have played havoc with the harried housekeeper's timetable.

Certainly Dora would have had to be wary of the house-keeper, but from the speed of Dora's climb it is clear that she was very good at what she did, and as long as she was discreet, she would have been left alone.

In choosing not to go upstairs Dora also held on to her own identity; she was known as Miss, or even Mrs., Lee, and not called the name of her employer, as lady's maids generally were. Not for Dora the hours spent packing and unpacking those huge trunks called "Noah's Arks," five or six times a day for the interminable changes of dress required of the country-house weekend, the hour-long ironing of an outfit that would be worn for an hour or two—and then changed once more. Dora was doing something far more creative with her life, and there is no doubt that is why she stayed in the kitchen; she loved to cook and she was very good at it. At Red Rice House, the shooting parties held for a distinguished roll-call of guests would give Dora a new and important area of expertise.

A not entirely facetious reason given for the popularity of the shooting party during the Edwardian era was that it had all the appearance and excitement of an outdoor sporting activity, without requiring even the amount of athleticism demanded of the fox-hunter—thus perfectly suiting a corpulent monarch. There is no doubt that shooting down vast numbers of birds specially nurtured for the purpose satisfied the blood-lust of a race who pursued that fever—whether it was slaughtering lions and tigers, or pigsticking—right across the rose-coloured colonial face of the nineteenth-century globe.

But the shooting party was more than mere slaughter. It was a leisure-time activity that had taken on the significance of ritual, with a language of its own, and customs all its own— more than customs, for they were incorporated into the laws of the land. In October and November, when everyone was back from Biarritz and Monte Carlo, the great houses organized their shooting parties—and they took a great deal of organization by a considerable number of inside and outside staff. In many of the great houses there were at least three or four servants for every family member, and for the shooting parties, guests travelled with an army of servants, thus doubling or tripling the numbers in the servants' hall.

Although it was considered helpful to have some expert guns along for the shooting party, the guests of honour were usually people whose favours or attention the host was hoping to attract, and it had become essential to provide not only good game, but good food. A diplomat or a member of a European royal family could be persuaded to put up with a dearth of bathrooms and a chilly bedroom, if he knew the table was excellent. Indeed, the intermingling of social and political life in Edward's reign now made it essential for a man such as Ernest Haliburton Cunard to provide outstanding cuisine for his guests, who were used to eating at the Ritz in Paris or Monte Carlo, the London Savoy—and, by 1909, the Carlton.

At Red Rice House, Dora would have been up at four-thirty in the morning, to make huge quantities of sandwiches for the beaters, the men employed to rouse the game out of the bushes and thickets. She learned how to cook and pack up the colossal luncheons that were taken out to the house guests—a specialized skill that would have required the organizational ability of Chevet's movable feasts. Sometimes the meal was served in the open, but occasionally a marquee was erected at some strategic point. The servants would have the repast there at the required time, complete with the silver, glasses and china, for the arrival of the shooting party and the ladies. Nothing disposable about this picnic—indeed, when the upper classes went on safari in the colonies or crossed the desert, they generally took canteens of cutlery and linen tablecloths with them.

The weather was often bitterly cold during the shooting season, but the hot dishes must remain hot, the wine must be at the perfect temperature—and certainly there must be no hunting around for a mislaid carving knife or bottle opener. Expectations had changed from the days when the long traipse from kitchen to dining-room excused the arrival of food and drink at the wrong temperature.

To retrace the steps of the servants at Chatsworth along those bare, stone-walled corridors and up the cellar slope from what were the kitchens, to the dining-room, is to realize the state in which the food would have arrived at table. The servants themselves would have eaten hotter food, for the servants' hall is far closer to the kitchens. At a dinner-party attended by Disraeli in the 1870s, he was heard to mutter when the champagne arrived, "Ah, at last, something warm." The host's honour and image depended on the servants' expertise. And not only would Dora have helped pack and prepare the feast; the gifted kitchen maid almost certainly went with the butler, the footmen and the parlour-maids to make sure everything was perfect, and as Monsieur Leronicu had ordained.

When the shooting party got back to Red Rice House, they would have handed over the day's bag to the servants, to be counted and plucked and hung in the game larders. There would have been two or three larders at Red Rice House, with the game larder either in a separate building or close to the gunroom. There, the game would hang until it was crawling with maggots and ready for eating.

Life would have been no easier for Dora if she had stayed with the servants left behind at Portman Square. This was the time when the major house-cleaning was undertaken. All the carpets were taken up, the curtains taken down. The furniture was cleaned with vinegar to remove all the old polish, then new layers of beeswax and turpentine were rubbed on until the wood was actually warm from the efforts of an army of housemaids. Ceilings were scrubbed with soda and water, including all the elaborate cornices and scrollwork.

Dora knew how things were going for the staff back in the London house, because they kept in touch by letter and card. Ruth was a new friend whose cards now appear in the collection, and also Ada—who will play a key role in Dora's life later on. There are cards from fellow servants in the other establishment, although they would have been careful to keep complaints to themselves. Only a few of the cards carry criticism of the employer—for obvious reasons. When the writer is in a distant household—beyond the London area, for example—she may risk such remarks. In 1911 Jessie writes from the country:

> Dear Dora: Here I am in the last place God made I should think & here I'm likely to remain. Plenty of work and nothing to use, no coppers at all. Oh what a sport we have contriving.

The beleaguered Jessie is not complaining about the lack of police force here, but the dearth of decent copper cookware in the kitchen—possibly the huge coppers used for steaming of all kinds.

It was far more useful for Dora's career to be in Hampshire, rising at four in the morning and going to bed after midnight, when the elaborate dinner-parties were over. During those late evening hours, she must often have looked at those children of the kitchen, the scullery maids, as they wearily scrubbed the black of the charcoal off the pots and pans before they could be washed, and thought back to shy little Dora at The Ferns, only three short years before. She was still only seventeen years old, still only a kitchen maid, but already she was being called upon to assist the star of the downstairs world. The skills she acquired at Red Rice House would be crucial to her rapid advancement over the next two years. For by March 1910, only a year after joining the Cunard household, Dora was on the move again.

Dora's frequent moves over the next five years might appear to suggest an employee whose work is less than satisfactory, or that Dora herself has difficulty with prolonged commitments. The truth, in fact, is quite the opposite. Both the frequent moves and the nature of the households to which she goes are a strong indication that Dora is considered a valuable commodity.

It must have been maddening to lose such a capable and gifted servant, but Dora by now has acquired something of a reputation, and the frequent moves have more to do with getting a better situation for herself and, above all, more money. Given Dora's adventurous and ambitious nature, she may well have become restless, but her motivation will have been far more concrete than a mere desire for a change of scenery.

During those first four years of Dora's life in London, Escoffier had transformed the public's concept of the kitchen and the image of the chef. Above all, by improving his working conditions, he had changed the way that the professional chef perceived himself. When the French writer and cook Pierre Hamp came to train with Escoffier at the Savoy in 1894, he could not believe that his room was free of bugs, and that he had the use of a bathroom. What was more, the kitchen was light and clean, and the staff were well-fed. The little man who was invited to sit at the same table as kings, princes and divas had not forgotten what it was like to be an apprentice.

The groundbreaking partnership of the remarkable triumvirate who had revolutionized London's social world ended in 1898 in a bitter quarrel. In the mid-1980s, British journalist Paul Levy was sent information that had been kept hidden in the files of the Savoy for over eighty years: signed confessions by Ritz and Escoffier, and also by César Ritz's *maître d'hôtel*, who were all fired in 1898. Ritz had been furthering his other interests at the expense of the Savoy, and Escoffier had been taking gifts and commissions from many of the suppliers. As the manager of Hudson's Grocers in the Strand put it, "Mr. Escoffier did not actually ask for the commission but he came and hung about and talked in a way that I knew exactly what he had come for."

The Savoy kept silent about the affair for various reasons, but principally because the two men were personal friends of the heir to the throne and many of the most powerful people in England. Undoubtedly the "commissions" were a way of life for Escoffier, learned at his uncle's restaurant in Nice, and he would have seen nothing wrong with it. After all, the suppliers were making good money from their connection with the Savoy, and were being patronized by the greatest chef in Britain and Europe. Inaccurate newspaper reports of increased profits at the time caused one shareholder to wonder out loud if D'Oyly Carte knew what he was doing. In fact, kitchen profits improved impressively after the departure of the two men.

Three years later, Escoffier and Ritz parted company, and it was the coronation of their most illustrious patron, Edward VII, that finally broke up the dynamic duo. All-day celebrations had been planned at the Carlton Hotel for Coronation Day, highlighted by a huge formal dinner to be attended by many of the coronation guests, still in ceremonial dress. Guests were coming from all over Europe and America, every room was let, every table filled. Anyone of any consequence in British and European society wanted to be seen making a theatrical entrance down the carpeted stairs into the Carlton's Palm court. The social hub of all activities organized around the coronation outside Buckingham Palace was the Carlton Hotel, and César Ritz had made quite sure that his kingdom was in order for the great day.

But what even this perfectionist could not control was the no-show of the main attraction. Just two days before the coronation Edward underwent an emergency operation for appendicitis and, as *The Times* enunciated it: "At the very moment of the last rehearsal, when we were all looking forward to the joy of celebrating the most solemn of national rejoicings with all the beauty and ritual which the Church of England can employ, the cup was, as it were, dashed from our lips."

The bursting of a bombshell, Ritz called it. He walked into the middle of the restaurant at lunchtime, made the announcement, dealt with literally hundreds of cancellations, then collapsed. It was a breakdown from which he never recovered.

Their personal *entente cordiale* may have come to an end, but the Carlton Hotel, which Ritz had conceived and opened with Escoffier in 1899, went from success to success, as did the quiet cook, who was all that was left of that brilliant triumvirate. The Carlton was the first hotel in London to provide a private bathroom for each bedroom, and Ritz planned to have a telephone in each room. But above all, it was the air of luxury and the marvellous kitchen that drew in the wealthiest people in the world. Escoffier's kitchen was staffed by a brigade of sixty, and could produce five hundred *couverts* at a single dinner. He himself had a flat on the fifth floor of the hotel, and it was here that he centred his life over the next eighteen years, also serving on the Carlton's board of directors.

Dora's postcard collection shows that the servant network ran between the great hotels and the staff in private homes. George, who is holidaying on the south coast of England in 1911, tells Dora he is having a "ripping time" and that the "Savoy girls" are on holiday too.

Escoffier's great work, *Le Guide Culinaire*, was published by Flammarion in Paris in 1903. The first edition in English was published in London in 1907, Dora's first year in the city, in a cleaned-up version that smacked more of Victorian than Edwardian sensibilities and with an eye, perhaps, to the female market. All references to "cocottes," famous or infamous, were expunged. Dora would not possess her own copy of *Le Guide Culinaire* until she worked with the great man, but she probably took a look at the versions owned by the French chefs she worked with—many of whom by now would have trained with Escoffier at the Savoy and the Carlton. And, of course, besides the creations in honour of princes and noblemen, their French versions would have contained all those dishes named for celebrated women—however risqué the reason for their fame. Dora would have watched Monsieur Leronicu prepare the fish course—poaching the sole fillets in a fish *fumet*, placing them in scooped-out baked-potato shells on top of a layer of shelled shrimp tails in a white wine sauce, and covering the whole dish with *sauce Mornay* before glazing in the oven. If she asked the name of the dish, *"filets de sole Otero,"* was the name she would be given.

And perhaps in his broken English laced with French, Monsieur Leronicu would tell his wide-eyed assistant stories of the Spanish dancer, *"La Belle Otero"* considered one of the greatest, and the most flamboyant, of the *grandes horizontales*. Many men had killed themselves over her—her nickname in the American popular press was "The Suicide Siren." Her jewels were extraordinary, among them the diamond *rivière* of Marie Antoinette, Empress Eugénie's pearl necklace, and a diamond bolero by Cartier that had stopped traffic on the Rue de la Paix when it was on display.

Caroline Otero was vulgar, she was avaricious, she was nervy. When her seat at the *Comédie Française* was taken by the unexpected arrival of the Tsar of Russia, she stopped in front of his box before making a magnificent exit and shouting, "From this day on, I'll never eat caviar again!" She once told Colette that the moment in the life of every man when you have him at your mercy—"when he opens wide his palm" —is not the moment of passion, but the moment when you twist his wrist. *La Belle Otero* was the quintessential new woman in a very old game.

The recipes in *Le Guide Culinaire* are a study in the power structure and the star system of the Edwardian Age. From Russia there was Prince Galitzin, who ate at *Le Petit Moulin*

Rouge with the *demi-mondaine*, Blanche D'Antigny, and for whom Escoffier created *Faisan Galitzine*, pheasant stuffed with truffles and minced snipe. Prince Anatole Demidoff would enjoy the *Consommé Demidoff* named for him, before going to the theatre to join the actress Duverger, who would appear covered in the diamonds he had given her. The French novelist Emile Zola adored talking food with Escoffier, particularly the regional dishes of his childhood in the Midi, and for him Escoffier produced *Consommé Zola*, a chicken and celery soup flavoured with pepper and tomato, garnished with gnocchi and the white Piedmont truffles the author loved so much.

On the menu of the Anglo-French banquet in Westminster Hall to celebrate the *Entente Cordiale* in 1904, two of the *pièces de résistance* created by Escoffier were *Chaud-froid de Caille à la Loubet* and *Poulard Edouard VII*. The third was *Truite froide Amiral Caillard*, honouring the commander of the French fleet, which was in Portsmouth. Escoffier, who disliked party politics and political conversations of any kind, but was fiercely patriotic to his native land, honoured the admiral and the king, but omitted direct dedication of the dish to the political figure, President Loubet!

As in the case of the Westminster Hall dinner, Escoffier's dishes sometimes commemorated events of world importance, or those that had captured popular imagination. When the Norwegian explorer Fridtjof Nansen came to talk to three hundred people at the Savoy about his expedition with his ship, the *Fram*, to the North Pole, Escoffier marked the occasion by recalling the tragic loss of an earlier ship, the *Jeannette*, by presenting *Suprême de Volailles Jeannette*. One wonders if the diners grasped the significance of the escalopes of cold chicken breast with their tarragon decoration on a bed of foie gras mousse and chicken jelly, imprisoned in a sculpted block of ice, which represented the terrible fate of the ship and the death of most of its crew.

From the world of the stage came *La Bombe Néron*, created for the actor-manager Sir Herbert Beerbohm Tree after the opening night of *Nero*, a verse-drama by the fashionable Edwardian writer Stephen Phillips. There were, of course, the dishes dedicated to *la divine Sarah*, and a plethora of creations dedicated to Adelina Patti, named after her or called, simply, *Diva*.

The dishes Escoffier created for Edward VII had a special significance for him, and he kept a record of them in a separate notebook, but—as he told Madame Duchêne, the wife of the manager of the London Ritz—his creations for the women of the era were dearest to his heart. Very early on in his career, when he was at the Monte Carlo in the 1880s, the mistress of Prince Kochubey, a highly successful *demi-mondaine* known as "Katinka," who travelled as part of the suite of servants and secretaries of the prince, came to visit Escoffier in his kitchens, to talk about the dishes of her native Hungary. Some he incorporated in his cookbook, and for her he invented *La Rêve Katinka*, a dish of shellfish she could eat without messing up her pretty fingers.

Princesses, kings of kingdoms long gone, opera singers, actors and actresses, all those *cocottes*, expurgated from the London edition of *Guide Culinaire*—from the pages of a groundbreaking cookbook the names still exude the glamour and the glitter of a vanished world.

BOMBE NÉRON

... it is harder to develop a love of food and an understanding of cooking from books that impose rules and regulations. Some of the best writers about food—the great English writer Elizabeth David comes to mind—are hopelessly imprecise in their attitude to measurement, knowing that you cannot evoke the way people actually make good food

in Provence or Liguria or Cyprus by measuring out ground
pepper by the grain.

John Allemang, The Globe and Mail, *August 23, 1997*

Using a dome-shaped mould, line the mould with vanilla
ice-cream and caramel. Fill with vanilla mousse into which
you have mixed small chocolate truffles. Turn it out on to
a bed of Punch biscuits (similar to ladyfingers), of the same
diameter. Cover the whole with a thin layer of Italian
meringue, and decorate, using a piping-bag of the same
meringue. Set the dessert in an oven to glaze quickly.

This all sounds deceptively simple, and it is worth noting that
a similar recipe, for *Le Saint-Cyr, glacé* (Frozen Chocolate
Mousse Molded in Meringue), in Volume 11 of *Mastering
the Art of French Cooking* by Julia Child and Simone Beck
covers nearly five pages. For a reader who has to copy everything at home, and cannot watch her work, Julia Child
details quantities and describes the techniques required for
every step of the recipe, unlike Escoffier. Italian meringue,
for instance, consists of a hot sugar syrup (made from
scratch), beaten into egg-whites, and the ice-cream, of
course, is not bought in a store. She also takes great care to
describe the techniques of lining a mould—and then getting
everything out in one piece.

The idea that a cookbook should take the reader through
step by step in an organized fashion was not a priority for
Escoffier, and many other great exponents of the art form.
It is a comparatively modern idea—Mrs. Beeton's 1860s
cookbook, *Household Management*, with its detailed recipes,
was much ahead of its time.

Mouth Wide Open

*Think this over carefully, the most charming hours of our life are all
connected by a more or less tangible hyphen with a memory of the table.*
PIERRE-CHARLES MONSELET

On May 7, 1910, King Edward VII died. His usual trip to Biarritz had not helped his health, as had been hoped —although, remembering the gigantic meal he had consumed on that last trip to one of his favourite haunts, one wonders how anyone could have expected otherwise. Outside the gates of Buckingham Palace, the crowds kept vigil through the sixth day of May and, shortly after midnight, the throne passed to Edward's son, George V—an entirely different kettle of fish from his father.

It is perhaps only in retrospect that the writers and survivors of that short Edwardian period remember sensing that the good times were over, and that "the clouds were massing for Armageddon," as the historian R.C.K. Ensor expresses it. But the changes that Edward had brought about when he included financiers, industrialists and women of all classes— as long as they could amuse him—in his social life would continue to affect the world of Dora Lee.

The Savoy and the Carlton had, in fact, seen less of Edward once he ascended the throne, but the members of the new, privileged class mingled in the dining-rooms with politicians and members of foreign royalty: the Duc d'Orléans, Léopold II of Belgium, Alfonso XIII of Spain. Book launches were held at the Carlton for risqué modern authors such as Elinor Glyn. And just before the death of Edward, Dora left the employ of Ernest Cunard in March 1910, to go and work for Thomas J. Barratt, the chairman of the Pears Soap Company, who had taken up residence in Stonor Park, the property of Lord Camoys, near Henley-on-Thames.

Stonor Park was an Elizabethan mansion in the Chiltern Hills, standing amidst three hundred acres of parkland, with great beechwoods that sheltered herds of deer. Stonor was the family name, but the ancient Camoys peerage went back to the Battle of Agincourt in 1415. It then fell into abeyance for four hundred years, to be revived in 1839 by a descendant of the ancient family. It would appear that Lord Camoys, a Catholic peer, was land rich and cash poor, for he had rented Stonor Park to Thomas Barratt, chairman of the Pears Soap Company, and Andrew Pears, the great-grandson of the founder of the firm. Andrew Pears died in 1909, so by the time Dora arrived, Thomas Barratt occupied the property himself.

On March 19, 1910, Mrs. Ballard, the housekeeper, writes to Dora from Stonor Park, "Shall expect you Monday, leaving by the 2.20 train from Padd. [Paddington] You will be met at Henley Station."

As the pony and trap rattled through the great beechwoods just coming into leaf that March day, the driver may well have told Dora about her new employers, and pointed out Lord Camoys's house in the great park: "There, that's the Warren, where his lordship lives now, nothing like as grand as the great house. Not that he's there much these days. They say he's going to marry an American lady who's got all kinds of money, lives on Fifth Avenue in New York City. And there, that's the chapel, Catholic it is, like the school over there that his lordship has, for ninety kiddies from the village—and there's the almshouses, five of them, for needy folks on the estate...." But it would be the disposition of the housekeeper, Mrs. Ballard, that would affect the kitchen maid's life far more than that of either Thomas Barratt or Lord Camoys.

This time Dora's motive for getting the job at Stonor Park was possibly personal as well as professional, because one of the postcards from this period asks her how the courting is going. She may have got the job through some link with the cryptically named "Whisker," whose signature appears on another postcard given to Dora by a girlfriend. The message is, in parts, illegible, but it reads, "… don't work too hard or worry, but use Pears soap from Whiskers What …"

Servants in the downstairs network frequently found positions for each other. Lucy, writing to Dora in about 1912, asks her if she has yet asked a Mr. Massoni about a first maid's place for Florence, and news of moves to new places are passed along the network. One card from Nell, in 1910, lets Dora know of her new "crib," using the Victorian underworld slang word for her new place. Sometimes the moves are so swift that the writer declares she thought Dora was dead, and sometimes Dora is reproached for not keeping in touch with her friends and family.

The move to Stonor Park appears to have brought even more work than usual; Dora describes herself as being "knocked up" in one communication—in England, this means she is exhausted. But, in moving to work for Thomas Barratt, Dora has made her first foray into the new, extended privileged class that surrounded Edward VII, and she knew this was a good move for her career.

Dora followed the trends in society that could affect her own life, and she followed the rituals of royalty. One of the twelve dated entries in Dora's handmade notebook reads, "Went to see Edward VII open parliament, January 29, 1909"—a state occasion that had fallen into disuse. Edward may have widened the circle of Marlborough House, but it would be a mistake to think of him as a populist; he understood very well the importance of panoply and symbol to the popularity of the monarchy. Dora had managed to get away from Portman Square long enough to watch the king go by in his gilded coach the first time that state occasion was reintroduced by the monarch. She knew that people such as the chairman of Pears Soap were now part of the upper crust and, what is more, that they could pay handsomely for an outstandingly talented cook. The stately home of Lord Camoys was occupied by two industrialists, who would once have been considered mere tradesmen.

The accepted interpretation of the word "gentleman" during the nineteenth century and the first few years of the twentieth century was someone who did not have to work for a living. In the series of books by P.G. Wodehouse about an upper-class gentleman and his butler, Jeeves, the name of Bertie Wooster's club is "The Drones," after those members of the hive who live on the labours of others. Nevertheless, Dora could hardly have chosen more elegant and acceptable examples of gentlemen who worked for a living than the occupants of Stonor Park.

Pears Soap sold itself on the refinement of its product and, by implication, on the exclusivity of its users. For most of the twentieth century, its advertisements featured illustrations of exquisite small girls painted after the manner of the most popular Victorian painters of small children, with translucent complexions and heads of golden, tousled curls. Their slogan, "Preparing to be a beautiful lady," survived for decades, and, for many twentieth-century girls, Pears was the bar of soap they most wanted to tuck into their sponge bags when they were sent off to boarding-school. Even the appearance of the soap was unlike the plebian white or green bars of more common soaps. It was (and still is) a translucent oval, with the appearance of a large, smooth piece of amber—more like a semiprecious stone than something so ordinary as a cleaning product. Dora's new employers may have been in trade, but it was very much the carriage trade. They held the Royal Warrant for the supply of toilet soap to a succession of monarchs: Queen Victoria, Edward VII, soon to be followed by George V.

Though they may have cultivated the carriage trade, the Pears Soap Company under Andrew Pears and Thomas Barratt moved their company elegantly but aggressively into the world of advertising in the early 1880s. At the end of the nineteenth century, British newspapers carried only a small number of advertisements; posters on hoardings were poorly designed, and few and far between. In what was a groundbreaking move for the period, Andrew Pears chose to use works of art as the vehicles for selling his product in newspapers and on walls. He paid £2200 for the rights to Sir John Millais's celebrated painting, Bubbles—a huge sum for the period—and purchased pieces of sculpture at such venues as the Paris Exhibition.

Even the partners' use of money had class. Thomas Barratt literally put the name of Pears into circulation in the early 1880s by buying up 250,000 French ten-centime pieces, which, at the time, were also used in Great Britain as pennies, stamping the name "Pears" on them, and putting them back into circulation. No question of defacing the coin of the realm, because it was someone else's coin. So numerous were they, and so persistent was their use, that the government finally bought them all up, melted them down, and declared the French coin illegal. Pears became the name to quote when talking about numbers, or size—or success.

Not content with the British market alone, Thomas Barratt crossed the Atlantic and persuaded the American evangelist Henry Ward Beecher to endorse his product—which he did, in a letter reproduced on the front page of The Herald. Probably taken by surprise—and possibly by other more mercenary means—the renowned preacher declared, "If 'Cleanliness is next to Godliness' soap must be considered as a 'Means of Grace'—and a clergyman who recommends moral things should be willing to recommend Soap." Small wonder the great newspaper magnate Lord Northcliffe once called Thomas Barratt "the father of Modern Advertising, from whom I have learned so much."

Nineteen hundred and eleven was a year of spectacle. Just before the coronation came the official opening of the Queen Victoria Memorial and Admiralty Arch and, if there was indeed a feeling of the clouds gathering, they may well have started to darken the skies over London on this occasion. Kaiser Wilhelm II and his empress were in London for the ceremony —their last appearance before Armageddon—and a naval build-up was underway in Britain, with the commissioning of three new and improved dreadnoughts, and a huge increase in the naval budget for the year.

The new king was not well known to his people. He was, in fact, the second son of Edward and Alexandra, becoming heir to the throne—and to the royal fiancée—on the death of his elder brother, Albert Victor. The death of "Eddy," as he was known, was fortuitous for Britain, since he was feeble both of body and mind. For many years ugly rumours swirled around the monarchy that Eddy had even been the notorious Jack the Ripper, but recent evidence has lain that particular canard to rest.

George was forty-five when he ascended the throne, and had spent most of his adult life in the Royal Navy, away from the British Isles. His wife, the former Princess Victoria Mary of Teck—and the former fiancée of Albert Victor—was a more chilly and austere version of Queen Alexandra, without a shred of the vulnerability that Alexandra's extreme deafness gave to her beauty. Although he was a model of decorum compared to his father, George had his own brush with scandal in his coronation year when a left-wing journal published the rumour, current in some circles, that George V had already contracted a marriage in Malta to the daughter of an admiral.

Marriage, of course, was a far more serious issue than adultery, because it involved the royal succession. The writer of the article was charged, put on trial, and sentenced to twelve months in prison—which resulted in more publicity than if the matter had been left alone. However, no smear of scandal stuck to this reactionary, ultra-conservative, clock-watching monarch, whose distrust of change extended to his diet of kippers for breakfast and roast mutton, boiled potatoes and brussels sprouts for dinner. As well for Escoffier that he no longer needed the British monarch in his dining-rooms for the success of his own kingdom; Tum-Tum's successor was a culinary lost cause.

The Duke and Duchess of Devonshire both had significant roles to play in the coronation: the duke, appointed as one of the Bearers of the Queen's Regalia, carried Queen Mary's crown, and Evie, of course, was Mistress of the Queen's Robes.

In his diary, Victor comments on the chaos at the coronation rehearsal: "Thursday June 8. Lovely day. Rehearsal. Nobody knew what to do. Good deal of confusion. People were rather stupid." However, all went well on the great day: "Most splendid sight and ceremony. Evie did her part very well and looked very nice. I managed alright."

As one of the greatest shows on earth, the coronation of a British monarch is a vast moneymaking proposition and business opportunity for everyone in London from the street vendor to the storeowner, and Dora's new employers were hoping to get a piece of the action for themselves. Joining forces with what *The Times* called "an influential committee of owners and occupiers of property in the West-end," a group that included the Gophir Diamond Company, the London Stereoscopic Photographic Company and Mappin and Webb, A. and F. Pears (Ltd) brought pressure on the Earl Marshall, the Duke of Norfolk, to have the Royal Progress, which took place before the coronation, pass along the streets on which they had their businesses: Regent Street, Oxford Street, New Regent Street, and Holborn. So much money was tied up in the event that, in the light of what had happened to the last coronation, concerned investors in the spectacle took out insurance. As *The Times* reported:

> During the last few days a fair number of insurances have been placed at Lloyds to cover the payment of a claim should the Coronation not take place before the end of June. From 20 to 25 per cent was the last rate quoted. The market in this class of risk is extremely limited, and so the rate is easily influenced by the amount of business offered.

Some historians suggest there was not as much excitement for this coronation as there was for Edward's, because his had been the first in most people's lifetime—given the long reign of Victoria. However, newspaper accounts reflect as great a public interest as ever. Around the shores of Great Britain three thousand coronation bonfires lit up the sky— from far southwest Cornwall the chain of fires blazed to Plymouth Hoe in Devonshire, on into Dorset and Hampshire, through Wiltshire and Gloucestershire. London itself was encircled by fire—at Hampstead and Shooter's Hill, Dulwich and the Crystal Palace, huge structures of coal, tinder, wood, and tar barrels were set alight. That chain of beacons would have delighted the heart of Dora's Neolithic ancestors.

Abroad, the dominions celebrated. Throughout India, coronation day was proclaimed a holiday, and in Calcutta there were special prayers for King George and Queen Mary in the Temple of Kali. Canada was singled out for special attention by being chosen for the new king's first public act after the coronation ceremonies: the laying of a foundation stone of a new Seamen's and Fishermen's Institute in Newfoundland, which was done from the King's Room in Buckingham Palace "by electric connexion." There were fireworks in Toronto, *Te Deums* chanted in Montreal, royal salutes fired in Niagara, and a great military parade in Winnipeg, where "the day was observed with exceptional heartiness."

All the world had come to London: Prince Chakrabonga of Siam, Prince Mohamed Ali Pasha of Egypt, Desjamatch Kassa of Ethiopia, Prince Tsai Chen of China. Dozens of state landaus carried the titled heads of Europe past the London crowds: Prince Philip of Saxe-Coburg, Prince and Princess Maximilian of Baden, Princess Frederic Charles of Hesse, the Grand Duke of Mecklenburg-Schwerin, the Crown Prince of Bulgaria, the Hereditary Prince Danilo of Montenegro, Prince Rupprecht of Bavaria, the Hereditary Princess of Saxe-Meiningen—the list goes on, column after column. Eighty-five years later, they read like the cast of an operetta, set to the music of Lehar, from a world as unreal as Pontevedro or Ruritania.

From the coronation in June 1911, through the following season in 1912, the social life of London society took on a frenetic pace. For the Devonshires, there were many opportunities in the course of the year for formal events—even without a coronation—because there were various honourary titles that came with the dukedom.

Among those honourary positions were the titles Mayor and Mayoress of Eastbourne—a seaside town on Britain's south coast that was a fashionable watering-hole for the quality in the nineteenth century. In 1910, the duke and duchess gave a great ball at Compton Place, the ducal property in Eastbourne, to which nine hundred guests were invited. So grand was the scale of the occasion that temporary buildings had to be constructed over a period of weeks before the ball.

The ballroom and supper-room were each a hundred feet long, and decorated in the style of Louis XV. In the ballroom, great banners of yellow-and-white Japanese silk decorated the walls and ceiling, and candles flickered in their sconces around the oval-shaped mirrors that lined the room. Installed halfway down the great room was the private orchestra of the Devonshires—or a section of it, according to *The Times*. The other section of the orchestra played in the supper-room amid green-and-white silken banners and beneath candle-shaped electric lights in the great chandeliers. The duke wore his chain of office and a scarlet robe trimmed with fur, and was accompanied by the Eastbourne Corporation mace-bearer with his massive silver-gilt mace. Evelyn wore a superb diamond tiara and a dress of blue-grey velvet embroidered in silver.

The elaborate display at Eastbourne was not just self-indulgent aggrandizement on the part of the Devonshires. In their symbolic role it was expected of them, and it would have been taken as an insult, or lack of interest at the least, if they had not fulfilled their duty: *noblesse oblige* indeed, in this case.

It is tempting to make a metaphor out of the Louis XV motif in the ballroom, and best to resist it. The catastrophe that was so very close at hand would certainly change the structure of many countries in the Western world, and symbolic displays such as the ball at Eastbourne would either be modified or disappear altogether, but the class that embodied those symbols in Britain would survive the deluge.

"Bread and circuses," however, is a reasonably fitting description for the role of the monarchy and the aristocracy at the beginning of the twentieth century. From the circus of Eastbourne the Devonshires returned to Chatsworth, and at Christmas they distributed among the poor of Sheffield, Buxton, Bakewell, Chesterfield and Derby the proceeds of the charges made for admission to Chatsworth during the summer —about £500 in total.

The viewing of stately homes is not just a twentieth-century phenomenon; a distinction was made on most great estates between the private apartments of the family and the state, or public, rooms, and Chatsworth has been on view to the public since the early eighteenth century. But whereas once the income was an extra that could be disposed of to others—

in this case what the Victorians called "the deserving poor"—it has now become vital for the survival of the estate.

One of the grandest circuses of the year 1911 was the Derby Night Ball held in June at Devonshire House. Unlike the Eastbourne Ball, at which the Devonshires did their domestic duty towards the prominent and noteworthy citizens of the area, this was an international circus ring celebrating the season's highlight of the sport of kings: the Derby. In spite of its name, the race is run in Surrey, on the magnificent expanse of Epsom Downs; the name dates back to its creation by the Earl of Derby in 1780. There are symbols, signs and portents galore to be found in the guest lists for those great spectacles of the ruling class. And in the year that bridged the death of one king and the coronation of another, parliament was embroiled in a constitutional crisis that carried portents of its own.

The Parliament Bill was a complicated matter, but essentially it addressed reforms to the House of Lords and its right to delay certain bills, which involved, therefore, a shifting of the balance of power. One of the most intransigent voices against change was Lord Lansdowne, who wanted no part of anything that might ease the way to Irish Home Rule. The acrimony over Irish Home Rule divided families, caused huge problems among the members of Brooks, Victor's club, and made for difficult weekends at Chatsworth and dinner-parties at Devonshire House when the Abercorns refused to speak to more liberal-minded guests.

The Constitutional Conference held twenty-one sittings and failed miserably after five months. At one point it looked as if King George would be required to create five hundred new peers to alter the balance of power in the House and force the bill through. An outraged member of the old guard, George Wyndham, wrote to his wife, the former Lady Sibell Grosvenor, "… now we are finished with the cosmopolitan press—and the American duchesses ... and all the degrading shams ... for the House of Lords today—tho' they did not know it—voted for Revolution."

By the end of July 1911, the Parliament Act was finally passed, and by then, Dora was working in the kitchen of one of those American duchesses. As she moves on from the Elizabethan mansion of a gentleman industrialist, Dora's career path continues to trace the trends of her times. For the next six months Dora Lee is employed by the ex–Duchess of Marlborough, Consuelo Vanderbilt, in the London home that was part of her father's wedding present to her. In the hands of this dollar-princess, the epicurean and social revolutions will be made to serve each other as never before.

Even by the standards of those turn-of-the-century American robber barons, William K. Vanderbilt was a wealthy man. His grandfather, Cornelius, had made his fortune in ships, roads and railroads. Yet William's wife, Alva, had difficulty penetrating the social enclave of the four hundred top families, as decreed by Mrs. William Backhouse Astor, doyenne of New York society at the turn of the century. So she had set her heart on marrying her daughter, Consuelo, whom she called "Baby," to the sort of man whose class could not be questioned, even by an Astor: a British peer.

It was strictly a business deal that Alva masterminded with the ancient House of Marlborough and with the Ninth Duke, whose sadly inappropriate nickname was "Sunny." Fifty thousand shares of the Beech Creek Railway Company, a profitable subsidiary of New York Central, worth two and a half million dollars, were transferred to the House of Marlborough, along with an annual income of £100,000 for the duke and Consuelo. A triumphant Alva gave her daughter the pearls of Catherine the Great, Empress of All the Russias, as a wedding present, and on November 6, 1895, the bride was let out of her locked bedroom, her eyes almost swollen shut with tears, to marry the

owner of one of the oldest titles and one of the most magnificent houses in Britain: Blenheim Palace in Oxfordshire. Like
Evelyn, Consuelo became a Ninth Duchess, married to an
aristocrat who, coincidentally, was Evelyn's cousin—again, not
surprisingly, for Consuelo was new American blood in that
almost incestuously interrelated gene pool. In fact, on a visit
to the Lansdownes while they were in India, Alva had at one
time considered Evelyn's brother as a potential son-in-law.

The marriage between Sunny and Baby lasted eleven years
before ending in divorce in 1907, when Consuelo was thirty
and the mother of two sons. By the time Dora came to work
for her at Sunderland House in 1911, the ex–Duchess of
Marlborough had put together a completely new life for herself.

Sunderland House was built on the site of what had once
been the Mayfair Chapel, which was demolished in 1899.
This time Dora had indeed moved into a palace, for the house
was considered the last of the great Mayfair mansions to be
built, and it cost Consuelo's father two and a half million dollars. Although purists judged the French Renaissance style of
its architecture would have been better-suited to sweeping
lawns and landscaped gardens, the confines of Sunderland
House must have seemed like a boundless horizon to Consuelo
after the miserable years among the splendours of the gardens
of the eighteenth-century landscape architect Capability Brown
at Blenheim.

Most significant of all for Dora was her new mistress's attitude towards her belowstairs staff after what she had seen at
Blenheim Palace, where—for all her privileged upbringing
—her democratic American soul recoiled at the downstairs
hierarchy and upstairs attitudes.

Although French ladies' maids were considered quite *comme
il faut* by most of the quality, Marlborough found his wife's
French maid unsuitable, because she didn't know English
ways. Indeed, *The Management of Servants*, published in 1880,

issued a stern warning: "A Parisian maid out of her orbit is not a treasure." Sunny Marlborough was of the same opinion, and got his mother to have a substitute ready when they got back to England. Ironically, the elderly Swiss maid chosen by Consuelo's mother-in-law turned out to be a man-hater, who promptly added Sunny to her list, and who devoted herself unswervingly to Consuelo, hectoring her, chiding her and loving her until she died—still in Consuelo's service.

When the new duchess arrived at Blenheim Palace, she acquainted herself with the household, starting with the butler, whose rule was absolute. The butler and the upper servants had their own dining-room, to which no lower servant could gain admittance, and that new addition to the servant hierarchy, the chauffeur, who would later become quite a glamorous figure belowstairs, was at first relegated to the bottom of the ladder, and the servants' hall.

The housekeeper managed the whole of that huge palace with six housemaids, whose quarters were up in a tower known as Housemaids Heights, where there was no running water. When Consuelo tried to improve their living conditions, she was told that this was the way matters had been for two centuries, so "I was not allowed to improve their lot." There were five laundresses, a still-maid who cooked the breakfasts and did some of the baking, and a French chef with a staff of four, who was at constant war with the housekeeper. No *entente cordiale* here.

When Consuelo first came to live at Sunderland House after her divorce, she added an original touch of her own. She had the architect create a bas-relief of the old commodore, Cornelius, and place it opposite that of the Great Duke of Marlborough, whose victory at Blenheim had won him his sovereign's undying gratitude and a palace. Such *lèse-majesté* caused raised eyebrows among some of her loftier guests. Could this American upstart be suggesting that her ancestry was as good as Sunny's?

The passive nineteen-year-old led to the sacrificial altar in tears had grown into an activist for whom, in her own words, "a purely social life had no appeal." At the time of her separation, Consuelo had endowed a centre called the Marlborough Relief Depot, for the Church Army, to help the families of men in jail. From there she would go on to associate herself with movements to encourage the higher education of women, birth control, publicizing the horror of sweated labour, and the enfranchisement of women. On March 9, 1907, *The Illustrated Mail* announced, "The latest aristocratic helper in the social work of the Church Army is the beautiful Duchess of Marlborough. Her Grace is the daughter of Mr. W. K. Vanderbilt, the American millionaire. On her marriage to the Duke of Marlborough she received a dowry of £1,000,000."

By 1911, the year that Dora joined her staff, Baby had come a long way.

Dora may have been having problems with a cheeky male member of Consuelo's staff while she was at Sunderland House, and complained about it to one of her girlfriends. "A.E.W." sent her a cartoon of a pretty lady talking to a janitor with a mop and pail. The message is brief and to the point: "Don't forget the keyhole." Whatever the problems might have been—and it may all have been just a bit of a giggle—Dora has by now been in service in six households and has been fending for herself for five years. She is more than likely a match for any Peeping Tom at Sunderland House.

Dora would have found her new employer very much to her liking. When she was at Red Rice House

with the Cunards she was sent a cartoon postcard of a suffragette waving
her umbrella from a dais as she speaks
to a group of women. The caption
reads: "Amid this mighty fuss just let
me mention / The rights of women
merit some attention." Beneath it is
hand-written, "This is you standing up
there." The message on the reverse of
the card is garbled, but the meaning
is quite clear:

> (P.S.) I see you go your mouth wide
> open. The sender is not known which
> is the one out of these. (C.R.P.)
> (C.L.P.) This will have this time
> (won't it) half time.

Another similar card sent to Rice
House has a caption that reads, "Suffragettes are going about sticking bills
in prominent places."

The first card in particular suggests
that, not only was the subject topical,
it held a special appeal for outspoken
Dora Lee.

Nineteen hundred and seven, the year
that Dora first arrived in London to
work at Queen's Gate Place, coincided
with a sudden increase in activity in
the arena of women's suffrage. Get-
ting coverage in a male-owned and male-dominated press was
always a problem, and the Women's Social and Political Union
discovered that an effective way of gaining public attention was
to organize extensive processions to the House of Commons,

and to demonstrate in large numbers—thereby forcing the police to make arrests in equally large numbers. Their first march resulted in the arrest of sixty-five women, the second, seventy-six, and the publicity they attracted drew large crowds to their meetings for the first time.

The newspaper coverage was sensational—but, then, so were the events they covered. They described women "assuming an aggressive demeanour," women "using their umbrellas against anyone who opposed their advance," women "met by a great body of police against which they flung themselves again and again," women "in a battle royal with the police that lasted six hours, and was characterized by scenes unparalleled in the history of Westminster."

More cautious members of the movement, who were originally known as "suffragists," felt that notoriety and public agitation would hinder the cause, and separated themselves from the more confrontational and aggressive suffragettes. The suffragettes had their own war song, which was sung on the hustings, and on the marches to the House of Commons. It was published in full, surrounded by pictures of the leaders of the movement, on February 23, 1907, in *The Illustrated Mail*. It had four verses and was to be sung to the tune of "John Brown's Body." The second verse is as follows:

> We storm'd the House of Commons with our little band so true,
> And we frightened all the statesmen till they trembled thro' and thro',
> They clapped us into prison and we gladly went for you,
> And the cause goes marching on.

The women of "the cause" were beginning to catch the public imagination. A week before the war song was printed, the same paper gave major coverage to the marriage of one of the leaders, Teresa Billington, to Frederick Lewis Greig, a Glasgow businessman, under the heading, "Courtship of a

Suffragette." Lavishly illustrated, it shows a suffragette complete with her "Votes for Women" banner, reluctantly pulling away from a gentleman with one hand outstretched towards her, the other gallantly holding his bowler aloft. Photographs of the pair are enclosed in beribboned hearts. Although the illustration suggests the difficulties inherent in such a union, the caption is not critical. It says that Teresa Billington "has … suffered imprisonment for the cause," and that she will keep her own surname, adding it to that of her husband— Billington-Greig—a form that would take about eighty more years to become common practice.

The article on the marriage also covers the two-thousand-strong march on the Houses of Parliament, and illustrates the extraordinary mix of classes in that procession: "Women of title, women of culture, and women of the workshops walked bravely through the rain to prove to the male population that they are entitled to votes." The writer creates a striking picture of the women in the procession, the majority of whom would have been totally unaccustomed to exposing themselves in such a fashion:

> Though motor-omnibuses lumbered by, splashing mud in their faces, though their skirts were streaked and stained with London's own particular street mixture, they struggled on heroically. The weather made it impossible for them to look their best, but for once they bowed to the inevitable. Their faith in the cause compensated them largely for the disorder of their hair, the muddiness of their clothing and the peculiar angle of their hats…. At one point, where the jeering was unusually loud, a well-dressed young man stepped forward and presented one of the Suffragettes with a bunch of violets…. The scoffing ceased in a moment and the ribald laughter changed to something like shame-faced silence.

At the head of the procession was Lady Frances Balfour, sister-in-law of Arthur Balfour, former prime minister and leader of the Conservative party, which had suffered one of the greatest defeats in British electoral history two years earlier—a year that saw the election of fifty-three Labour members of parliament.

Among the women who elected to go to jail was Mrs. Despard, the sister of General French, one of Britain's leading military figures during the Boer War. He was quoted in the press as saying, "We have tried all we could to keep Mrs. Despard from mixing up with these people. If she will join in this foolish agitation she must expect to suffer. My own opinion is that the police have been far too lenient. This business ought not to have been allowed to go on as long. The women have simply been made bolder by the policy of the authorities." The military neanderthal, who publicly castigated his own sister, would eventually be held accountable for far greater human tragedies than the breaking of a few umbrellas over the heads of the unfortunate police he judged too lenient.

Consuelo chose a different way to move mountains on very different terrain. She herself quotes a contemporary account as saying that "the Duchess of Marlborough understands the British public. She is in closer touch with the thrifty spirit of the nation, which abhors the house-burning and window-breaking methods of illuminating grievances, than any of her radical co-workers." This is, of course, a barb aimed at those violent, undignified women who were betraying their class, but it is also an unusual compliment from the notoriously chauvinistic British press that this American duchess had a better grasp of what would bring about change than did many of the British themselves.

Only, it was not her understanding of the British public that made Consuelo so effective; it was her understanding of the elite class into which she had married. She knew where the power lay in Britain, and she knew that two apparently trivial stratagems were the most powerful weapons in her particular arsenal: flattery and fine dining. It was now not only acceptable, but *de rigueur*, for women to be seen in public entertaining guests, particularly if it was at the Carlton. And the Carlton was not the only place where Consuelo used those same formidable weapons to sway the opinion of all those "bishops, politicians, butterflies of fashion, industrial captains and bigwigs," as the same contemporary account puts it. She brought the fight for the rights of the underprivileged to her dining-table in Sunderland House.

The example in her memoirs dates from 1913, after Dora's time with the Duchess of Marlborough, but it is only one of many. On the pretext of entertaining them, she assembled a powerful group of leaders from the church, industry and politics at her home who came "in the expectation of passing a pleasant hour or two exchanging trite moral reflections over tea and strawberries and gratuitous champagne," only to find that the entertainment also included listening to the stories of twelve old women who had been employed in the sweatshops of Britain.

The Sunderland House conference may be an extreme example of the method used by the ex–Duchess of Marlborough to influence the powerful elite, but the one ingredient all such invitations had in common was a good cellar and fine cuisine. It is uncertain when Dora first worked with an Escoffier-trained chef, but it is more likely than not that the Sunderland House chef had trained with "*Le Maître*." By this time, Escoffier was training up to sixty chefs in his kitchens, some of whom would move into private homes, others to hotels in which he had an interest. He was not only a propagandist about food, but he loved teaching (for which he was handsomely paid), and it seems more than likely that the fine French chef in Consuelo's kitchen, who had personally hired Dora, came from the Carlton.

Not all were won over by the American duchess with the swan-like neck and the deceptively gentle eyes of a fawn—and certainly not all women. Headed by Lady Jersey, and championed by influential men such as Lord Curzon, Lord Cromer and Sir Edward Tennant, the Women's Anti-Suffrage League rallied their troops to oppose the monstrous army of women who sought to liberate themselves from the patriarchal yoke.

Undoubtedly, what was as disturbing for Lady Jersey, Lady Robson, Lady Desart and their class was the presence in the suffrage movement of women of their own class marching side by side with ordinary working-class women—such as the eight women who had travelled from Lancashire to represent fifty thousand women workers, and who spoke on the second great march of 1907 to two thousand people in Trafalgar Square.

They were right, of course, to be disturbed. As soon as the lines were not firmly drawn, then that narrow, privileged world was under siege. All change had to be resisted, all the protocols had to be observed. Even the omission of a single word could shift the balance of power—as in the wedding service.

In 1912, Una Dugdale, a suffragist and the niece of a viscount, married the secretary of the Men's Political Union for the Enfranchisement of Women, Victor Duval, in the Chapel Royal, after a fight to have the word "obey" removed from the wedding service. She failed, because at the last minute the Archbishop of Canterbury intervened to say that the marriage would not be legal if that one word was left out. Before a congregation that included leaders of society, and of the women's movement, including Christabel Pankhurst and Lady Pethwick Lawrence, the marriage service was read "as prescribed in the Prayer-Book." However, *The Times* informed its readers, "it was stated afterwards by a relative of Miss Dugdale's that the word 'obey' was not uttered by her."

Of all the silences that Dora kept, perhaps the most to be regretted is the silence about her time at Sunderland House. It was one of the briefest of her stays, but it was probably the most influential in terms of her advancement in her profession.

Although she never told her family she had once worked for Consuelo, Duchess of Marlborough, in her two-million-dollar Mayfair mansion, there is one tangible link between Dora and Consuelo, and all those bigwigs and butterflies of fashion.

In Dora's hatbox there is a collection of dozens of exquisitely printed, gilt-edged menus, with coats of arms at the head. Among them is one from Sunderland House, dated "23 *Mai, 1911*" and the title reads, "*Souper de Bal.*"

Although the sandwiches included in the menu suggest this was probably set up buffet-style, the menu bears various hallmarks of an Escoffier-trained chef. First, there are no hors d'oeuvre, as such: Escoffier was not a fan of hors d'oeuvre, because strong flavours ruined the subtle taste of the soup or fish that followed. Oysters, caviar or smoked salmon were acceptable. Secondly, there are Russian salads; every chef trained with Escoffier came away with a good arsenal of Russian dishes, just as there always was a good selection of Russian cuisine in his writings, dating from his years at *Le Restaurant Français*. Thirdly, there is the use of fresh fruit —always Escoffier's favourite ingredient. On this menu, cherries are used with the duck and, as always on an Escoffier-influenced menu, the sweet course features fruit in some sort of alcoholic combination, as it often was, in this case, some of that "gratuitous" champagne. Escoffier also frequently used ices and ice-cream in some form or another to end the meal.

This one menu suggests that nineteen-year-old Dora was very much involved with the preparation of Consuelo's *Souper de Bal* that spring, and begged a copy from the chef to keep as a memento. Later on in her career, Dora will follow the lines of this supper party when she is cooking for the most distinguished of all her employers.

Dora's arrival in London corresponded with a seismic shift in the way women were beginning to perceive themselves. It was not so much that they were yet beginning to question their roles as wives and mothers, but their place, legally and politically, as wives and mothers in that society. If she went to see the king open parliament, Dora likely went with a girlfriend or two to watch all those women marching by with their banners and their war cry, "Vote for Women!" Standing there in the rain, huddled under their own umbrellas in Trafalgar Square, the little kitchen maids heard women expressing views that seemed even more startling and inspiring, coming as they did from women in society who appeared to have the world as their oyster.

Even in the servants' hall, there were changes that affected both men and women and their right to protection under the law. In 1907, the year that Dora came to London, the new Servants' Compensation for Injury Act was passed. The act affected about a million domestics in Great Britain, and *The Times* recorded that "Wise householders are already taking out policies with the insurance companies to cover the legal obligations of the new Act."

Besides the practical benefits of such a law, the fact that their class finally was considered entitled to such protection must have given servants a moral boost. In the past, there had been no legal recompense if they could not work for a while, or if injuries ended their livelihoods. They could still be let go at a moment's notice if they were deemed unsatisfac-

tory—or immoral—but now they could not just be turned out the door if they were injured during the course of their duties.

Dora and her fellow servants obviously shared their delight in this new-found recognition of their worth. Her friend Mary sends her a chatty card about going to help her father collect the rents at Thornton Heath, and about buying the material for her costume (perhaps her maid's outfit) in Croydon. She hopes Dora is getting on all right on her "lonesome" and admonishes her, "Dear, if you can't be good be careful of this motor … sent this for a joke."

The times were changing, and an impressionable teenager belowstairs listened, and drew strength from the courage she saw displayed in the streets of London by her own sex, and the example set in a Mayfair mansion by an upstart American duchess. The refusal of so many women, from so many different social classes, to accept the status quo must have played a major role in Dora's own refusal to accept that someone of her abilities should always remain merely a kitchen maid. For, in September 1911, Dora made a quantum leap in her progress up the downstairs hierarchy. She moved from the London home of an American dollar princess to work for the descendant of an Irish beer baron: Walter Edward Guinness.

RECIPE FROM DORA'S COLLECTION
Punch Biscuits

16 oz sugar	12 egg yolks
3 whole eggs	lemon rind
12 oz flour	10 oz melted butter
8 whipped whites	

These are the biscuits (cookies) that Escoffier used as the base for the vanilla mousse with chocolate truffles in his *Bombe Néron*. This hand-written recipe therefore probably dates from somewhere around 1911 to 1913.

In some of her recipes, Dora gives basic instructions on how to work with the ingredients. In this one, she clearly felt no need to do so, because she had either worked with an Escoffier-trained chef, or had watched Escoffier himself, and knew what to do. All she needed to do was to make a note to herself of that intriguing balance of whole eggs, yolks and whites. The recipe is in her Escoffier cookbook, but the fact that she wrote it out suggests she was making these biscuits before she acquired the cookbook.

The egg yolks and whole eggs are first beaten with the sugar; lemon rind is added next, followed by blending the flour into the mixture. The melted butter would then be stirred in. Lastly, the whipped egg-whites would be gently folded in to give lightness to a very rich concoction—which itself is only a small part of an even richer mélange. Escoffier's recipe also uses rum and some orange zest with the sugar. The mixture is baked in buttered moulds, cases or rings, "according to the purpose it is intended for."

The finished product is more like a shortcake than a cookie, or biscuit, and makes a great base for fresh fruit, such as strawberries.

PART THREE

Cook

Six

Beer and Baronets

*Some said it started as an accident, that his father burnt the malting
barley and the caramelized result was better than had ever been
brewed before... Others suspected there was magic in the water of the
St. James' Gate Well and it was the Liffey which gave Guinness
porter its distinctive taste.*

MICHELE GUINNESS, *THE GUINNESS LEGEND*

In a land of leprechauns and Blarney-stones, there are few
more far-fetched fairy tales than that of Dora's new employers. The origins of the family have their own share of myth
and legend, but it all seems to have begun when a fun-loving
cleric, the Archbishop of Cashel, in County Kildare, died in
1752 and left a hundred pounds each to his servant, Richard
Guinness, whose dark, home-made brew had made the archbishop's parties such a hit with the local gentry, and to Richard's
son, Arthur. Arthur first started a small brewery in Leixlip,
just over the border of County Kildare, and then headed
for Dublin. He bought a small brewery at St. James' Gate,
turned it into a going concern, married an heiress, and never
looked back.

The Guinness family tree is a complex sight to behold. Not
only were Arthur's descendants prolific, but they moved with
such skill and circumspection up various social, political and
industrial trees that there is a banking branch, a brewing
branch, and even an evangelical branch.

Politics in Ireland have always been a dangerous game,

even before Oliver Cromwell took possession of the great estates in the seventeenth century and handed them over to his Protestant followers, thereby creating an Anglo-Irish aristocracy of landowners who cared little or nothing about their tenants. Arthur Guinness used his wealth judiciously, strengthening his position in local government and endowing various influential and prestigious institutions. About twenty years after arriving in Dublin, Arthur was Master of the Corporation of Brewers, and official brewer to the English Viceroy in Dublin Castle. Finally, he was in a powerful enough position to persuade parliament in Dublin to abolish the crippling excise tax on Irish beer.

The main thrust of Arthur's argument was certainly original: he proposed that beer should be encouraged as a healthy alternative to the heavy whisky drinking that caused such devastation among the Irish. By the time he died, his sons had leading positions in the church, the army, the lawcourts and the brewing industry. The Guinness brewery was Ireland's biggest single business enterprise, and the largest porter brewery in the world.

A generation later, Arthur's grandson, Benjamin, who had taken over the brewery, became Lord Mayor of Dublin, and the richest man in Ireland. By 1890 *his* youngest son, Edward Cecil, was a multimillionaire, and the firm of Arthur Guinness and Son had now gone public, with Edward keeping one-third of the share capital for himself and his family. The gift of a quarter of a million pounds—a vast sum of money at the time —to be held in trust for the construction of housing for "the working poor," paved the way to a title: Baron Iveagh of County Down. His marriage to his distant cousin, Adelaide, adds further complexity to the Guinness family tree, by linking the banking and the brewing lines that had more or less divided by this generation.

In fact, it was matters of marriage and class that gave Edward Cecil control of the brewery business. Edward bought out his older brother Arthur, whose wife, the daughter of the Third Earl of Bantry, found the connection with trade distasteful. Arthur purchased a title with some of the proceeds, and when he died, well before his wife, one of the *bons mots* out of Dublin was that she wanted to give him time to make the right connections up there.

The right connections were everything—and often not enough. Looking at the evolution of the Guinness family, one can only marvel at the brilliant manipulation of their wealth that enabled these "dollar princes"—called by some "the beerage"—to penetrate one of the most exclusive clubs in the world: the British aristocracy.

It was one thing to "buy" your way into that coterie—once in, you had to be able to behave to the manner born, and Edward Cecil's great advantage in the battle between beer and baronetcy was his wife. "Dodo," as everyone called her, knew how to play the aristocratic role, because she had been groomed in the courts of Napoleon and Eugénie for a noble marriage. At Farmleigh in Ireland, and Berkeley Square in London, their parties became the stuff of legend. Socialite Augustus J. Hare noted in his diary in June 1879: "… I was with the Prince at Mrs. E. Guinness' ball, on which £6000 are said to have been wasted. It was a perfect fairy-land, ice pillars up to the ceiling, an avenue of palms, a veil of stephanotis up to the staircase, and you pushed your way through a brake of papyrus to the cloakroom."

The death of a maharaja provided them with the perfect country seat. Elveden Hall in Suffolk had been the home of the Maharaja Duleep Singh—his compensation for having his estates in the Punjab annexed by the British army. Edward Cecil turned the heathland around his mansion into the finest pheasant and partridge shoot in England, attracting both Edward VII and his son, the Duke of York, who was a crack shot.

Walter Edward Guinness, Dora Lee's employer for the next two years, was the third son of Edward and Dodo. Educated at Eton, he had served with distinction in the Boer War, and had then entered parliament. He married into the old British aristocracy in 1903 by taking Lady Evelyn Erskine, the third daughter of the Fourteenth Earl of Buchan, as his wife. He and his brothers, Rupert and Arthur, owned three great mansions on Grosvenor Place, facing the west wall of Buckingham Palace, and it was here that the Guinnesses entertained the most powerful people in Britain.

Walter's house at Grosvenor Place was in many ways an extension of the powerful Carlton Club, and he entertained ministers of His Majesty's government across one of the best boards in London. From September 1911, Dora's London address would be 11 Grosvenor Place, and she would be one of the chief architects of that "best board." Her other addresses during that period would be Knockmaroon House, the family seat in Ireland, not far from Dublin, and Rue de Poitiers, Paris, Walter Guinness's Paris *hôtel*, or town house. This is the only period of Dora's professional life in England that she spoke about at all with her family, and then it was for only one reason and about only one fact: that it was the Guinnesses who had sent her to train with the great Escoffier in Paris.

Dora spent the winter in London with the Guinnesses. Taken from *The Times* for March 16, 1912, the guest list for just one of those dinners that Dora helped put on the table—under difficult circumstances—includes the Marquess of Lincolnshire, the Marquess of Londonderry, the Countess of Kerry and Viscount and Viscountess Churchill. In April 1912 Dora made her first journey to Knockmaroon House, her first trip outside the British Isles and her first experience of Irish country-house life.

It was also her first experience of the Irish Sea—"a beastly crossing," as one of Dora's correspondents described it. Those stormy crossings were so unpleasant that they are among the few reminiscences she shared with her family. The Irish

Sea was no respecter of class; in his diary, Victor Cavendish records being thrown out of his bunk in the middle of the night during one particularly wild crossing.

One of the disadvantages of working with the Guinnesses was having to endure the discomforts of seasickness on that "quickest and best route," while in charge of all the equipment that was transferred from one house to another. It was somewhere around this period in her professional life that Dora started using the leather-bound "Ladies' Elegant Pocket Souvenir for 1856."

Very few of the entries are dated, and do not appear to be in any chronological order. It is as if a harried Dora whisked out her little almanac and hastily jotted down what she needed to remember—the writing is rushed and often unclear—but there is a dated entry that reads, "Ireland 26 July 1912," which is in three parts. The first is an expense account for the trip that includes taxis, travelling and porters, and adds up to fourteen shillings and sixpence. Alongside it Dora has written "£1," which may be the amount she was given by the housekeeper to cover her costs. The second part reads, "1 cutter, 8 knives, 2 bags, 1 steel," followed by "Casserole, brass covers, copper covers." Obviously Dora has taken along with her various pieces of kitchen equipment so that she will not be in the position of poor Jessie when she found herself in "the last place God made." Quite why she took only covers with her is strange, but perhaps she means something different by the word—in French, *couvert* means a main course, or a dish. The bags are almost certainly piping bags for sugar and icing decorations.

Other lists in the almanac include clothes lists, and Dora often had to pack up without warning and take off to London or Paris whenever the Guinnesses' social and political life demanded it. One list includes twelve aprons, four white dresses and two pairs "combs" (combinations). The large number of aprons suggests that Dora is meeting on a regular basis with her mistress to discuss the menu—when she would have put on a fresh apron over her dress.

There are other entries that suggest Dora was given greater responsibilities, involving not only recommending new servants, but actually being involved in hiring them. One reads: "May Ford, 19 years old 11 months, under parlour 2nd 12 months, wages £20–22, laundry [illegible] found. Town and Country." The next is as follows: "Ada Sergeant, aged 23 years. Scullery maid 2 years singlehanded. Wages £24, inexperienced kitchen maid. Town and Country." Given the lifestyles of the rich and famous of the period, it was undoubtedly an asset to have experience of city and country routines. Later on, when her friend needed help, Ada did not forget that Dora had given an inexperienced kitchen maid a push up the downstairs hierarchy.

The Guinnesses may have become members of the aristocratic class by marriage, but they had roots in Ireland that were far removed from those of the Anglo-Irish aristocracy or the Devonshires. Although the Guinnesses appear from Dora's record to have been in Ireland in July, the usual time for the aristocracy to return to their Irish properties was between January and April, generally to entertain vast numbers of guests with hunting and shooting. As in Britain, shooting was restricted to men only and subjected the women to hours of tedium. One bored wife, Lady Clodagh Anson, in an almost Chekhovian description, remembered shooting parties as "awful things ... The men went off after breakfast, and all the wives sat around in the drawing room making unattractive things in wool ... dinner [was] a very long affair with six or seven courses. How does one live through such things?"

As the wives sat, bored to death inside, the death-toll outside in the fields and woods rose to obscene levels. Pheasants, hares, rabbits, woodcock, snipe and grouse were all sacrificed to the gun, their deaths duly and diligently noted in the estate records. On one of the estates, Charleville Forest, the death-toll on December 9, 1873, was recorded as seven thousand, one hundred and thirty-one. Not all wives remained unmoved and merely bored. One member of the Anglo-Irish ascendancy, Shane Leslie, remembers his mother sitting in the car, weeping at the sight of heaps of gleaming, feathered bodies. But then, being American by birth, she was not bred to this particular form of butchery.

Knockmaroon House was a plain, Georgian-style house that looks from pictures to have been roomy and serviceable, rather than grand or imposing—the house of a gentleman, in fact, rather than an aristocrat. While servants such as Dora, or personal maids and valets, who had particular skills, commuted between the various homes of their employers, there would have been a staff who remained behind in Knockmaroon.

Dora was a young woman with a strong sense of humour and a love of fun. Her girlfriends reminisced with her about jokes shared on their days off, and giggled about their employers or their boyfriends, and she would have got a charge out of the Irish servants she met in the kitchen and servants' hall. Many of them never got the hang of the decorum and deferential demeanour expected of a ducal servant. Queen Victoria's son, at one time governor-general of Canada, on a visit to Ireland shortly after his mother's death, was assured by the butler that the blinds were still down in nearby Portadown "in mourning for your royal highness's ma'." Two Irish valets, rashly taken to London for Queen Victoria's Jubilee, got drunk and ran down Oxford Street shouting, "To hell with your bloody old queen."

The Guinness family had a long tradition of treating their servants with more than usual consideration, rewarding excellence among those who waited on them. And among those who now waited on Edward and Evelyn Guinness was a gifted and hard-working nineteen-year-old kitchen maid called Dora Lee.

The postcards from France in Dora's collection begin with two cards from Alice to Grosvenor Place. One has a photograph of the Louvre Museum, the second is of the Eiffel Tower, which Alice has marked with an "X":

Thanks so much for the letter and P.C. I am afraid I shall not know you. You are getting nice looking "Eh what." Will write soon. With love to both, Alice. We are going up that tower one day.

In Dora's collection is a sepia-tinted photograph of *Le Grand Palais*, Paris, addressed to the mews attached to Grosvenor Place, where once the coachmen and grooms lived, close to their horses. By now it was occupied by the

drivers and mechanics employed by the Guinness family to look after their automobiles:

Dear H. This is the place where the Paris motor show is held every December.

Thought you would like a card of it. You can tell Ede from me that she need not think I don't know who sent the Torquay post-card. I'm Sexton Blake. Write again soon. Yours, Jack.

"H"—Harry—gives Dora five cards for her collection. They provide a picture of the good time some of the Guinness staff are having amidst the popular pleasures of a new century, celebrated ten years earlier by the 1901 Universal Exhibition of Paris in a landscape of iron and steel, amid the five thousand multicoloured lights of the Palace of Electricity on the Champ de Mars. Forty million people came to see this exposition of a brave new world, described in the inaugural speech by Prime Minister Alexandre Millerand as a world in which "the machine is crowned Queen of the World. Automatons of iron and steel are driving out the worker of flesh and blood, turning him into a mere auxiliary." Such a pronouncement from one of the privileged class—himself a leading industrialist—does not sound reassuring for the masses in the new century.

There were, in fact, ominous portents everywhere: the Russo-Japanese War from 1904 to 1905 had given everyone a glimpse of the horrors of the new weaponry—machine-guns, mines, torpedoes—and yet most people would still have endorsed the euphoric statement of the kaiser at the beginning of the new century: "I lead you towards a splendid era."

None of this would have bothered Jack or Alice. She would have gone up the Eiffel Tower, thrilled and overwhelmed by that bare-bones structure, so alien to her Victorian-Edwardian sensibilities. He would have marvelled at the huge, vaulting iron ribs of the great cupola in *Le Grand Palais* that arched over the magnificent steel beasts beneath. Henry Ford's assembly line in Detroit was still two years away, but two years after the 1901 exposition, there were already thirteen thousand automobiles on French roads.

The Sexton Blake Jack refers to is a detective of popular fiction who first made his appearance in 1894—a stock character for all seasons, infinitely changeable to suit the fads, fancies —and fears—of more than one generation. Like many of his nation, for instance, his relationship with the kaiser was ambivalent, and in a chain of adventures involving the two— who are on first-name terms—Sexton and Wilhelm call on each other from time to time for help.

In a card with a picture of the Paris Hippodrome sent soon after, Jack writes:

> Dear H. Here is a card you can show 'em. THE AB-SO-LUTE largest and finest picture show in the world. Gaumonts Picture Palace. IT IS fit to beat the band. Yours Jack.

Jack was right. Gaumont's Palace was indeed "LE PLUS GRAND CINEMA DU MONDE" which were the words writ large over the portals of the 3400-seat Hippodrome in the Place

Clichy, first opened in 1900. Léon Gaumont, founder of the cinema chain, purchased it complete with its magnificent Cavaillé-Col organ, then refurbished and reopened it in October 1911, when an enthralled Jack was among the earliest patrons.

It was a popular practice to turn photographs into postcards, and Dora had many in her collection. One is of a garage in Paris showing four men with two

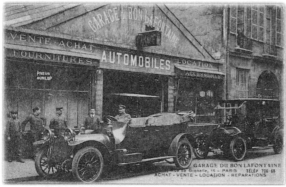

cars, one with a chauffeur at the wheel, which is on the right-hand side. The caption reads, "Garage du bon Lafontaine. 16, Rue de Gienelle, Paris. Telep. 706-68. ACHAT—VENTE—LOCATION—REPARATIONS."

By 1911, when those postcards were written, the automobile was a common enough sight in the stables and garages of the wealthy in Britain and France. About ten years earlier, most repairs outside the main capital cities had to be done by the local blacksmith, and for any major repairs requiring spare parts, the manufacturer had to send out not only the parts, but mechanics who understood what to do with them. An American motor journalist, writing in 1905, felt that no sensible driver would leave home without carrying seventy spare parts with him. Understandably, this gave a great deal of prominence to that new member of the servant class: the chauffeur.

In his peaked cap, buttoned-down jacket and breeches, the chauffeur stood out from the rest of his class, but his position was not an enviable one. The popular press jibed that all he did was ferry the mistress of the house to and from the stores, and take parlour-maids out for a spin. He was, in many ways, neither fish nor fowl, because in many cases he did not drive the car. The owner drove the car, keeping his liveried attendant around in case an emergency arose that might require such messy manual labour as changing a tire, or crawling underneath the vehicle. Since proximity with a servant was unusual, to say the least (although many a gentleman's gentleman must have removed the clothing of a drunken master, the only servant to touch anyone sober would have been the lady's maid), in some cases the chauffeur had to sit on the floor out of sight until needed. From the postcards Dora was given, it was clear that the mechanical side of things loomed large. There are no cards about carefree jaunts along the *Routes Nationales* of France.

Those messages arriving at Grosvenor Place gave Dora glimpses of Paris that made her feel envious during that winter in London, when she begged Harry Day for his cards to add to her collection. The Guinnesses' social and political life always kept their staff on their toes, but Dora was having to pick up more than her usual share of the load. Lizzie, writing from the Earls Court area of London on Christmas Day, 1911, to wish Dora "a very Happy Christmas and a bright New Year," also says that she is very sorry to hear about Ada and hopes "she is going on alright."

Round about the busiest time for family celebrations, Dora's right-hand woman has taken ill and, to make matters worse, Dora herself has a problem. Jessie, as has happened before, has to forgo a meeting because her employers are having a lunch and dinner-party, and she adds, "I do hope your poor arm is alright today considering you are on your own."

Perhaps, besides out of self-interest, it was in recognition of services rendered in difficult circumstances that the Guinnesses rewarded their talented kitchen maid by sending her to Paris to train with *"Le Maître,"* Escoffier.

On April 24, 1912, an exuberant Dora sends Ada a card— rather aptly in the circumstances—of the Arc de Triomphe:

Dear Ada: How are you sagaciating Tut Tut. I have just got a nasty gash on my Phisog the result of a beer bottle, not a word. Love Fatty.

The majority of the cards in the collection, not unnaturally, are those received by Dora. So it is particularly fortunate that

Ada Sergeant kept this rollicking sample of Dora's writing style, with a glimpse of her life in Paris, and returned it to her friend. The message is brief, but it reveals a great deal about the nineteen-year-old who sent it.

Significantly, it gives the reader a look at Dora's managerial style in that hierarchical structure. Ada is her subordinate, but Dora is not the least concerned about telling her she has been in a drunken brawl, however peripheral her role in it may have been. The Guinnesses, presumably, are in Paris with other senior staff members so, although Dora asks Ada to keep it to herself, she is not worried about them finding out from her card.

Dora's writing style is juicy, her vocabulary entertaining and original. "Sagaciating" obviously means, "Are you being a good girl?" which Dora herself is *not*.

"Phisog," from "physiognomy" (face), is a slang expression far more likely to have been used by someone of her employer's class. It is not the only example from the cards of Dora and her friends aping such expressions and using them tongue-in-cheek: in October 1911 Alice had used "eh what," when she talked about how good-looking Dora had become, and vacationing George had spoken of having "a ripping time" in Ramsgate. Their use conjures up scenes of great mirth and hilarity in the kitchen, as the servants mimicked their masters' and mistresses' accents and behaviour. A good laugh is a great way to deal with injustice, or just plain condescension.

And "Fatty"? Fatty is definitely Dora, because the handwriting is hers. Nice-looking Dora is living it up, and putting on the pounds, as she cooks and eats her way through one of the most extraordinary experiences of her young life.

In 1908, Escoffier posed for a photograph on the roof of the Carlton Hotel with his staff—all fifty-two of them. Here, too, there is a clearly defined hierarchy. The *chefs de partie* sit on each side of Escoffier in his black frock coat and, in the back row, stand the dishwashers, *les plongeurs*, minus the white coats and chef's hats of the rest of the staff. But, in spite of the pecking order, there is a sense of the new pride and honour that Escoffier had given by his own achievements to the members of a once-despised profession, which they now proudly called *le métier*.

There is one other striking detail: the fifty-two members of the Carlton staff are all men. By 1911, when Dora was sent to train with Escoffier at the Ritz in Paris, that particular statistic would not have changed much, if at all. Most of the British cooks who trained with Escoffier went to the Carlton, and it is unlikely that there were many British cooks in that Paris kitchen, and even more unlikely that there were women. In the light of that alone, it cannot be stressed enough just how amazing was the achievement of nineteen-year-old Dora Lee.

What would Dora have seen, that memorable day in April, when she walked into the kitchens of the Paris Ritz? Before her stretched a vast room, divided into sections that dealt with different areas of expertise, and various stages of the meal. Just in front of her was the *table chaude*, where the waiters picked up the plates of food. Beyond that was a huge cast-iron stove in the middle of the room, near the *rôtissoire* with its army of spits. On each side of the ornately decorated chimney of the charcoal-burning grill, the walls were lined with dozens and dozens of plates of all sizes, and pots and pans hung from the ceiling above the stove. On one side of the room was the *plonge*, where the dishwashers (lowest of the low in the pecking order) worked ceaselessly, and in a separate area alongside was the white coolness of the *garde-manger*—its high walls covered with sides of beef, lamb, pork, venison and game. From their different stations, dozens of men eyed this comely rare bird in their midst—the waiters in their ties and tails, the *chefs de partie* in their trademark whites, the *plongeurs* with their powerful arms crossed in a precious moment of relaxation over their thick leather aprons.

Dora, aged two, on the knee of her mother, Annie, with her
father, Samuel, and other family members. Even at this age, she
looks the world straight in the eye.

Sir Walter Edward Guinness, Dora's employer from 1911-1912.
It was the Guinness family who sent Dora to train
with Escoffier in Paris.

Auguste Escoffier. A photograph taken about the time
Dora trained with him in Paris.

STANLEY G. VINCE

Dora Lee, aged about twenty-one, in male Highland costume.
Taken in a photographer's studio in Aboyne around 1913-1914,
when she was working for the Neumanns
at their hunting lodge in Scotland.

STANLEY G. VINCE

An upper servants' dining room, possibly at one of the
Neumann or Guinness homes, with the table laid for an
important dinner and two of the staff posing in formal dress.
The room is pleasantly decorated, with even a piano
provided for entertainment.

STANLEY G. VINCE

Eight footmen in the Devonshire livery, their hair powdered,
posing in the formal dining room at Rideau Hall around
1918-1919—a similar mirror hangs there today. One can see how
vital it was to have well-turned calves and a good head of hair.

STANLEY G. VINCE

Dora, first cook, with her staff in the kitchens of Rideau Hall,
1918-1919. She is pouring herself a glass of wine.

STANLEY G. VINCE

Dora in the centre of the Rideau Hall staff. Since everyone is
well wrapped up, it is probably the winter of 1918-1919. Her
front-and-centre position in the photograph reflects
her status in that downstairs hierarchy.

STANLEY G. VINCE

Dora, her victorious women's hockey team and their coaches
pose proudly with their trophy. This probably dates from
around the winter of 1918-1919, but nothing is
known of the league in which they played.

STANLEY G. VINCE

Dora enjoying the pleasures of a Canadian
winter, on her toboggan.

STANLEY G. VINCE

Dora, Get Your Gun. The gun looks like a Martini-Enfield rifle, modified for target practice with a peep-sight at the rear.

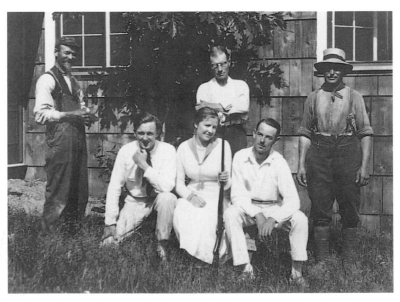

Dora with gun and a group of male staff. The cedar-shingled building behind them appears in other photographs—perhaps it was staff quarters at Meech or Blue Sea Lake.

The gasometer in the grounds of Rideau Hall:
it has housed gas cylinders, militia and maidservants.
It now holds the Rideau Hall archives.

STANLEY G. VINCE

Dora with her staff and the first of a long line of beloved fox
terriers. This obviously commemorates some sort of celebration
—the Red Ensign Dora is holding suggests perhaps Victoria Day.
This is the only photograph of Dora in her *bonnet*.

STANLEY G. VINCE

A laughing Dora in a sombrero, a clay pipe in her hand.
The photograph shows the vitality and spirit that carried her
through to the top of the downstairs tree.

STANLEY G. VINCE

This man appears in a few of Dora's photographs, and may well
be the mysterious Bert. Here he is dressed for his role as
postillion, in which he adorned the Devonshires' state
carriage and controlled the horses. The ribbons along
the pocket of his jacket mark him as a veteran, as
were most of the young men who came to Canada
on the Devonshires' staff. He appears in
another photograph in naval uniform.

STANLEY G. VINCE

Dora showing off her well-tailored suit and her white fox fur,
the marks of her new-found affluence in Canada.
Taken on the grounds of Rideau Hall—there is a glimpse
of the gasometer in the background.

STANLEY G. VINCE

The brooch given to Dora by the Prince of Wales in 1919.
Twenty rubies and eight pearls surround the Prince of Wales
Feathers in the centre, and the crown that holds the feathers is
studded with emeralds and rubies. The actual size is about
one and a half inches in width and length.

STANLEY G. VINCE

Dora and her husband, Archie Vince, on their wedding day,
March 10, 1921. She was twenty-eight years old;
he was twenty-one.

STANLEY G. VINCE

Lady Evelyn Fitzmaurice. A very young Evie, possibly
photographed when she came back to England from India
to be presented at court in 1890.

lady Evelyn Cavendish Copyright about 1891 ?

Victor Cavendish and Lady Evelyn Fitzmaurice. The handwritten
caption at the bottom suggests the date as 1891, and it was
probably taken on the occasion of their engagement.

Victor, ninth Duke of Devonshire. Whether standing alongside his
fiancé, his family, or a slaughtered tiger,
Victor's expression never changes.

Evelyn Cavendish, exquisite in eighteenth-century costume for
the great costume ball at Devonshire House in July 1897.

Victor and Evelyn Cavendish with Li Hung-Chang, the Chinese War Minister, on his visit to Barrow-in-Furness in August, 1896. The interpreter stands on Evie's right.

Evelyn, ninth Duchess of Devonshire, in her ceremonial robes.
From the age she appears to be in the photograph, it was
probably taken to mark Victor's assumption of the title in 1908.

Evie, the mother, reading to three of her younger children:
Dorothy, Rachel and Charles. Although the photograph is
obviously posed, she shared her children's life more than
many women of her class and era.

The vice-regal family in the grounds of Rideau Hall, probably the
winter of 1919. From left to right: Charles, Dorothy, the Duke
and Duchess of Devonshire, Anne, Maud, Rachel, Blanche.
The duchess and Blanche, who had a foot operation, do not wear
skis, and the duke wears snowshoes rather than skis. With his
gouty foot, both must have been painful and given him difficulty:
getting up after a fall on skis was a challenge, and Maud says he
used to trip over his own snowshoes because
his feet turned in. This photograph is in the Chatsworth
archives, but Dora had a copy of her own.

The arrival of the Duke and Duchess of Devonshire in Ottawa to
take up their vice-regal post on November 13, 1916.
Note the newsreel cameras in the foreground. The bald-headed
gentleman in the background is Lord Richard Nevill, the
Comptroller, and the uniformed man saluting is
Aide-De-Camp Angus Mackintosh. To Lord Richard's right
stands Maud, her face "bright blue" with cold.

A formal photograph of the Devonshire Household, most likely
taken on the occasion of Maud's engagement to Angus
Mackintosh. The young couple stand between the duke and
duchess, with Dorothy and Blanche to their right. Charles
stands behind his father. Rachel holds a little white dog, and her
sister Anne is in front of her, in a hat. Harold Macmillan,
who would later marry Dorothy, stands at the back on the
left in his military uniform. Dora had obtained a copy of
this photograph for her collection.

Stanley G. Vince

A formal portrait of the ninth duchess. The ribbons and badges
she is wearing appear in all formal pictures, and are not purely
decorative. They represent various ceremonial orders and titles.

Lady Evelyn Cavendish, painted by John Singer Sargent, that quintessential portrait-painter of the British aristocracy of the period. Victor Cavendish saw Sargent's work at the Royal Academy in May 1902, and asked him to paint his wife. The work was done at the artist's studio. Sargent has captured perfectly the shy aloofness of the young Evie but, although Victor liked the work-in-progress "very well," in July he found the finished result "rather stern."

Fifteen-year-old Dora took her courage into her hands when she made her solitary way to smoky London, and she would need every bit of that courage now. It is startling to think of her, walking into the kitchens of the Ritz, aged nineteen, facing that roomful of tough males. She did not speak much French—only cooking French—so she would not have understood most of what they said about her, or the foul language they used when tension mounted during the two daily *coups de feu*, but that attractive and lively nineteen-year-old would have had to fend them off. There was an old superstition among French chefs that it was unlucky to have a menstruating female in the kitchen, and some will have been openly hostile. She saw them lose their tempers, and she witnessed the fights that broke out. Again, that was one of the few details she told her family. They not only threw dishes, they threw the great knives they carried in leather scabbards around their waists—the knives that were their badge of office and their pride and joy. But she was where she had hoped to be, face to face with the little man who had given her this extraordinary chance, and Dora was going to seize the moment that fate—and a considerable fee paid by the Guinnesses had given her.

By the time Dora went to train with Escoffier, he was sixty-six years old, and had built up a staff of *chefs de partie* skilled in his methods. The chances are that most of her training was with these aristocrats of the kitchen, and she would have been moved from one area to another: from the *rôtissoire* to the *garde manger* and, finally, to work with the *chef saucier*, Escoffier's second-in-command. Escoffier, however, was very much in evidence; this was his kingdom, and he ruled it with a diminutive iron hand—"severe and minuscule" is the description of him given by Pierre Hamp, who trained with Escoffier at the Savoy. By far the biggest thing about him was his massive chef's *toque*, which towered above those of the rest of his staff.

To advance in the way Dora wanted to advance took more than being a good cook. Even in a private home as opposed to a hotel, it required the ability to organize and coordinate a huge body of subordinates, all of them working to create wonderful food that arrived on the table at the right moment, and at the peak of perfection. Escoffier will always be known to posterity as the man who created dishes such as *La Pêche Melba*, but perhaps his greatest achievement was the major overhaul of how a team creates such dishes. Although there had always been specialists in the kitchen—*le rôtisseur, le saucier* and so on—the general practice was to have one chef put together one dish. Years before Henry Ford's assembly line in Detroit, Escoffier started using mass production methods to create some of the most exquisite meals on the planet.

By the old method, a classic dish such as *Oeufs sur le plat Mayerbeer* took about fifteen minutes for a skilled chef to prepare, and there were problems keeping the various components at the peak of perfection. Under Escoffier, *l'entremettier* cooked the eggs, while the *rôtisseur* grilled the kidneys, and the *saucier* prepared the truffle sauce that completed the dish—thus reducing the time needed to about five minutes. To a generation three-quarters of a century beyond the dawn of the assembly line it sounds glaringly obvious—like cleanliness and adequate bathrooms in hotels—but at the time it was a true revolution of that hidebound kitchen tradition, and had much to do with Escoffier's success at the Savoy, the Carlton and the Ritz. To her natural gift as a cook Dora now added the ability to organize and control a team of between fifty to eighty people, with varying degrees of skill and different areas of expertise. In addition, she learned how to plan a menu and arrange the perfectly balanced meal. "Fatty"'s twenty-inch waistline became a thing of the past, as she sampled the legendary dishes she was learning to create.

Ever since the days when he learned to fashion flowers in wax, the chef who had wanted to be a sculptor had developed skills with ice and icing sugar that would have astonished Carême himself. He could sculpt ice, using a chisel, and polish it with a hot iron into a finish as fine as marble or alabaster. It is likely that the Guinnesses sent her to Escoffier to learn some of the more rarified techniques for which he was famous, which would adorn their dinner-table and impress their guests. In a world in which everyone could afford the finest champagne and the best caviar, style was everything.

In the 1890s, Pierre Hamp watched the brilliant *chef glacier*, Monsieur Eberlé, make mountains and castles out of huge blocks of Norwegian ice in the basement of the Savoy. These were then taken upstairs to be decorated with sugar figures cloaked in meringue, such as Escoffier's beautiful swan with its mist of *sucre filé*, the most sensational feature of the first *Pêche Melba*. Watching Escoffier or the *chef glacier*, Dora would have learned how to create baskets, flowers, birds—decorations and ornaments of all kinds—out of icing sugar. Years later, Dora would continue to decorate cakes with a skill and imagination far beyond most professional decorators. Years later, she would still have a collection of piping bags, like the ones she took with her on her travels between her employers' houses.

The culinary education of Dora would have taken her from the icing on the cake to the quality and selection of the raw ingredients in the *garde-manger*, which Escoffier considered indispensable to his art. Some of the entries in the Ladies' Almanac for 1856 are shopping lists which, although undated, give an interesting look at what Dora bought for her employers. One of the recurring items is sugar of different kinds and in huge quantities—one list reads, "7 lbs castor, 7 lbs demarara, 7 lbs loaf." Here, she has purchased a range of textures—castor sugar being the finest—for what appears to be a sizeable dessert dish. She also distinguishes between cooking salt and freezing salt—the latter, presumably, for use with the hundredweight of ice that appears on one shopping list.

As one would expect on the shopping list of a top chef, other recurring items are the ingredients for the basic stock indispensable to every good cook. Dora would already have learned about the creation of good stock without which, as Escoffier said, "no good cooking can be achieved." Many of the lists have various meats, including "stock meat" (on one list, 14 lbs) and fillet beef, rib ends of beef, best end neck lamb, shoulder lamb, mutton chops, ox tongue. There is fresh fish—plaice, sole, flounders—and the meat required for "barding" roasts of meat of various kinds: streaky bacon, side bacon and "lard." This could either be cooking lard, or fat, in the English sense, or the French word for bacon.

Another prominent grouping on the shopping lists is fruits of all kinds, from the humble to the exotic: bananas, pineapples, apricots, figs, plums, pears, oranges and masses of lemons. Such variety is taken for granted at the end of the twentieth century, but at the time it would indicate the shopping list for someone of considerable means. Dried fruits also appear: currants, raisins, sultanas. There is a wide range of vegetables, from watercress to turnips. There are the staples: cream of tartar, arrowroot, semolina, pearl barley, gelatine, oil, vinegar. There are pastas such as macaroni and vermicelli, and different kinds of rice—Patna and Carolina. There are the basics such as coffee and tea, although the make and type are not mentioned, as it is with cocoa, which is always Van Houtens'.

The cheeses listed are two generally used in cooking: Parmesan and Gruyère. And although Dora lists yeast (there is a recipe for rum babas in her collection), she obviously bought a good deal of the bread used, for she mentions French rolls, dinner rolls and even Hovis. She makes a distinction between "cooking eggs" and "fresh eggs," "cooking butter" and "fresh butter." In both cases, it will be the age of the ingredients that classify them, with salt possibly being added to the cooking butter. Most exotic of all are truffles and foie gras.

Truffles and foie gras are wonderful, but just as desirable was the basic hygiene that Escoffier also insisted upon. A kitchen had to be clean, and "scrubbing soap, soft soap, toilet soap, dish cloths, scrubbing brush, stove brushes, ammonia, Brasso" appear on the pages of the Ladies' Almanac. Presumably the ordering of all cleaning materials at one point was also the responsibility of this Escoffier-trained chef.

The days were long—sometimes as long as eighteen hours—but outside the kitchens of the Ritz, there was Paris. Renoir, the painter-chronicler of that turn-of-the-century city and its women, was long gone from its streets to his country paradise in Cagnes, but how he would have loved Dora! With her strong, supple hands, full lips, beautiful skin and lush curves, like the girls in *The Boatmen's Luncheon* or the young women in *Dance at the Moulin de la Galette, Montmartre*, Dora would have attracted many admirers. There would be plenty of friendly natives to show her around the Hippodrome, the bistros around the Moulin de la Galette, the smart shops along the Rue de la Paix, puppet shows, *le Guignol*, on the Champs Elysées and in the Tuileries gardens.

Unlike London, the classes mixed more freely in their pleasure-palaces and places of entertainment, and Dora would have seen society women and actresses, *demi-mondaines* and members of the middle-class at places like *La Grenouillère*, the restaurant on the Seine that is the setting for *The Boatmen's Luncheon*. At Porte Clichy, the street gangs, *les Apaches*, in their peaked caps and their tight trousers, still hung out with their girls who wore narrow shiny silk skirts and kept their money in their stocking-tops. The *café-concerts* (*les caf-concs*) of the *Belle Epoque*, such as *La Scala* on the Boulevard du Strasbourg, or *l'Eldorado* on the Boulevard Saint-Denis, continued to thrive, where Mistinguett and Maurice Chevalier began their careers. Was it there that Dora got hit in the phisog with a beer bottle? Or was it in a kitchen mêlée? We will never know, because she never said, in her later, respectable, middle-class years.

A rare bird she was indeed, in those Paris kitchens, but there was one woman who preceded Dora in the culinary world: the legendary Rosa Lewis, known as the Duchess of Jermyn Street. Rosa was twenty-three years older than Dora, so her career coincided with the heyday of Edward, Prince of Wales, but there are some striking parallels between their stories.

Rosa was put into service at about the same age as Dora, and her first place of work, 3 Myrtle Villas, sounds quite like The Ferns—a prosperous, middle-class home, where Rosa was the maid-of-all-work. Like Dora, she used her cooking skills to move up the downstairs ladder. She got herself a job as an under–kitchen maid with the Comtesse de Paris—leaving 3 Myrtle Villas unexpectedly and much against her parents' wishes. Dora probably did exactly the same thing when she left for London. And Rosa, like Dora, made it her business to pick up as much French as she could from the countess's French chef. Like Dora later on in her career, Rosa decided to freelance, using the services of an agency, and was hired by Lady Randolph Churchill (American Jenny Jerome, the mother of Sir Winston Churchill).

Did the two women ever meet? It seems possible they would have coincided at some point in that tight-knit, rarified world—two women who had beaten the odds, and who had both worked with the great Escoffier. Rosa trained with Escoffier ten years earlier than Dora, so by the time Dora had achieved any prominence in her profession, Rosa was a considerable property owner, and a personal friend of many of the aristocrats she served. They were both gifted and intelligent; they were both tough, earthy, humorous, unafraid—and successful in a male world. This alone ensured that Rosa would not have taken kindly to Dora. By 1909, "Mrs. Lewis, the well-known cook," was making the front pages of *The Times* organizing ministerial banquets for the Foreign Office. Rosa was unique, and she wanted to keep it that way.

By the time Rosa trained with Escoffier, she was around thirty years old and already well-known; when Dora trained with Escoffier in Paris, she was an unknown nineteen-year-old kitchen maid. Rosa reached professional prominence at the height of the glittering Edwardian era; Dora benefited from the golden afterglow. Both women married, but Rosa's marriage when she was twenty-five was a failure, and she never again let love or a personal relationship affect her professional success. Dora Lee, on the other hand, would one day allow her heart to rule her head.

RECIPE FROM DORA'S COLLECTION
Sabayon

1 lb powdered sugar	12 egg yolks in basin
1 quart dry white wine	

Whisk until finished.

These are all the details Dora needed to create one of the classics of French cuisine, the Gallic version of the Italian *zabaglione*. This would make a large quantity of *sabayon*—the average recipe for four people uses three egg yolks, so this presumably would serve about sixteen people. There are other versions of this sauce—some using the sugar syrup for the fruit it covers, some using champagne—

but one procedure they all have in common is the whipping of the ingredients over a *bain-marie*, or double boiler. Dora does not need to remind herself of that basic step. And, of course, the whisking would be done with a wire whisk, not with an electric beater. Years later, her son Stanley and his wife Beth gave her a Mixmaster for Christmas. She never used it—she still tucked the bowl under one arm and beat the mixture with her whisk.

Sabayon is the wine-custard used in the dish created by Escoffier for the Empress Eugénie, wife of Napoleon III. He placed pitted and peeled Montreuil peaches, interspersed with wild strawberries, in a silver dish set on ice, sprinkled them with sugar, and added a touch of kirsch and maraschino. Just before serving, he covered the peaches with the *sabayon*, which could only be made shortly before, but which had to be as cold as possible.

This sauce is usually served on fresh fruit of all kinds, and doubtless Dora used it on some of those exotics on her shopping list.

SEVEN

Butterflies and Bigwigs

Nostalgia is a natural emotion, and it is hard not to sympathize with those who regretted the passing of an era after 1914 ... Between 1900 and 1913 the world was close-knit as never before or since ... It was the Belle Epoque; *but it was also* l'Epoque Ephemère.

MALCOLM FALKUS

The list of guests in *The Times* for the Derby Night Ball at Devonshire House in 1911 reads like the cast list for some vast tableau of that watershed of time between the South-African War and the Great War so soon to come. At one long table decorated with pink malmaison carnations sat titled heads from virtually every kingdom and dukedom in Europe, from Princess Victoria of Schleswig-Holstein to Princess Victor of Hohenlohe, and there were dukes, earls and marquesses from every county in England. Ambassadors from Germany, Russia, Austro-Hungary, Sweden, Denmark, Belgium, France, Greece, Italy, Spain and the United States sat alongside prime ministers. Wilfrid Laurier, the prime minister of Canada, was there, as was Viscount Kitchener, the hero of Khartoum. There were four Guinnesses—among them Dora's soon-to-be employers—and four Rothschilds. Queen Mary was there, but the king was not present, because of court mourning.

The list of players for the Derby Night Ball of June 6, 1912, is very much the same. Little has changed in that upstairs world: pink and blue hydrangeas adorned the entrance hall, trails of Dorothy Perkins roses entwined the famous crystal

147

staircase. Evelyn, Duchess of Devonshire, received her guests at the entrance to the ballroom, and supper was served in a marquee lit by a myriad of electric candles, amid a host of carnations climbing giant bamboo plants. Out in the three acres of garden, hundreds of fairy lights twinkled in the trees, in the very heart of the city.

Once more, Devonshire House is the setting for the Derby Night Ball of 1914. A larger crowd attended than usual, because the queen had asked her friend Evelyn to invite guests whose court ball on May 14 was cancelled—again because of court mourning. Again there were Dorothy Perkins roses, hydrangeas and malmaison carnations. Again there were ambassadors and ministers—even a minister from China this time—and everyone danced to the music of Herr Boxhorn's orchestra. Whatever had happened beyond the walls of Devonshire House, nothing much had changed, it seemed, in that privileged world, between 1887 and 1914.

The course of Evelyn's life also seems unchanged, even more predictable than the lives of those at the other end of the social scale. Unlike Dora downstairs, there was nowhere for her to climb, for she was already at the top. The marquess's daughter had fulfilled her destiny and had done her duty. She had been fertile, and was now the mother of seven children, including the heir and a spare—the ideal combination in her world. She was a conscientious chatelaine of the dukedom's great homes, overseeing everything from balls to drains. On the death of the dowager duchess, Louise, she had taken on, albeit reluctantly, the ceremonial role of Mistress of the Robes for her queen, whom she had known since their dancing-class days. From contemporary accounts and the columns of *The Times* it appears a life with some frustrations, but without too much conflict, a path strewn with pink malmaison carnations and—apart from giving birth seven times—very little pain.

Later recollections paint a picture of a distant, haughty woman, who left her humanity behind when she took on the mantle of duchess. Those who knew her, then and now, would largely agree with that assessment. But behind the scenes is a different woman, the product not only of her class, but of her times.

Whatever reservations Evie had about her role as wife of Victor Cavendish, heir to one of the greatest titles in England, she would never have questioned the role society decreed for all women, whether God had made them high or lowly: motherhood. In fact, it was her inability to spend time in that role because of her official responsibilities that she most regretted. Indeed, the women who marched in the streets, or attacked policemen and politicians, would generally have agreed that motherhood was still one of the supreme achievements for a woman, even if it were not her only purpose in life.

When a woman gives birth to seven children in fourteen years, it seems unlikely she has had any troubles at all in fulfilling that destiny. However, a year after her marriage, Evie spends a month at a spa in Germany called Bad Schwalbach, which specializes in "diseases peculiar to women," and, even more specifically, in the treatment of uterine disorders in women returning from India.

The climate of India had taken its toll on Evie Cavendish. Simla was a respite between April and October, but for the other half of the year the viceregal headquarters were in Calcutta, where the heat was far more trying. The Lansdownes' letters are full of references to the difficulties of coping with the climate—from the dangers of malaria, typhoid and dysentery, to the unpleasantnesses of ringworm and prickly heat. In 1880, the wives and children of British soldiers stationed in India had a three times greater chance of dying before their time than if they had stayed in Britain.

India was hard on the women of the Raj; the numbing boredom of a life in which they did not have to lift a finger led to the mindless, gossip-filled days and desperate liaisons chronicled by Rudyard Kipling in his *Plain Tales from the Hills*. The Lansdownes' function in the Raj protected them from boredom, but it did not protect them from the dangers of the climate.

When Evie came back from India to marry Victor Cavendish, she was anaemic and underweight, and at some point had had an attack of jaundice, which had left her liver enlarged. London doctors had been of little or no help at all, and she was still unwell when she married Victor. After a year of marriage she either had not conceived, or had had at least one miscarriage. From evidence in her mother's letters, Evie's monthly cycle had been affected by her anaemic condition, and certainly her journey to Schwalbach suggests this. Evie knew what was expected of her, and she was not going to wait around any longer for nature to take its course.

By the middle of the nineteenth century, "taking the waters" had become part of the yearly routine of the privileged and the wealthy. For many, such as "Tum-Tum," it was a necessity—a period of recuperation from the excesses of the rest of the year. For most, it was merely a delightful and self-indulgent way of filling time.

There had always been a water culture of some kind, and eighteenth-century travellers took the waters after undergoing difficult and uncomfortable journeys, staying in flea-ridden accommodation to do so. But when those ancient springs so beloved of the Romans were patronized by the nineteenth-century upper crust, *le gratin*, the entrepreneurs moved in to provide first-class railroads, casinos, theatres and hotels. Even a spa water stinking of sulphur seemed more palatable when sipped from a Lalique glass. A night at the roulette table helped one forget the discomforts of the douche bath, the gargling bath and the slime bath—to name but a few of the tortures devised by doctors to keep the wealthy happy and, hopefully, healthy.

There were spas in many European countries—Evian-les-Bains in France; the Russian spas in the Caucasus; Marienbad in what was then Bohemia, patronized virtually every August by Edward VII—but some of the most glamorous spas were in Germany, and among them the most fashionable were Baden-Baden and Wiesbaden. It was to the Kursaal restaurant in Wiesbaden that Escoffier was seconded in 1870, when he was a prisoner of war. West of Wiesbaden lay the spa of Bad Schwalbach, where Evie Cavendish went to take the waters for a month in the summer of 1893.

At the time Evie visited it, most of the clientele was English and, according to one nineteenth-century writer, it had not been "sufficiently aristocratized" to have acquired the gorgeous trappings of Wiesbaden. One contemporary account declares that "in the way of amusements Schwalbach has not much to boast of; excellent bands play at stated hours in the Allee; there is a pretty park and miniature lake, reading and billiard rooms in the village ... " Even the setting was not as picturesque as that of "the romantic and secluded charms" of Wiesbaden, according to one dismissive traveller. However, Evie was not there for the scenery; she was there on a vital mission.

Mineral waters vary in composition. There are iodated and bromine saline waters, sulphurous mineral waters, and simple and saline chalybeate waters. Bad Schwalbach was particularly noted for its "ferruginous" chalybeate waters, rich in iron, and it had three springs, one of which, the *Paulinenbrunnen*, was only discovered in 1828. The other two were called the *Weinbrunnen* and the *Stahlbrunnen*. Iron-rich springs were considered a specific for gout, an inflammatory disorder that some doctors thought showed up in the limbs of men and in the uteruses of women, but very few men came to Schwalbach.

In ancient times, water was worshipped as the source of life, the mystical fluid that flowed from the earth's womb, but nineteenth-century Evie would have cared little for such fancies. All she cared about was getting back her health so she could become pregnant. Chronic inflammation of the womb was listed as one of the chief afflictions suffered by the women of the British Raj, according to Edward Tilt, a doctor writing in the 1870s, causing "abdominal pains, nervousness, depression of spirits, and perhaps hysteria."

In a chapter devoted to "Mineral waters in the treatment of diseases peculiar to women," Thomas More Madden, vice-president of the Dublin Obstetrical Society, writing in 1876, describes the values of the three springs in this female place of pilgrimage. From his account Evie probably favoured the *Weinbrunnen*, which was higher in iron and easier on the stomach. Its name derived from its earlier reputation as a cure for hangovers, and it is described by the doctor as "agreeable, piquant, and ferruginous in taste." He also tells the reader that "three-fourths of the invalid visitors to Schwalbach suffer from some form of anaemia ... nearly all authorities on the subject speak of the powerful action of this spa in certain forms of functional derangement of the female system."

The eminent doctor's description of various female disorders is accompanied by a striking paragraph on the mental aspect of such disorders: the phenomenon of hysteria:

> Hysteria in some form is generally associated with chronic uterine disease, and this underlies and complicates most of the symptoms for which gynaecologists are consulted. Counterfeiting every malady, acting through and upon the nervous system, attended with groundless apprehension, depression of spirits, and morbid irritability of temper, oftentimes rendering the patient herself as miserable as she renders those about her, this disease is closely allied to that graver nervous lesion which constitutes insanity, and, if unchecked, may pass into it.

Evie's pilgrimage to Schwalbach in 1893 takes place two years before Sigmund Freud goes to study in Paris with Jean-Martin Charcot at *La Salpetrière*. Cardinal Mazarin's old gunpowder factory was now a hospital where Charcot was carrying out his groundbreaking research into female hysteria and hysterical paralysis, and it was not until 1895 that Freud wrote his first monograph on hysteria. But "the ritual dance around the fetish of the hymen" was already being observed by medical experts as a dance that brought mental suffering, and even madness, to the women whose lives were centred around that ritual.

For women in general, and in particular for women like Evie Cavendish, society had decreed it was the only dance that mattered, and that the failure to produce a child should result in unhappiness, depression and mental instability seems entirely logical. So Evie journeys to Schwalbach, a town full of unhappy women, to bathe in the *Maisons de Bain* of the *Salon de Promenade*, to take the mud and vapour baths and to drink litre upon litre of those magic waters.

The relationship between Evie and her mother is close and surprisingly frank for those Victorian times. Writing from India, Lady Lansdowne counsels patience, begging her daughter not to worry if she can, for she has heard that fretting only makes such matters worse. While Lady Lansdowne would certainly have hesitated to say anything connected with the sexual act that brings babies into the world, she felt quite free to talk to her daughter about her menstrual problems. To comfort her daughter she tells Evie that she comes from a family who often have problems when young, but grow stronger as they age—words that will prove true in the case of both mother and daughter.

Looking out from the windows of her suite of rooms in the Villa Gutenberg, a small and exclusive establishment in the town, a desperate, unhappy Evie watches the women drinking at the fountains from dawn to dusk, hears the bands playing in the *Allee*, and reads her mother's letters from India. She must have written to her husband of her loneliness, because Victor joins her for a few days in August, causing a shocked Lady Lansdowne to comment that she didn't think they even allowed men to be there. Certainly he is the only man shown among the Villa Gutenberg's eleven women guests. But there Victor was, by the side of his wife. And perhaps if he had known that he would be suffering from gout fifteen years later, he too would have taken the waters in Schwalbach that summer of 1893.

Whether it was the chalybeate water, whether it was psychological, or whether it was just a question of getting over India, Evie finally gives birth to a son and heir, Edward Cavendish, on May 6, 1895. A year later, Eddy is joined by a sister, Maud, named for her grandmother, Lady Lansdowne. Blanche, Dorothy and Rachel follow at two-year intervals, Charles is born in 1905, and Anne in 1909.

Victor Cavendish was devoted to his wife. He called her "My own darling," and signed his letters "Ever your Victor." But he did not treat his "own little one" as the typical Victorian wife, kept in the dark about his parliamentary life and his financial affairs. He counselled her to read the papers regularly and to keep up on such matters as the Irish question, discussed politics with her, and gave her details of House of Commons debates and local meetings in his Derbyshire constituency. There is evidence in the diaries that his wife did a considerable amount of work on some of his speeches. His diaries refer frequently to how much he misses her when he is in London, or when she is away with their ever-growing family visiting her parents—now back from India—in Dereen in Ireland, or at Lansdowne House in London.

When they were first married, he discussed in detail with Evie the financial intricacies of getting a loan from the bank on their new London home. Cash flow would always be a problem for Victor Cavendish, even when he became Duke of Devonshire, and from the beginning Evie kept meticulous accounts of expenditures. She was particularly careful to note the bills paid out of her own personal allowance—to various members of the staff, for example—that should have come out of other funds. This suggests that servants and tradesmen, such as the National Linen Company, were paid promptly by the mistress of the house out of her own pocket, and were not kept waiting around—a common problem for those dealing with the carriage trade.

They spent a great deal of time apart, for Victor took his parliamentary duties seriously. Between 1900 and 1905 his attendance at parliamentary divisions in the House of Commons stood at 2346 out of a possible 2396 appearances. During those five years he was treasurer to both Queen Victoria's and King Edward's households, financial secretary to the Treasury, and was appointed a member of His Majesty's Privy Council in 1905. During those years, his wife went through three pregnancies, and would often have been on her own, secluded at Holker Hall.

But when Victor was with Evie, the pattern of their lives was different from what is perceived as the normal pattern of Victorian upper-class and aristocratic families. Although there were nannies and governesses galore in the nursery and school-room, there was not the demarcation one would expect to find, with the children sequestered in one area and brought down to meet their parents for an hour or so each day. Both Victor's diaries and the memoirs of Maud, their eldest daughter, paint a picture of a family who enjoyed being together. Maud recalls:

> We invaded my parents' rooms to say good morning, before they went down to breakfast. We had luncheon with them ... we "came down", dressed in muslin frocks and sashes, every evening before going to bed. My father often rode with us at Holker, and he took us for long walks every Sunday, giving the most exhausted child a pick-a-back, if one could walk no further.

In his diaries, her father gives as much space to his family activities as he does to his parliamentary and ducal responsibilities. He worries about his children's health; Sunday after London Sunday is spent taking the children to the zoo:

Sunday, March 25 (1906) Cold. Sleet showers. Evie and I with the three children went to Westminster Abbey. Nice service. Walked home. Blanche was sick after luncheon. Evie and I took Maud, Rachel and Dorothy to the Zoo. Saw the Lemurs there which Bertie [Evie's sister] brought back. They seemed very fit and well.

Victor records Evie's worries over breast-feeding problems, and it is her husband she wakes, every time she goes into labour. Touchingly, he records his reactions—and Evie's—to the birth of all those little girls:

Aug 30 (1909) Evie woke me a little before six. Got really underway about seven. Baby born eight minutes to nine. Got through v. well. A little girl. Evie wanted a boy but it is a great thing to get it safely over. A very satisfactory baby. Weighs 7lb 6oz.

Disappointment is still Evie's reaction, even though by the birth of Anne in 1909 she has produced the "spare," Charles, in 1905. The diaries do not start until 1899, so there is no record of how he felt about the birth of the long-awaited first child.

It is an almost idyllic life, the sylvan and city life of the Cavendish family in the early, Holker years. Evie encouraged the children to put on a play every Christmas, complete with professional-looking, printed programmes for the event. In 1904, *The Sleeping Beauty* ran for three performances, with versatile Maud playing both a princess and the bad fairy, Malvolia, and cousin Evelyn Cavendish appearing as Chief Mistress of the Ink Bottle. Christmas at Holker Hall has all the appearance of those English family Christmases portrayed in delicious Dickensian detail on Christmas cards all over the world.

Having achieved the family she had wanted, and had been expected to provide, Evie Cavendish would have been quite content to run Holker Hall and bring up her children—within the context of her class, that is, and a support staff of nurses, undernurses and French, German and English governesses. But, even before becoming Duchess of Devonshire, part of the job description was her attendance at other occasions besides balls and state dinners, when she was expected to play an official role alongside Victor. There is a striking photograph of one such event, taken during the visit of Li Hung-Chang to Great Britain in July and August 1896.

Li Hung-Chang had various titles: Senior Guardian of the Heir Apparent, Classical Reader to his Majesty the Emperor, Senior Grand Secretary of State, Minister of the Foreign Office, and Earl of First Rank. As he was "charged with authority as to all the armaments, both on sea and land, of the Chinese nation," his visit to Britain was of particular interest to those in the business of producing arms, or warships.

The British government treated him like royalty, conveying him in the royal yacht to Cowes, after which he visited Queen Victoria at Osborne, on the Isle of Wight, to present his credentials from the Chinese emperor. August 17 finds him arriving in Barrow-in-Furness by special train, to be greeted by the Eighth Duke of Devonshire, chairman of the Furness Railway Company and the Barrow Steel Company. There, "with a large party of gentlemen," which included Victor Cavendish, he looked over the blast furnaces and the steel-rolling operations of the Barrow Steel Company which, at the time, were turning out steel rails for the Indian government. After the steel works it was on to the Naval Construction and Armaments Company.

There was little difficulty discussing the official and business matters at hand through an interpreter, but small talk at such affairs was always a problem. The duke had just been shooting grouse at Bolton Abbey and asked his distinguished guest if he had ever done so. "No," replied Li, "but I have often shot rebels." The exchange, which caused much amusement in Britain, certainly encapsulates a significant difference in the means available to the ruling classes of East and West for subduing opposition.

The viceroy's speech, through an interpreter, is also significantly different from the kind usually heard on such occasions. Not only does it demonstrate the fusion in Li Hung-Chang's society between the practical and the metaphysical —the war minister who is also the royal classical reader—but it has an unmistakable tongue-in-cheek quality to it:

> China is a nation of literature and philosophy [cheers]. Literature and philosophy are rather abstract subjects. The English people, being the most practical nation in the world, have produced such eminent men in your literature and philosophy as Lord Bacon, Shakespeare, Herbert Spencer, Darwin and Huxley ["hear hear"], who arrived at the same conclusions as our Lao-tse and Confucius. Their principles … and the ultimate object of these industrial pursuits which the Viceroy has seen is peace ["hear hear" and cheers]. For people to make ready for war is the best guarantee for peace ["hear hear"].

Li's toast to the Duke of Devonshire, his host, is a subtextual delight:

> The Chinese empire is a liberal one, and I trust that [my] visit … will enlighten the [British] people, not only literally and philosophically, in order that they may survive in a world that they call a world of evolution and a world in the material advantages of which the Duke of Devonshire is very well represented. The Viceroy begs you to lift your glasses and drink to the Barrow Hematite Steel Company and the Naval Construction and Armaments Company, and to couple with that toast the name of their president in the person of the Duke of Devonshire.

One wonders if any of the "large party of gentlemen" picked up what appears to lie beneath the oratorical surface. Could it be that Li Hung-Chang is saying that, for all Britain's much-stated moral superiority over such nations as his own, they have the same vested interests: winning wars and maintaining the security and privileges of the ruling class?

What would Evie Cavendish have made of all of this? For she is there, shortly after the birth of her second child, to present the Chinese viceroy with a bouquet, "a floral representation of the Chinese flag, with a blue dragon and the sun, carefully depicted." In one of the official photographs she is seated alongside Li Hung-Chang, with the second interpreter standing so close that the sleeve of his ceremonial robe brushes the sleeve of Evie's dress. It is difficult to tell what she feels, because in this case the cliché of the inscrutable oriental is not only politically, but racially, incorrect. No one's face is more difficult to read in the photograph than the face of that inscrutable occidental, Evie Cavendish.

In January 1899, between the births of Blanche and Dorothy, Evie accompanies Victor on a trip to the United States and Canada. They are to be away for about a month and Victor notes in his diary: "Sat Jan 7. Left Holker by 9.34. Felt very miserable going away especially leaving the babies. I shall never have been away from them for so long a time before. Sailing on Servia from Liverpool." He does not record what their mother, Evie, must have felt about the separation.

Ten days later they are in New York, and they attend the opera in Mrs. Vanderbilt's box and have lunch with Andrew Carnegie. Victor's entry for Thursday, January 19, reads: "… met Evie going to luncheon with Carnegie. Went with her. Interesting man though snobbish."

For a duke to call a self-made man a snob seems particularly inappropriate. Perhaps this son of a Scottish handloom weaver, put out of work by the Industrial Revolution and forced to leave his country, felt the need to show this English lord that his friends and contacts in Britain, among them

British Prime Minister William Gladstone, were as stellar as Cavendish's.

But the more likely reason is that Carnegie felt no need to show any form of deference to a member of the British ruling class, and thus appeared to be acting in a superior manner. Carnegie despised inherited wealth and advocated abolishing the monarchy and establishing a British republic. His "Gospel of Wealth" had caught the public imagination in both countries, and his belief that the duty of a rich man was first to provide for his family, and then to return his surplus wealth to the community, did not jibe well with the concept of aristocracy.

"Interesting man" as a description of Andrew Carnegie is a typical Cavendish understatement. By the time of their meeting, the production of American steel had surpassed that of Great Britain, almost entirely because of the genius and foresight of that Scottish immigrant, and Victor and Evie's luncheon date had less to do with philanthropy or social imperatives than it had with business. Within the week Victor and Evie are in Pittsburgh, which, according to its City Charter in 1901, two years after the Cavendishes' visit, "illustrates more clearly than any other city in America the outcome of democratic institutions. There are no classes here but the industrious classes; and no ranks in society save those which have been created by industry."

Looking round Carnegie's great Homestead Works in Pittsburgh, Victor describes them as "far in front of anything I had seen." A day later they are touring the railways in Chicago, and the blast, bessemer and open hearth furnaces of the Illinois Steel Company. It is little wonder that the entry for that day concludes, "Evie rather tired."

Four days later they are in Toronto, staying at the Queen's Hotel, and Evie is still not in top form: "Evie rather seedy. Expect it is the bad oysters. Very sick and uncomfortable. Great bore."

Victor Cavendish may not have written his diaries in code, but his repeated use of certain adjectives and phrases are a clue to his feelings, and he always goes for understatement. "A great bore" does not mean he is inconvenienced by Evie's indisposition, but that he is upset by her suffering. So, when they go on to Ottawa to visit Lord and Lady Minto, the governor-general and his wife, and Victor describes the hockey match between Ottawa and Montreal as "quite wonderful," one knows he was extremely impressed. "I have never seen such a hard and fast game," he positively enthuses—for Victor. It is with reluctance that the Cavendishes leave Ottawa on February 10, 1899. They would be back, seventeen years, and four more children, later.

Back in England they found the children "very satisfactory and well," and soon Evie was back in Holker Hall "busy with patterns of wallpaper etc.," picking up once more the fabric of her domestic life. Indeed, those years at the beginning of the new century must have been as happy as any for her. Dorothy was born in 1900, and Rachel in 1902. But in 1904, the happy family was split up—not by death, and certainly not by divorce, but by the traditions of their class. Eddy was sent off to prep school—in his case, Ludgrove School—from where he would go on to Eton. Just as Dora was sent away to make her way in the world while still virtually a child, Eddy was sent away at an even younger age from the bosom of his family, to make his way through the British preparatory and public school system. The girls, of course, stayed at home with their nurses and governesses.

Andrew Carnegie would not have approved. He believed that "any education that separates man from man is not wholly good," and certainly most countries view the British boarding-school tradition as barbaric. In fact, the main purpose of the tradition was to do exactly what Andrew Carnegie deplored: to make sure that the future heirs of a privileged society were kept with those of their own kind and taught by

those who understood their mandate. The virtues—and vices
—of the boarding-school system vary a great deal, depending
on the individual nature of the child involved. Some take to it
like ducks to water, and some do not. Eddy Cavendish did not.

Eddy was a gentle little boy, according to his sister Maud.
Although she was a girl and a year younger than him, she
could boss him around mercilessly—not a good candidate for
the British boarding-school system. Unlike most such children, who kept a stiff upper lip and a stoic silence, Eddy shared
his emotions with his unhappy mother and father. At first he
seemed to be adapting to the separation from his sisters,
whom he adored, and from the comfortable nomadic life of
his class: the Irish countryside at Lismore, the seaside at
Compton Place and Cromer, the bucolic pleasures of Holker
Hall. But, from about 1905, he begins to express his unhappiness outwardly in his behaviour, in poor marks at school and
in letters home to Evie, who is deeply distressed. In 1905
Victor writes in his diary:

> Sept 20. Wednesday. In the afternoon went with all the nurses
> and the children to Windy Hills ... Tea and bonfire. Eddy very
> cheerful, but I think he will be very sorry to go as he had happy
> holidays. We shall miss him terribly, but he is very happy at
> school ... Eddy had not got any of his things together, but we
> managed to collect most in the course of the evening. He
> seemed very cheerful, although he whistled a lot. He will be
> alright when he once starts.

It would seem that Eddy was not the only one whistling
in the dark. The entry for the next day reads:

> Sept 21. Thursday.... Eddy went back to school. Very sad part-
> ing with them all, but he was wonderfully good and made no
> fuss. I went up to London with him. He was rather tired but
> otherwise alright.

Victor spends the rest of the day trying to put the image of that sad, drooping ten-year-old out of his mind. He goes to the Treasury—"not much going on there"—he dines at Boodles (one of the oldest London clubs, to which the Regency dandy Beau Brummel once belonged) and then he goes to the theatre—"not a very good show. London seems empty." Finally, he tries to cheer himself up again: "Altogether a very trying day and feel quite knocked up, but Eddy will be very happy when once he gets to school."

On the contrary. At one point Eddy writes to his mother, virtually accusing her of cruelty. Evie is so distraught that even Miss Tonge, the girls' governess, writes to Eddy to reproach him, and his response is not to write any letters at all. His father confides to his diary: "Both Evie and I are very unhappy about Eddy. He has not written to any one for a month. Evie has written two letters almost begging him to write. Most unsatisfactory." At one point, Victor uses the word "painful"—it is as powerful an adjective as he ever employs.

However distressed Evie was, it is unlikely she asked Victor to bring Eddy back. In the eyes of many, the fact that he was a gentle little boy would have been added reason to send him away to be toughened up—to remove him from the petticoat tails of an adoring mother. This is what duty decreed must happen to that beloved child it had taken so long for her to conceive. For Evie, just as for Eddy, there is no escape.

Nineteen hundred and five was a difficult year for Evie Cavendish, and it should have been a particularly happy time. On August 29 she gave birth to the second son she had so longed for, two days after her own birthday. She had been strong during this pregnancy, and the day before she went into labour she had gone for a long walk with Victor. Charles weighed eight pounds, four ounces, and was born after rather a long labour of nine hours, the last three of which were "pretty bad" for Evie, according to her husband. Indeed, he notes the various times—when the footman ordered the coachman to fetch the doctor, when the labour accelerated—so precisely, that one has the feeling he was either in the room or certainly close by.

Clearly, Victor is euphoric. The baby is fine and strong-looking, Evie is wonderfully strong and well. The telegrams are pouring in. The other children have seen their new brother and are "very pleased with it." Yet, by the beginning of October, something happens that changes the nature of the marriage and the relationship between Victor and Evelyn Cavendish. What happens is confined to two diary entries.

The first is dated October 3 and it reads: "Left for London by 9.27. Tedious journey. Went to the Ty [Treasury]. Very quiet there. Evie got a letter blackmailing me. Very bothersome. Hope it will be nothing. Not many people about. Long talk with [scratched out] Fellowes in the evening. He is rather bad with tooth ache."

On October 4, Victor records the meetings he had during the day and his return home by eleven-thirty at night. On October 5 he writes: "Long talk with Evie about the blackmailing letter. Told her all about it. Dreadful, but she took it very well, but I feel that things will never be the same again."

Somewhere around the beginning of October, someone had written a letter to Evie at Holker Hall accusing Victor—of what? If it was a "blackmailing" letter, it sounds as if Evie was being asked for money, but it is more likely Victor means that the letter was the result of his own refusal to pay someone off. The "long talk" suggests Victor took legal advice immediately after he heard from his wife because, although part of the name is scratched out, the "Fellowes" mentioned is possibly a lawyer.

There were two likely candidates practising in London at the time: an Evelyn Napier Fellowes in the city, and a William Gordon Fellowes at Lincoln's Inn. A shaken Victor had taken legal advice from someone recommended to him at one of his clubs, or possibly from a member of one of his clubs, but he had not gone to the Devonshire family's legal adviser, whose name was Currey—for obvious reasons. So urgent was the matter that he had called upon the poor man in the evening at his home or office while he was suffering from terrible toothache. There is a tragicomic quality to the scene: a desperate Victor, usually so controlled and monosyllabic, having to reveal his misdemeanour—whatever it was—to a comparative stranger in agony himself.

Whoever it was knew where to write to Evie, but that sort of information was easily obtained from the court and society columns in such newspapers as *The Times*. If Victor's transgression was something to do with money, it is more likely his colleagues in the House of Commons, or in one of his clubs, would have received the letter. The explanation that makes the most sense is that Victor had been unfaithful to his wife, had put an end to the affair—or whatever it had been—had been asked for money in return for the woman's silence, and had refused to pay it.

For many men in Victor Cavendish's position, such a revelation would not have been earth-shattering. Their marriages were business contracts, an arrangement understood by both partners. But Evie's and Victor's marriage had been different. In the early days of the marriage they did not keep to the separate bedrooms that would have been the accepted arrangement for their class, for Victor writes about how lonely and empty their bed seems without her when she is away. Presumably the unknown woman knew that Victor cared for his wife, and knew that telling Evie would hurt the man who had deserted her, or who had refused to go on paying.

Even in Victor's minimalist style it is evident how difficult and distressing the scene was: "dreadful" is the adjective he uses. Most telling of all is his realization that, however well Evie has taken it, something between them has changed for ever. And, although he never again makes any mention of the incident, the entry for October 8 gives some idea of just how deeply Evie Cavendish has been hurt by the blackmailing letter.

There is surely never a good moment for a blackmailing letter to arrive, but the timing of this one was particularly trying. Charles's christening was to take place on October 8, and the baby was registered on the day of Victor's revelation. Members of the family were beginning to arrive, among them Lady Lansdowne, who arrived the day after Victor had told Evie "all about it."

Somehow, Evie had to maintain a front that nothing was amiss, because the last thing in the world that proud woman would have wanted would have been disclosure. So she took refuge behind the weakness and tiredness commonly felt by women after childbirth—particularly by a Victorian woman after the birth of her sixth child. The entry in Victor's diary for Sunday, October 8, reads: "Fine but grey ... Afraid Evie was not quite right & could not come to the christening ... All went off well. Lot of people there."

So Evie's much-longed-for second son was christened without his mother in that church full of family members. It is unlikely she was genuinely ill—physically, at least. After the birth of Charles, Victor's diary is full of references to how wonderfully strong and well his wife is. Either she was afraid of breaking down in such an emotional setting, or she was punishing Victor. She had given him two sons, and all the personal, social and ceremonial support for which he could have hoped. But more than that, she had given him something that, contractually, she was not obliged to give: she had apparently given him her heart.

On that grey day in October, after all the carriages had left for the church with the aunts and uncles, her brother and her mother, her children, her husband and her baby, Evie Cavendish must have felt as lonely as she ever had in her entire life. Lying in bed, listening to their voices, hearing the clatter of the carriages as they went down the driveway, she must have allowed herself the luxury of tears in the only private time she had had since the blackmailing letter.

Evie had always had the potential for the kind of chilly hauteur her father was known for, and it had served as a shield for her shyness. Only her husband knew that she was a far more emotional woman than she allowed the world to know, and her anger and hurt at his betrayal would indeed make a difference in their lives. John Singer Sargent, who painted Evie's portrait in 1902, picked up that remote quality even then. Evie looks out at the world with her shy, fawn-like eyes, causing Victor to observe in his diary on July 17: "Went with Evie to see the picture. Think it looks alright but it is rather stern."

She also appears to have lacked the sense of humour that humanized her mother's character. Lady Lansdowne's sense of the ridiculous caused her to break into uncontrollable fits of giggles at inopportune moments. Her son-in-law once caught her eye across the table of a large formal dinner at Devonshire House when, he told Evie, "Uncle Cav filled his beard with crumbs, so I looked at your mother and she began to giggle."

The blackmailing letter was certainly no laughing matter, but Evie had to find something to protect herself from the hurt it had caused her. Humour is a good weapon and a wonderful shield, but Evie did not have it in her personal armoury. So she called upon the Lansdowne characteristic that had protected her in the past: she drew around her the aristocratic grandeur of her position.

Who was the woman—if indeed it was a woman? *Cherchez la femme* is of more than prurient interest, because it is not so much the individual woman who is intriguing, but to which class she belonged. If Victor was having an affair with someone of his own class, discretion would have been essential, and the last thing a woman of his class would consider was to tell the wronged wife.

There was much turning of a blind eye in Edwardian society

and, even if the mystery woman's husband was carrying on his own affair, there would have been little to gain, and much to lose, from his wife sending a letter to Evie. It is more likely that Victor had somehow become involved with a woman who was *not* of his class, and who tried to make some money out of the affair.

There are various possibilities for the sender of the black-mailing letter. The *demi-mondaines* were not as cohesive a group in London as in Paris, where they formed a social class of their own. If it was not a woman of Victor's set, it was possibly someone from that other demi-world: the theatre.

Victor loved the theatre. At Trinity College, Cambridge, he had been president of the Amateur Dramatic Club. When he was in town he went to the theatre almost every week, and he kept up the habit after his marriage. His diaries have frequent references to the plays he attended, sometimes with Evie, and he took his children when they were older. Even when he and Evie went to America he found time to fit in a visit to the theatre, besides the socially required visit to the opera. In Washington they "went to a play called the French Maid. Rather amusing, but extremely vulgar." One wonders what Evie must have thought of such a piece of boulevard theatre!

Most men of Victor's class lived another life, which was separated from their domestic life, but which was not necessarily duplicitous. It was an exclusively male world occupied by those of their own kind with whom they spent a great deal of time, and it centred around the clubs to which they belonged. Victor used various clubs—the bachelors' club and the amusingly named Boodles—but his principle *pied-à-terre* was Brooks in Pall Mall.

While clubs like Brooks were oases of all-male comfort where the privileged could gamble and drink to their hearts' content, their chief purpose was to bring together like-minded men of political influence. Brooks was Victor's club, and also

the club of the Eighth Duke of Devonshire—Harty-Tarty,
Uncle Cav—and his father-in-law, Lord Lansdowne. So central
was the political factor to such clubs, that the fight over home
rule nearly caused a split in the ancient establishment, with a
quantum leap in attempts by members to blackball each other.

To that world gravitated a Bohemian mix of characters who
crossed class lines, actors and actresses, bookies and chorus
girls. All would have been shown the door at Brooks, but there
were other clubs in the West End only too happy to admit
them, and the wilder members of the aristocracy who enjoyed
their company.

Victor Cavendish loved his wife and family, and he was not
wild. But he had friends who were, and one of his theatre
companions was Sunny Marlborough, Consuelo's husband.
Later on, when the divorce proceedings were underway
between Sunny and Baby, Lady Lansdowne suggested in a
letter to Evie that possibly Sunny was being so surprisingly
acquiescent because he had his own reasons to keep quiet.

Together, Victor and Sunny went out to the legitimate theatre, or to its naughty relation, the music-hall. Together they
might have seen comedienne Harriet Vernon promenading
and singing on an imitation crystal staircase in a parody of
the Duchess of Devonshire, and looking not unlike Georgiana
in her great, plumed, Gainsborough hat. Wistfully, one of
their fellow clubmen later recalled those glorious turn-of-the-
century days:

> The clubs were in their heyday, most of the eighteenth-century
> dignity and charm of Mayfair and St. James were still unim-
> paired, and there was a light-heartedness and sense of well-
> being that has now entirely vanished. How pleasant it was to
> get into a smart hansom and drive down Piccadilly on a June
> evening when the trees in Green Park were gilded by the rays
> of the westering sun ... dinner at White's, then the opera with
> Melba and Caruso, and supper at the Savoy or the Carlton.

From entries in Victor's diary, this was often the pattern of his London evenings, when his family was not at Devonshire House. After a day in the House of Commons he would relax by going to see a drawing-room comedy starring Charles Hawtrey or Gerald de Maurier, or perhaps a musical comedy put on by George Edwardes, who knew that good tunes and pretty girls were far more essential to success than a strong story-line. Some of those girls would go on to marry men like Victor—Gertie Millar, a Gaiety Girl in the early years of the twentieth century, would leave the stage to become Countess of Dudley. And sometimes Victor and Sunny went to the Alhambra Theatre of Varieties in Leicester Square.

By the turn of the century the Alhambra had become one of the leading venues for variety performers from all over the world. Victor and Sunny may well have seen *La Belle Otero* when she performed there and, later, the legendary Gaby Deslys—legendary because her beauty would change the course of history in Portugal. Public dislike of the Portuguese monarchy was kept at the boiling point by accounts of the king's ransom in jewels showered upon her, and in particular, her priceless rope of pearls—a rope extravagant enough by which to hang, or for which to murder, both the king and his heir.

Ballet at the Alhambra took on a *louche* and less classical patina than Anna Pavlova's performances, as pretty girls posed and pranced twice-nightly in a range of costumes. There were busby-crowned ballerinas holding guns, their waists tightly cinched into their tunics, their legs seductively encased in flesh-coloured tights and calf-hugging boots, depicting "The Armies of All Nations." One extraordinary flight of culinary fancy illustrated "All the Ingredients of a Salad," complete with the mustard pot and slices of boiled egg.

Perhaps the unknown blackmailer came from this world—a woman hoping for a more permanent arrangement than Victor was prepared to give. His character does not suggest a man who would care to set up a nice little alternative establishment somewhere in London for a mistress. Or perhaps the blackmailer came from the circle surrounding Uncle Cav and his wife, Louise.

Old age and marriage had not freed Harty-Tarty from some of the more disreputable friendships of his youth. Lord Curzon, no straitlace himself, described the Eighth Duke's circle in censorious terms: "That fashionable card-playing, race-going lot are an idle set, and their life is empty and vapid." Lady Lansdowne disliked many of Uncle Cav's friends, and sympathized with her daughter's sense of unease in their presence. After all, this was the man who had openly invited Edward and Alice Keppel to Chatsworth together, without the usual attempt to maintain outward appearances. Victor Cavendish saw a lot of his uncle, both because of their respective parliamentary roles and because he was the heir to the dukedom, and had no problems with the raffish group around him.

Whatever happened, there is no doubt that Victor deeply regretted what the blackmailing letter had done to his domestic happiness.

Nineteen hundred and six began on a sad note for Evie, when in February she lost a precious bracelet, containing locks of the children's hair—possibly the bracelet in the Singer Sargent portrait, which appears to have pendants of some kind. Evie and Victor went to Scotland Yard which, after an investigation that took all summer, uncovered the culprit. The clasp had come loose in a hansom cab on her way back from attending the opening of parliament, and the cab-driver decided to keep this windfall for himself. On October 11, Evie went with her mother to the Police Court in Lavender Hill to give evidence. "Great bore," noted Victor in his diary.

It must indeed have been very trying because, two days before her husband's trial, the cabby's wife wrote to Evie in great distress. However, Detective Pritchard, who had tracked down the bracelet, assured Evie the cabman was "a bad lot." The police report seems to indicate this was indeed the case: cabby James Smith had a record for assaults and drunkenness, was driving without a licence, and was wanted on a warrant for earlier offences. The bracelet—gold, set with diamonds, with four pendants, and valued at £40 (about £1500 today)— was long gone. It had taken a circuitous route through London's underworld.

First, the cabbie had obtained a loan of thirty shillings against it from William Dabbs, son of the innkeeper of the Duke of Wellington Public House in Battersea. Some months later he redeemed it, by getting a labourer with a better reputation than his to borrow money for him. One wonders also if the labourer, Walter Barrett, was sweet on cabby Smith's wife, because he gave her two of the pendants. Smith was picked up while trying to pledge one of the pendants at a Battersea pawnshop. The bracelet and the remaining pendant had already been sold for two shillings.

Smith's explanation of how he had come by the bracelet is colourful; he said he had found the bracelet fifteen years ago while serving with the army in Burma. It looks as if the cabman was a former soldier of the Empire, who was having problems surviving back on his native soil. The Honourable John Augustus de Grey, the presiding judge, was unconvinced. He sentenced James Smith to four months' hard labour.

It is not likely that Evie Cavendish would have spoken up in court for the cab-driver out of pity for his wife, whatever the circumstances of the theft. But the fact that she had lost something so personal as the locks of her children's hair would have finished any chance Mr. and Mrs. Smith might have had. Forty pounds meant nothing to Evie, compared with the riches it represented to James Smith. But the hair from her babies' heads—*that* she could never replace. The sad truth is that the cabby might have got far more from the grateful Cavendishes if he had turned the bracelet in to the police.

But then, life had probably taught James Smith never to trust a swell.

Whatever her earlier misgivings about her official role, Evie was now doing what was expected of her. Since Victor had come into the dukedom, she had devoted herself to putting Devonshire House to rights. The place had been left in disarray by the Eighth Duke and his Duchess—two priceless Kent tables had been sent out for repair and had never come back. In fact, one had somehow got into the showroom at Gillows, and had been sold to Mrs. Potter Palmer, the doyenne of Chicago high society. A huge chandelier had been rented for a special occasion, never returned, and rent had been paid on it for about eighty years. In effect, it had been bought many times over.

When Victor started discussions about the possible sale of Devonshire House, things became difficult for him with his wife. On October 18 he writes: "Got home about 8.15. Evie very tired and cross—quite hysterical. It makes everything very difficult. Expect it will be best not to sell D.H., although it is obviously the right thing to do."

Evie stayed in bed with a headache the next day, but "was calmer on other matters." However, the heavy artillery was again ranged against her, this time in the shape of her father, with whom Victor talked on October 24. Perhaps on the advice of his father-in-law, who knew his daughter well, Victor apparently chose not to tell her that Lord Lansdowne advised him to go ahead with the sale, but to bide his time. Lord Lansdowne may well have been surprised that Victor kept his wife informed about financial matters and involved at all in such decisions.

Evie, kept in the dark, went back to one of the tasks she loved, keeping herself "very busy with tapestry and pictures" at the house to which she had devoted so much of her time. Losing Devonshire House would mean a loss of face in the world that was now as much the centre of Evie's life as her husband, or her children. For the new Duchess of Devonshire, Devonshire House represented the aspects of aristocracy she had been expected to embody, and for which she had now given up so much of her personal life.

BREAK FAST ON 5TH APRIL 1892

Fish Pumplett
Eggs poach & Bakem frye
Kitney shootind
Muttenchap mix pattatoes
Cold Meat

It is probably superfluous to say that this is not a menu from Dora's collection. It had been kept by Evie among her papers, and there it has been for over a century. It is hand-written by someone with a good, clear hand, but a foggy grasp of English culinary terms.

Translation is a challenge: the poached eggs and fried bacon are clear enough, also the mutton chops and pota-toes—although "mix" is puzzling. Over the word "shootind" is written "sauté?" in another hand, as someone—the mis-tress of the house, perhaps—attempts an explanation. But "fish pumplett"? Two possibilities occur: pancake and omelette, but neither are methods of cooking usually asso-ciated with fish. Another possibility is "dumpling." And one can imagine the relief as the writer finally hears an item he recognizes: "cold meat."

The date 1892 suggests that it may have been a break-fast menu from the Lansdownes' Indian period. The writer has a good hand, but is thrown by those alien English dishes. Later colonials have memories of similar approximations— "miner's sauce" for mayonnaise, for example. Or it could

174

possibly have been one of those wild Irish servants from Dereen.

One thing it illustrates for sure: good help is very hard to find. Whoever it was, it amused Evie enough for her to keep it among her papers all those years.

EIGHT

Desperate Acts

Beneath even the luxury of the social country house it was evident
that the upper classes were not as secure as they had been ... many
[members] were not merely new, but so conspicuously arriviste
that Society shuddered to read the court circular.
CLIVE ASLET, *THE LAST COUNTRY HOUSES*

In December 1913 the monarch and his queen came in
royal progress to hunt at Chatsworth. Against the night
sky torches flamed in the hands of three hundred and fifty
estate workers, members of the National Reserve and boys
from the Scouts and the Church Lads Brigade. Like a scene
from a novel by Count Leo Tolstoy, the lights from the great
flambeaus flickered and crackled in the wind along the winding
private road through the rolling parkland.

As King George and Queen Mary drove into view, the
church bells in the village of Edensor pealed out a royal welcome that mingled with the cheers of the assembled crowd.
The royal party crossed the pretty stone bridge that arched
over the river, and saw ahead of them against the evening sky
Wyatville's lofty belvedere, built for the Sixth Duke over the
estate's private theatre. A chorus of children's voices rose
from the quadrangle outside the house, singing the national
anthem. Evelyn, Duchess of Devonshire, awaited her guests
in the Painted Hall with her son and heir, Lord Hartington,
who had just returned from Cambridge, and her eldest
daughter, Maud.

Already Chatsworth was beginning to reflect the changes brought about by its new chatelaine. In the Painted Hall Evelyn and the architect W.H. Romaine-Walker had replaced the smaller steep staircase of the Sixth Duke with what the present Duchess of Devonshire describes as a "grandiose affair." Certainly, the red-carpeted flight with its gilt ironwork balustrade serves as a fitting metaphor for the new Evelyn, a statement in gilt, iron and stone.

The programme for the visit had been announced in *The Times*: the king would go grouse-shooting in the morning and pheasant-shooting in the afternoon; the queen would visit Derby Infirmary, Lyme Hall and Haddon Hall and, *en route*, would partake of the waters at Buxton.

All appeared to be well, and immutable, in the best of all possible worlds. But in December 1913, there were signs of revolution in the playgrounds of the rich and the privileged, and the freedom-fighters were women. Not only were the roads lined with cheering, torch-bearing villagers, but with a strong force of police. The reason given by *The Times* was "rumours of possible suffragist outrages." This time, the royal progress passed without incident.

The authorities had reason to be concerned about suffragist—or suffragette—outrages. Earlier that same year, on June 4, 1913, Emily Davison threw herself in front of the king's horse, Anmer, during the running of the Derby at Epsom. The Duke of Devonshire was in attendance with Maud, his eldest daughter, whose presentation at court would be marred later that year by "a screaming girl [who] threw herself in front of the Queen's feet, asking her to help get votes for women. The courtiers removed her hastily, but the poor Queen went white as a sheet." Even within the palace walls, at that most exclusive of ceremonies for the chosen few, women of action were making their case.

The Derby drama was covered at length in the newspapers, although the press was equally concerned over the disqualification of the winner, Craganour, in favour of a hundred-to-one outsider, Aboyeur. The tone of the press reports is, predictably, one of outrage. The "desperate act of a woman who rushed from the rails on to the course as the horses swept round Tattenham Corner, apparently from some mad notion that she could spoil the race" was first thought to be an accident, until a sign saying "Votes for Women" was held up in the crowd. Any further doubts were dispelled when the woman's identity became known.

Emily Wilding Davison had been agitating for the vote for thirteen years. Her record was lengthy. Her first hunger strikes were in 1900, in Limehouse Prison, London, and in Manchester. She was imprisoned for stone-throwing, breaking windows in the House of Commons, setting fire to pillar-boxes, and attacking a Baptist minister who found himself in the wrong place at the wrong time—Davison thought she was attacking Liberal Cabinet Minister Lloyd George. She had been forcibly fed, often with great brutality, particularly on one occasion at Strangeways Prison. She had been close to death in the past. This time, she died for her cause.

The Times, deploring the fact that the general public was more likely to remember Emily Davison's act than the disqualification of the winner, opined:

> A deed of the kind, we need hardly say, is not likely to increase the popularity of any cause with the ordinary public. Reckless fanaticism is not regarded by them as a qualification for the franchise. They are disposed to look upon manifestations of that temper with contempt and disgust ... They say that the persons who wantonly destroy property and endanger innocent lives must be either desperately wicked or entirely unbalanced. Where women are concerned, the natural gallantry of the public always inclines them to take a favourable view, and accordingly they are gradually coming to the conclusion that many of the militant suffragists are not responsible for their acts.

Regardless of Emily Davison's state of mind when she sacrificed herself for the movement by dying beneath the hooves of the king's horse, it is clear that women who were politically active, or who pushed themselves forward into the spotlight, were looked upon as not being in possession of their faculties. They had lost the very qualities that made them female: passiveness, submissiveness, acquiescence and resignation. It would not have been that outlandish a conclusion to the column if the reporter had written: ... *accordingly they (the general public) are gradually coming to the conclusion that many of the militant suffragists are not really women.*

On the other hand, they could just have been behaving hysterically—a very feminine quality, after all. But hysteria is the resort of the powerless when a situation is unbearable and there is no chance of change, or escape. These women threatened to bring about changes to the system, so they had gone beyond being hysterical women and had passed into "that graver nervous lesion": they were madwomen.

The threat of change was in the air, and it came from an unexpected source. It came from the disenfranchised female population, whose vows of matrimony—the state to which every woman aspired—encompassed not only love and honour, but obedience. Even the most reasonable of males were uncomfortably aware of it.

Two years before the incident at Tattenham Corner, *The Times* covered the opening by the duchess of a new girls' school in Chesterfield in 1911. Evelyn opened the school and was presented with a golden key by the architects, but the two speech-makers were men: the headmaster of Repton, a well-respected boys' school, and the Duke of Devonshire.

The headmaster told the assembled guests he thought it vital that the problem-solvers of the day should be "of cultivated minds and trained judgement," thereby implying that, since the presence of women in public life seemed inevitable, better they should be educated. Victor, Duke of Devonshire, took a slightly more facetious approach. *The Times* reported it thus:

> While bearing testimony to the benefits of muscular develop-
> ment, he hoped that the gymnastic training given in the school
> would not induce any of the students to take part in the various
> movements which were better confined to the opposite sex. As
> a strong opponent of the Girls' Scouts movement, he trusted
> that the gymnastics would not induce them to take part in
> demonstrations of force in Westminster or elsewhere.

The news item was not headed, "The Duchess of Devonshire Opens a New High School for Girls," but, "The Duke of Devonshire and the Girl Scouts' Movement." Although Victor has taken a humorous approach, as a way of defusing or debunking the subject, he is quite serious about his opposition to Girl Scouts. Clubs are all right for men; similar organizations for women, or even girls, are downright dangerous, because they are dangerous for the world of men. They bring about change.

Change was certainly in the domestic air in 1913, unsettling and threatening to the status quo. Whether ensconced with her children at Chatsworth, or fulfilling her ceremonial role that played a vital part in maintaining ancient and, some were beginning to say, outworn symbols, Evie had become only too aware of the changes that threatened the security of her class. Devonshire House was no longer as solid and substantial a symbol of that immutable, God-ordained way of life as it once had been, and the Derby Night Ball was not held there that year. But there was a fancy-dress ball, a "Fête at Versailles," held in the Albert Hall and attended by the queen and an aristocracy still secure enough to have chosen that particular theme without a *frisson*.

The Devonshires did not attend. The reason is not clear, and there was certainly no intention on their part to withdraw from the social expectations of their class. For in December

1913 George V is demonstrating his brilliant marksmanship at Chatsworth, and Evelyn is at the foot of the splendid staircase she and her architect have created in the Bachelor Duke's Painted Hall. If the marble and alabaster staircase of Devonshire House, with its crystal rail and the sardonyx tiger's head at its foot, was ephemeral, then Evelyn would create another. The show must go on, and go on it did, in splendour.

And what of Dora Lee? As the suffragettes became more violent and disruptive, did she continue to open her mouth wide, as she had in her teenage years? However she may have felt privately, it is unlikely she was as outspoken as she had been when she was on the bottom rung of that kitchen ladder. No employer wanted a revolutionary under the same roof, and Dora by now knew what she had to do to get on. By Christmas 1912 she is back in Axbridge taking a holiday, and staying with a Mrs. Morrish on Cheddar Street, and for the next year Dora is not tied to one establishment, but lives in lodgings around London. She has taken what she could from her year with the Guinnesses and used her new status as an Escoffier-trained chef to make the next move in her career.

Dora may well have left the Guinnesses because, for all her training and her talent, she was not getting the recognition, or the money, she deserved. There were two strikes against her: one was her youth—she was still only twenty in 1912—and the other was her sex. Virtually all the great houses preferred to have chefs who were both French and male. There was nothing Dora could do about her race or her sex, but there was something she could do about her age; she could say she was older than she was. The only evidence that she added years to her age is from later on in her story, but she may have owed part of her major breakthrough to saying she was thirty when she was still only twenty-four. And she may have started lying about her age much earlier.

There was a great deal more money to be made in catering to the rich, or in cooking for them during the height of the various seasons. There are no records of what Dora earned at this time, but the figures available for Rosa Lewis give a good idea of what an Escoffier-trained chef with a good reputation could make—even if she was only twenty years old. By 1914 Rosa Lewis's catering alone was giving her an income of £6000 a year—approximately £84,000 today. Even allowing for a substantial reduction in the amount—after all, Rosa Lewis was a star in her own right—the sum gives an idea of what Dora could expect to earn on her own.

So, somewhere around November 1912, Dora again took her courage in her hands and left the Guinnesses. Although no letter of reference has survived from that period, it is not likely she left under a cloud, for her employers continue to be among the wealthiest and most distinguished in the land. She had her *bonnets* (her chef's hats, also known as *toques*), she had her own beautiful knives, purchased in Paris, and she had no ties. As well as her hand-written recipes, she now had her own Escoffier cookbook, the 1913 edition. From the changes that occur over the next three years, it looks like Escoffier-trained Dora Lee took her show on the road.

There was another advantage to being a freelance cook that may have appealed to twenty-year-old Dora quite as much as the money. She escaped the eagle eye of the housekeeper or the butler, the lack of privacy, the constant scrutiny and the controls that were put on those downstairs lives. By the early 1900s, many servants were given an afternoon and evening off every week, but a day off was never perceived as a right, and a curfew was imposed on even middle-aged servants. As long as she cooked brilliantly, Dora's private life was just that: private, and her own. Of the seven postcards that remain from this period, possibly five are from men—possibly, because not all are signed. On November 27, 1912, "Sardine" writes:

> Dear old Darling. Many thanks for letter, so glad to hear from you, will you meet me where you said quarter to four Friday, am looking forward to coming, so glad about Sunday, ever your loving old Sardine. Best love to all.

Could it be that Dora and "Sardine" were thrown together during a belowstairs Christmas party—when the servants were playing Sardines, and they both found themselves closeted in a cupboard or a pantry? This, of course, is the gentleman who sent Dora the flirtatious postcard about "tea at the Pap" to Knockmaroon.

Whoever he was, he had competition. On a card wishing Dora a happy new year, someone who signs himself "Till" writes: "Dear Dora, I have arranged to meet you this aft. at 3 p.m. Hoping you will." And someone, writing to Dora during her Christmas break in Axbridge, sends her a card that advises: "Yours with the old wish. A Very Happy Christmas. And many on em. (Now downt [sic] do it)."

If the sender is counselling Dora not to get married, she took the advice. By January 16, 1913, she is at Buscot Park in Faringdon, Berkshire, the country estate of Sir Alexander Henderson, who had been created a baronet in 1902, and who would shortly become Baron Faringdon of Buscot Park. Her good friend, Nell, may have got her the job, because she worked at "Kitemore" in Faringdon, the home of Harold Greenwood Henderson, the son of Dora's new employer.

This is Dora's first job with a titled family and the title is, of course, only recently acquired. Sir Alexander Henderson had an impressive curriculum vitae. He was Member of Parliament for West Staffordshire for eight years, and in 1899 became chairman of the Great Central Railway that ran like a spine from Marylebone, London, to the north, fanning out to the east and west coast of England and linking the Yorkshire and Nottinghamshire coal traffic with the ports. In the same year he purchased the rights to the ancient manor of Faringdon, which had been held in the eleventh century by Earl Hugh of Chester, son of the half-sister of William the Conqueror.

In a sense, Sir Alexander achieved prominence in the same way as the Cavendishes—only he did it about three hundred years later. First, he acquired influence and wealth, then he was ennobled. Buying the rights was the only way left to become lord of the manor in the twentieth century, and certainly the only way to graft modern shoots onto ancient roots.

The house itself was not very old. Built in 1870, it had acquired a new wing in 1899 when Sir Alexander became its owner and made it home to his collection of paintings by the Pre-Raphaelite artist Sir Edward Burne-Jones. Dora, the hired gun, would work here for about ten months before moving once more. The move was sudden, for months later Sally's card in April 1914 reads: "Yes, you bounder, you will see that I have found out where you are. I read a letter from Ma [possibly May or Mary, rather than "mother"] this morning, was very much surprised at the news."

It is addressed to Raynham Hall, Fakenham, Norfolk, one of the homes of Sir Sigismund Neumann and his wife, Anna Allegra. For about a year Dora's postcards will travel, like Dora, between Raynham Hall, Cecil Lodge in Newmarket, 146 Piccadilly in London and Glenmuick, the Neumanns' lodge on the banks of the River Dee in Scotland.

~ℰ~

"Conspicuously *arriviste*" is a description that fits the Neumanns like an expensive kid glove. Not only were they new to the ranks of the privileged, but they were not even British. Bavarian-born Sigismund Neumann had made his fortune in the diamond fields of Kimberley, South Africa, before retiring to Britain and opening his own banking house, Neumann, Lubeck and Company, in 1910—a banking house with a capital greater than the gross national product of Australia and New Zealand. He was also a director of the London Joint Stock Bank.

During his years in South Africa "Siggy" Neumann—as he was known to his friends—had been the most significant and successful fringe operator on the Rand, a thorn in the side of many of the principal financial houses. Ernest Rhodes, the younger brother of Cecil Rhodes, described him as "a jackal [who] picks up what he can after the lions have fed themselves." He arrived on the Rand in the 1870s, and by the early years of the nineteenth century his private company controlled eight Rand properties with an issued capital of almost five million pounds. In the years after the South-African War, when the boom years on the Rand were over, Siggy Neumann withdrew most of his fortune from the gold-fields and transferred his attention and his talents to Great Britain and to merchant banking.

Like the Sassoons and the Rothschilds, Sir Sigismund was Jewish, but, unlike them, he seems to have distanced himself from his racial roots quite early on. Given the prejudices of the time, which show up repeatedly in the letters and diaries of otherwise humane and reasonably enlightened members of the class he is entering, his decision is understandable. Although the spelling of his name is not officially changed until 1939, from a note in Dora's almanac it appears the pronunciation had already been anglicized, for Dora spells it as "Newman." His wife, Anna Allegra, was the daughter of a prominent banker in Alexandria, Jacques Hakim, and they had two sons and three daughters.

The gold and diamond millionaires of the South African Rand, the Randlords, were a dazzling new element of that extended court circle embraced by Edward VII. That the British members were viewed with suspicion by the old, established families was hardly surprising, for their antecedents were humble to the point of dubiety. A prime example was Lionel Phillips, the son of an Aldgate pawnbroker, to whom John Buchan dedicated *Prester John*. He returned to his native soil as a millionaire, bought a magnificent country home, Tylney Hall in Hampshire, and entered county politics. Barney Barnato, a diamond millionaire, was born in the slums of Whitechapel, and became famous enough to be included in a popular song.

One advantage of Sigismund Neumann's foreign roots was that his hosts did not hear the sounds of Aldgate and Whitechapel when he opened his mouth. But in the new court circle, first expanded by King Edward, it was wealth above all that counted—and Sir Sigismund Neumann was vastly wealthy. He established himself and his family in the hunting, shooting, fishing and racing seasons by entertaining at his various homes quite as lavishly as the Marlboroughs or the Devonshires. These new "gentlemen," however, had to be in the City during the week, and it was for their sake that the "weekend" was invented.

Not that it was often called a weekend, for that would have been middle-class, and destroyed the illusion that these were men who had time, as well as millions, in their pockets. The "Saturday-to-Monday" phenomenon meant that hosts now had to hold shoots on Sundays, in order to "get guns." But the traditional pattern of the season was maintained, and Dora moved between the Neumanns' homes following the lifestyle of her employers.

As a general rule, spring and summer were spent in London, autumn and winter in the country, with breaks for visits abroad, and a racing season that continued all year. On December

28, 1913, Dora is at Raynham Hall in Norfolk, where the Neumanns are spending Christmas and entertaining guests for the hunting season.

Raynham Hall, the seat of the marquesses of Townshend, was probably rented for the hunting season by Sir Sigismund. Its Italian-inspired Venetian windows, elegant Ionic columns and Dutch gables dated from the seventeenth century; the marble entrance hall soared one and a half storeys above the black and white diamonds of its marble floor on Ionic pilasters, fringed with garlands. There was a State Bedroom, prepared for Queen Anne but never slept in by her, and the Princess's Room, which actually was slept in by Queen Caroline when Princess of Wales. Sir Sigismund had rented a marble hall to dream of, a stately home on a grand scale.

Everything the Neumanns did was on a grand scale. Among Dora's papers are two dance cards, complete with their metal-capped pencils, for a Christmas ball, held on December 29, 1913, at Raynham Hall. The decoration on the cover is a wreath with holly berries, with "The Dances" printed in the centre of the wreath, and the date and the name of the house appear on the inside page. It is unlikely to have been a ball for the Neumanns, for the dance cards would have been embossed and gilded, probably with the Neumanns' newly acquired coat of arms, with its ostrich, springbok's head and antique coronet. These are Dora's keepsakes of one of the grandest servants' balls of her professional life.

There are fifteen dances in all on Dora's dance card, and they begin with a waltz, unlike the old tradition which usually had "Sir Roger de Coverley" as the opening dance. The musical choices are an interesting mix of traditional tunes and a piece representing the new cultural phenomenon of the movies:

1. Waltz   Nights of Gladness
2. Waltz   Schone Risette
3. Waltz   Girl on the Film

 4. Two Step   King Chanticleer
 5. Waltz   Dorfkinder
 6. Waltz   The Jewels of the Madonna
 7. Waltz   Puppenmadel
 8. Cotillion
 9. Waltz   Rosenkavalier
10. Waltz   Fidele Bauer
11. Waltz   Laughing Husband
12. Two Step   Wedding Glide
13. Waltz   Eva
14. Lancers   Girl on the Film
15. Galop

Ballroom dancing today among the general public has gone the way of the horse and carriage, and this all looks pretty tame, but appearances are deceiving. The lancers could be positively dangerous, and was often danced "like a football match," according to Violet Asquith, daughter of a British prime minister, in a letter to Archie Gordon, the son of Lord Aberdeen, a former governor-general of Canada. She writes: "Instead of ambling sedately around ... one was swung horizontally in the air. I felt my heels tinkling among the chandeliers." On another occasion she describes Edward Horner (the seducer of the Cunard maidservant) as swinging his partner so violently that her tiara flew off, and the band stopped playing "in mute amazement."

Servants' balls had a long history. When Georgiana, Fifth Duchess of Devonshire, returned home after a long exile in Europe in 1793, she gave a great ball for her servants at Devonshire House, which was also attended by her young children. The tradition was carried on by the Ninth Duke and his duchess, who turned over the theatre at Chatsworth for the occasion. Georgiana had a reputation for treating her servants well, and so had Sir Sigismund Neumann. His will shows that he instructed his family to make provisions for his servants, as well as asking them to continue to support various charitable institutions, as he had in his lifetime.

The servants' evening would have mimicked their master's celebrations, with the strict protocol of the hierarchy observed, the senior male servants leading in the women servants to supper on their arms. It would have been the perfect occasion for Dora to wear her beautiful black dress again—with a little bit of extra buckram let into the waist. Since Dora, for all her skills and responsibility, is still being called "first kitchen maid" at the Neumanns, she would probably have been escorted to dinner by a valet, or by one of those gorgeous footmen.

Among Dora's photographs is one of a long table set for a formal meal, with two servants in dinner jackets standing at the far end in front of a mirror. There are wine glasses, a cut-glass cruet and bread rolls on the table, which is covered with a white tablecloth. The room is pleasant, with floral wallpaper and pictures, an embroidered fire-screen, an upright piano, and ladder-back chairs around the table—but it is far from being an upper-class dining room. It is more likely to be the dining-room of the upper servants in the servants' hall, the kind of room that would be provided for them by the Neumanns. Clearly, it was an occasion worth recording, for Dora took the picture with her Brownie box camera and kept it with her other memorabilia.

Dora's employers and members of the family would have put in an appearance at the ball, and danced with various members of the staff. In many aristocratic households it was customary for the lord to lead off the dancing with the house-keeper, and the lady to do so with the butler. Just before the dawn of 1914, Dora dances the night away in the arms of valets, footmen, coachmen and chauffeurs.

There was a ghost at Raynham Hall, known as the Brown Lady. She was Dorothy, sister of Sir Robert Walpole, a prime

minister of Britain at the beginning of the eighteenth century. And if ghosts do indeed appear as warnings and portents
before the advent of terrible catastrophes, then surely the
Brown Lady must have walked that particular winter on architect William Kent's splendid oak staircase, where she was
sometimes seen.

It is likely that many of the entries in Dora's almanac date
from this period of her life. There is the pencilled "Newman,"
and some notes that refer directly to 146 Piccadilly. Alongside the word "Newman" in Dora's almanac is the name
"Cobbett," underlined. Morel Bros, Cobbett & Sons Ltd, were
grocers and Italian warehouse merchants whose place of business at 210 Piccadilly West would have been very convenient
for deliveries. From them Dora got a wide range of goods, from
sugars of various types to red currant jelly, patna rice, ox
tongue and chocolates. She got much of her meat from Allens
on Mount Street West, which had held the royal warrant for
the regal gourmand "Tum-Tum" and his wife, Alexandra. Bread
came from Stewart, Bakers, Biscuit makers and Confectioners at 50 Old Bond Street, and ice came from Richard Jordan
and Company at 29 Augustus Street. Her fish she ordered
from Gilson Ltd. on New Bond Street. From Gabriel Sandset
Ltd. on Swallow Street came coffee, and from Mrs. Mary
Segalant, fruiterer on the Brompton Road and Sloane Street,
Dora obtained a wide range of fruits and vegetables—from
plums and pears to turnips, parsley and French beans.

On more than one occasion Dora travelled up to Scotland
to cook for Sir Sigismund's shooting parties. There, the target of choice would be stag, and Sir Sigismund entertained
the highest in the land, including King George, who would go
anywhere—even to the hunting lodge of an *arriviste*—if it
provided a good shoot.

The owner of the nineteen thousand acres of the forest of
Glenmuick and Bachnagair, Sir James Mackenzie, had planted

the low-lying moorland with larch, spruce and Scotch fir—
an excellent winter shelter for stag and deer. The ground was
tricky, and the wind fickle, but careful management had
increased the kill to sixty to sixty-five stags a season. An account
of the time on the deer forests of Scotland has this to say
about the hunters' prey: "Sad to relate, the big stag is a self-
ish fellow, for not until he has had his fill will he allow his
weaker kin to join in the feast." The sentiment resonates
tellingly for both hunter and hunted.

On one of her days off, Dora got her photograph taken at a
studio in Aboyne. There she stands, against the photographer's
decorative backdrop in kilt and sporran, looking very young
for her years; her costume is, in fact, male Highland dress.
Among the snippets of information she shared with her family was how she loved to dance the Highland fling—the
national dance of Scotland, and traditionally a male dance.
In more primitive times it was probably a victory dance, performed after battle and—like the reel and the sword dance—
was forbidden to women until the twentieth century. In Aboyne,
where Dora had her photograph taken, that ban was still in
effect well into the latter half of the twentieth century, so—
although the costume may have been one of his own props—
this kilted kitchen maid may have been a somewhat unusual
subject for the studio photographer.

There, in the Neumanns' baronial Scottish manse, between
the long hours in the kitchen and on the moors, they would
push back the chairs in the servants' hall and dance the night
away. Young Dora would watch the Scottish gillies, gardeners and footmen on Sigismund Neumann's staff whoop-
ing and kicking up their heels and she would join them, just
as she had her kitchen confrères in Paris, dancing in the
rowdy *boîtes* and *caf-concs*, her exuberance and animal spirits
undefeated by years of drudgery and endless days of hard
physical labour.

In her little leather-bound almanac she noted her twenty-first birthday briefly, without comment: "D.L <u>21</u>." She kept no cards or reminders of that coming-of-age, but surely some of that postcard parade of friends—Ada, Nell, Ruth, Lily, Alice, Florrie—remembered to write to her on her special day. Of course, turning twenty-one was truly only a symbol for Dora, who had come of age when she entered the working world eight years earlier.

> To Dora: Her ladyship has re-considered her arrangements and now wishes me to write and ask if you will kindly arrange to go down to Cecil Lodge on Friday next (for perhaps a few weeks) to cook for the young ladies. Her ladyship would be greatly obliged if you will do this. Yours truly. L. Caton.

Cecil Lodge was the Neumanns' property in Newmarket, home of one of the most prestigious racetracks in Britain. The Jockey Club, which was founded in 1870, had its headquarters in Newmarket, but the racing history of the town went back to the seventeenth century and the reign of James I. Sir Sigismund and his brother, Ludwig, were very much involved in the sport of racing, and Dora's services were needed during the spring when the Two Thousand Guineas was run.

The tone of L. Caton's letter is quite different from that of any other similar letter in Dora's collection. If Dora were on the full-time staff of the Neumann household, no one would have written asking if she would "kindly" go to Newmarket to cook for the three Neumann daughters (Sybil Neumann had "come out" the year before). Nor would Lady Neumann have been "greatly obliged" if Dora would do this; her command would have been enough. Dora has changed the way she works, as a lengthy document among her papers proves. It is a certificate from Mrs. Massey's Agency for Servants that is accompanied by two letters of reference—one from L. Caton (Secretary), dated March 17, 1914, and the other, written in French, from Eugène Mangonnaux, the Neumanns' chef, dated April 8, 1914.

L. Caton was presumably Lady Neumann's personal secretary, and her letter follows the usually accepted form for such references: "Dora Lee has been in Lady Neumann's service at 146 Piccadilly as Kitchen Maid and not having been discharged for any grave misconduct, is, so far as I am aware, sober, honest and well conducted." However, in the space left for additional remarks, Miss Caton has added, "Can be highly recommended, thoroughly capable. L.C."

Chef Mangonnaux's letter was just as positive: "*Je n'ai qu'à me louer de son travail, de sa conduite et suis pret à lui donner les meilleurs renseignements … (elle) était avec moi première fille de cuisine.*" (I have nothing but praise for her work, for her conduct, and will readily give her the highest recommendation … her position with me was as first kitchen maid.)

It looks as if Chef Mangonnaux was also a gun for hire, because Dora has kept his business card, on which he gives two addresses: rue de Chazelles, presumably his home in France, and Savoy Chambers, Private Hotel, 19 Gerrard Street West. These were private apartments in Soho, where most French staff and chefs lived, run by an Italian, Antonio Vercesi.

The head office of the Massey Agency for Servants was in Derby for "customers corresponding from the country," but they had an office in London at 10 Baker Street for their city clientele. Mrs. Massey charged a shilling on the pound for temporary work on any wages earned as a result of her placement, and "Fourpence in the pound on first year's wages if no clothes are provided by the employer, and fivepence in the pound if any clothes are found." She was fair to young servants who earned less than fifteen pounds, for she took nothing, and asked for a one-time-only payment of two shillings and sixpence from servants who earned less than twenty pounds.

Dora was with a top-flight agency. In 1914 it had been

established for over sixty-nine years, and the nature of Mrs. Massey's business was stated as "Best Private Service only. Servants have been supplied for H.M. the King; H.M. the late King Edward VII, and H.M. the late Queen Victoria." Dora is also registered with an agency called "Richard Thomas Hutchinson, Servants' Registry Office."

Most of the evidence of what Dora cooked and how she put a menu together comes from later in her career, but there are two menus from the Neumann period: one headed *Dîner du 21 Mai, 1914*, the other headed *Souper du 21 Mai, 1914*. The menus have no decoration, no coat of arms, and are not well placed on the paper, so they are probably mock-ups by the printer. There are also errors. *The Times* lead report in the section entitled "Dances" is of a dance given by Lady Neumann at 146 Piccadilly on May 21, 1914, for her daughter Sybil.

For the occasion the house was decorated with pink rambler roses, and a green and gold-trimmed ballroom was built out into the garden, and festooned with pink sweet peas. Before the dance the Neumanns regaled grand dukes, counts and countesses, the Spanish and Italian ambassadors, and honourables galore to the following dinner:

Caviar d'Astrakan.

Consommé Polonaise.

Filet de Soles Marie Louise.

Suprêmes de Volailles à la Godard.

Jambon de Prague glacé au Cidre.

Salade Caprice.

Selles de Chézelles aux Primeurs.

Brochettes d'Ortolans.

Coeurs de Laitues Gauloise.

Asperges Lauris, sauce Délice.

Ananas Soufflé aux fraises des Bois.

Friandises.

Ramequins à l'Alsacienne.

From the caviar to the ramequins, it is an elaborate and costly bill of fare. The meal starts with Russian caviar from the Caspian Sea. *Consommé Polonaise* is a vegetable soup, predominantly using cauliflower and asparagus, sprinkled with finely chopped hard-boiled egg-yolk and parsley, or *fines herbes*. The fillets of sole have an unusual choice of garnish. Dedicated to Napoleon I's second wife, Marie-Louise, it is traditionally used with lamb or mutton, and has two principal variations: either potatoes and artichoke hearts stuffed with mushroom *duxelles* and onion purée, or small tarts filled with tiny balls of carrots and turnips.

For the poultry dish, *volaille*, the chef has chosen a classic accompaniment. Probably named after a chef at the Elysée Palace, *Godard* usually consists of braised and glazed lambs' sweetbreads, kidneys, truffles and mushroom caps in a sauce made with white wine or champagne and ham *mirepoix* (finely minced). The sauce alone requires great skill. The ham has been glazed with cider, and the following salad is probably a mixture of fresh greens.

It is the next dish that is puzzling: *Selles de Chézelles aux Primeurs*. Nowhere does *chézelles* appear in Escoffier, or *Larousse Gastronomique*, and even the acute accent over the first "e" would not be found in French spelling before a "z." It could be a printer's error, because it possibly means *selles de chevreuil*: saddle of roebuck. It could also be a dish Dora acquired from chef Mangonnaux—a creation of his own, named for the street on which he lived in France: *Chazelles*. There are many classic ways of cooking a haunch of venison, and the chef has chosen a simply perfect way, enhancing the quality and flavour of the meat with the young, fresh vegetables of the spring season.

Considered a great delicacy, *Brochettes d'Ortolan* uses this tiny species of bunting. They would have been wrapped in fatty bacon, placed on skewers with croûtons and roasted. There is a memorable scene in the movie *Gigi*, based on

Colette's novella about the upbringing and training of a young girl destined for the world of the *demi-mondaines*, in which her Aunt Alicia instructs Gigi on how to eat an *ortolan*: one must put it into one's mouth whole and crunch it up, bones and all.

The lettuce following the little birds would have cleared the palate. *Gauloise* has a wide range of possible ingredients, but usually involved kidneys, truffles and mushrooms. Presumably the lettuce hearts were stuffed with a sauce made with all or some of these ingredients. In many classic presentations, cocks' combs were used as decoration.

There is no entry in either Escoffier or *Larousse Gastronomique* for *Lauris*, but the chef has chosen asparagus here before the sweets. *Délice* is a term used loosely in cooking for many sauces, so it is impossible to tell what it means here. *Larousse Gastronomique* describes it as "exploited for its very vagueness implying in advance that the dish offered is delectable."

The sweet features a soufflé using fruits, pineapple with wild strawberries as garnish, followed by a choice of sugary delights. And, of course, no meal would have been complete without a savoury for the gentlemen to top it off. Here, individual dishes (ramekins) have been prepared for each guest. *Alsacienne* has a wide range of meaning, but usually the dish is garnished with sauerkraut, ham or salted bacon. It also is used for timbales, pies or terrines containing foie gras and, given the extravagance of this meal, the latter is the more likely interpretation.

The supper menu is lengthy, with four hot items under the heading, *Chaud*, and ten savoury and four sweet choices under the heading, *Froid*. The structure may be less formal, but many of the dishes are as extravagant: *cailles royales flambées, poulets diablés, délices de foie gras Tosca*, as well as a lavish spread of cold chicken tongue and ham. There is also a postscript to this particular menu headed "2 a.m," at which time an undoubtedly weary kitchen staff served devilled kidneys, poached eggs, bacon, marrow bones and Pilsener beer! At two a.m. fairy-coach French apparently changed into pumpkin English.

Dora may well be working with chef Mangonnaux, who apparently had not trained with Escoffier. Although the cuisine is classically French, there is virtually no dish that corresponds directly with any in Escoffier's cookbook. The menus, and the prestigious occasion they served, show Dora performing at a level few could match—man or woman.

It was a busy and successful time for Dora the freelance cook. One menu among her memorabilia, dated June 11, 1914, uses many of the same dishes as the Neumann dinner-party, so Dora may have had a selection of dishes that she offered prospective clients. Unlike all the other menus, it is not printed on card, but on good-quality bond paper, with a decorative border that suggests an engagement or wedding celebration. And on June 9, 1914, a countess was seeking her services:

> The Countess of Albemarle is in London for a few days and would like to see Dora Lee here tomorrow at 12.30 to 1 o'clock, or at 6.30. She will remember she heard particulars of the place before.

The Countess of Albemarle was having a servant problem. It sounds as if the two have negotiated in the past, and that she already knew Dora Lee. She asks Dora to use that servant network to get her "a thoroughly experienced good kitchen maid accustomed to [illegible] parties ... as I want her at once ... wages £26 to £28."

Dora has now landed a job as cook with a countess, who is herself the daughter of an earl. Her husband, the Eighth Earl of Albemarle, is the older brother of George Keppel, the unfortunate husband of King Edward's *"La Favorita,"* Alice Keppel. Formerly an aide-de-camp for King Edward, the Earl of Albemarle now served King George, so there will have been many occasions at their Windsor home when the countess will have needed a superb cook—war or no war.

Finally, Dora is being recognized for what she has actually been for her employers for the past two years: a cook, and not a kitchen maid. Finally, someone else will be doing all the kitchen work she had been expected to do in the past—and she has made sure of that before agreeing to come. The countess assures her that she has a "suitably experienced" kitchen maid in the letter arranging Dora's arrival.

Events in that month of June, when Dora began negotiations with the countess, will make it easier for Dora Lee to reach the heights of her profession, and to receive the recognition she has seen given to others, particularly if they were men—and particularly if they were French.

On June 28, 1914, Archduke Franz Ferdinand, heir apparent to the Austro-Hungarian throne, was murdered in Sarajevo in the Balkans. The assassin was an eighteen-year-old Bosnian Serb, a member of the Secret Society of the Black Hand. Over a crucifix, a dagger and a revolver he had sworn "by the sun that warms me, the earth that nourishes me, by the blood of my ancestors, on my honour and my life," to do what was asked of him. Witnesses said he was looking away when he fired the shot that would change the world of Dora and her employers for ever.

Archduke Franz Ferdinand may have charmed the Devonshires at a Chatsworth luncheon in the autumn of 1913, but he had not been a popular figure in his own country. His murder was a useful pretext for an attack on Serbia, to which the kaiser gave his full support. In Britain, attention had been focused once more on Irish affairs and on amendments to the Home Rule Bill, and the momentary diversion of attention to events in Europe was looked on as a breathing space for all concerned—a chance to unite a divided government and a squabbling country. Gradually, the general public became aware that something was happening in Europe that might affect them.

The splendid and arrogant isolation of "this earth, this realm, this England," was not much of a reality any more by 1914. The general hostility of Europe towards Britain after the Boer War had been tempered by King Edward's visits to Paris and the creation of the *Entente Cordiale* with France, to which was added a similar understanding with Russia. France, Britain and Russia now stood on one side of the chessboard facing the Central Powers—Germany, Austria and Italy.

But it was trade and colonial rivalry with Germany, above all, that dominated British consciousness, and the focus of that rivalry was naval domination. Britannia must always rule the waves, and the German naval build-up at the beginning of the century threatened that assumption. It was somehow viewed as a frivolous indulgence of the Germans, who were merely being ambitious, whereas it was considered imperative—a divine right of sorts—for the island of Britain to hold command of the sea. Therefore, the growth of naval expenditure from £31 million in 1901 to £52 million in 1914 was accepted as an absolute necessity. As the monstrous dreadnought battleships grew in number, so did the jingoistic fervour of the nation, spread by the popular press and even the music-hall. From the stage of the Alhambra, comics and comediennes belted out the songs that fired and fed war fever:

> We don't want to fight, but by jingo if we do
> We've got the men, we've got the ships
> We've got the money too.

Dora's perception of the war and what was happening to her country would be transmitted through those purveyors of popular opinion. What would matter most would be the changes to her country that would affect her profession, her friendships and, by 1914, her feelings for one man. The intricacies of Balkan nationalism, Anglo-German naval rivalry, or the ambitions of Austro-Hungary meant little or nothing to her. Yet, even for those in high places, there is a sense of a war that crept up on them unawares.

The weather was beautiful in May, as it was to be all that glorious summer. Evelyn, Duchess of Devonshire, held the Derby dinner and ball at Devonshire House the night before race day. *The Times* noted that it was "a bigger affair than originally intended." In fact, Evie had been given what amounted to an order by Queen Mary to take over the guests from a ball cancelled for court mourning and, according to Victor's diary, it was only with reluctance and at short notice that she agreed to hold the Derby Night Ball that year. Since there was no question of her refusing a royal command, Evie did it in style.

Along the great table, among the Princess of Wales malmaisons, sat the Russian ambassador, the Austro-Hungarian ambassador, the French ambassador, the Italian ambassador, the Turkish ambassador, the American ambassador. Up the crystal staircase, amid the lilium longiflora, the blue hydrangeas and the Dorothy Perkins roses, mingled Battenbergs, Desboroughs, Spencer-Churchills, Curzons and Rothschilds. Herr Boxhorn's orchestra played for princes and diplomats, marchesas and ministers, and one doubts that anyone swung their partner up to the Devonshire House chandeliers. The Countess of Albemarle was there. There were no portents. If ever a tableau illustrated the grotesque unreality of what would erupt in only three months, it was that final Derby Night Ball at Devonshire House.

Dora was with the Countess of Albemarle in Windsor, as events in the month of July inched the country towards war. The Home Rule Bill again preoccupied parliament, and was originally due to come up before the House of Commons on July 28.

It was finally postponed on July 30, when Russia mobilized. Before the Monday of the August Bank Holiday weekend, there was a run on the banks and the interest rate rose six percentage points in forty-eight hours. The government countered by keeping the banks closed until August 6. All those August holiday-makers returning home must have been only too aware that the country was on the brink of war when they found that the railways had been taken over for troop movements.

Under the general heading "The War Day by Day," the headlines on one page of *The Times* for August 1 read in large capitals: "ENGLAND'S DUTY ... THE PRECAUTIONS AT HOME ... EUROPEAN FLEETS BEING REINFORCED ... THE MENACE OF WAR ... THE STRENGTH OF THE NAVY." The impression given to the man in the street is one of firm resolve and quiet confidence: his leaders were at the helm, in control. The only note of dissonance on the page comes in a letter from a Mr. Norman Angell.

Norman Angell was the author of *The Great Illusion*, a book first published in 1909, which had been translated into French, German, Italian and Russian and, by the time of his letter and the declaration of war, had been reprinted ten times. Angell maintained that even the victors of war would suffer serious economic and financial losses. He reminded readers of the horrors of the Crimean War—now agreed to have been "a monstrous error and miscalculation"—and concluded: "We can best serve civilization, Europe—including France—and ourselves by remaining the one Power in Europe that has not yielded to the war madness." War madness would win out and, in the months to come, younger men who felt like Norman Angell would be branded as cowards, and handed white feathers by the womenfolk of England.

There was no reply to Britain's ultimatum to Germany, demanding that they withdraw from neutral Belgium, which they invaded on August 4, having first declared war on France. In the south of France there was a hurried exodus of German chefs, waiters and *maîtres d'hôtels*, who now found themselves on enemy soil. When Big Ben struck eleven on August 4, exultant crowds gathered outside Buckingham Palace singing the songs they had heard from the stage of the Alhambra, and cheering the king, who appeared on the balcony with the queen and the Prince of Wales to acknowledge his almost-hysterical people. On the same day, *The Times* reported that Russia had been invaded, railways attacked, and frontier towns occupied. It also announced the imminent signing of the proclamation of mobilization, which would affect both the reserves and the territorials.

Such was the upsurge of patriotism that even deserters were returning to the recruiting offices, declaring that they could not stand by and betray their country in her hour of need. Under the royal coat of arms *The Times* proclaimed, "Your King and Country Need You," exhorting "every patriotic young man ... [who is] unmarried and between 18 and 30 years old ... answer your Country's call." Concerned that their readers should not miss out on "The War Day by Day," the same newspaper carried an announcement in gigantic typeface urging them to reserve copies with their newsagent, because "the demand for THE TIMES greatly exceeds the supply." Others, besides arms manufacturers, would do well out of the next four terrible years.

In Paris, the city where Dora had worked and trained with Auguste Escoffier only two years earlier, there were no steamers on the Seine, no tourists. Most private cars, buses and taxis had been commandeered by the War Office, and most of the shops were closed. The only lights in the *ville lumière* were the searchlights that raked the night sky looking for zeppelins. By the end of August there were French casualties in the thousands. (Three months later, on November 1, Auguste Escoffier's second son was killed in action.) By the end of December 1914, the death-toll was already staggering: there were more French dead than all the British dead in the whole

of the Second World War. There were a million German soldiers on the soil of France, yet still there were those who
talked of a swift conclusion.

In Britain, where Dora was about to make another move,
the newly appointed Secretary of State for War, Lord Kitchener,
the hero of Khartoum, pointed an accusing finger at all young
males from every hoarding, and thirty thousand men a day were
enlisting. Among them was someone very special to Dora.

From the postcards we know him only as Bert. His postcards
to Dora start in October 1914, from Colchester:

> Dear Dora: have made all arrangements for you to come down
> here Saturday. Will write tomorrow morning Friday ... have got
> a nice place for you to stay. Love Bert.

There is then a gap in the postcard collection, and she will
not receive another card from Bert for six months—they have
probably been communicating more privately, by letter. In the
interim, Dora has left the Countess of Albemarle and gone to
work for a Mrs. Baer at 13 Maresfield Gardens in Hampstead.
However, it looks as if she had difficulty finding a job after
the countess. On one of her chatty postcards brimming over
with information, Dora's old friend Lily writes:

> Queen Annes Mead. My dear old girl: You will see by this I am
> back at the old place. This is the second weekend I have been
> here but they have all gone awa'. So we are very quiet. I am
> just off for byke [sic] ride. Wish you were here to come too. Is
> there any danger of seeing you? before the 12? I suppose not!
> Have you heard of anything yet. I do hope you will be lucky. I
> met Miss Williams last week. She has a place. She asked me
> to go round to tea but I would not do that. Only I said I would
> go out with her Saturday and then she was too busy, and I came
> here. I should like to have seen old John, as bad as he is. But
> I did not feel swanky enough for Fathers. Different if you had

been there. Do let's know where you get to, old dear. I shall come to London sometimes, if I don't leave at the end of the month. Give my love to everybody with fond love and a glass of port. If I had it. From Lil. XX.

Obviously, all those servants who have known each other over the years still get together on a Saturday night, with Dora right in the centre of things, never doubting for a moment she is swanky enough for "Fathers." "Fathers" is probably a pub or club in the London area, and the name may well be the servants' own name for it—much as a bar nowadays might be called "The Office." ("And where are you spending your evening off, Lily?" "At Father's, madam.")

Mrs. Baer is not an *arriviste*, for it is unlikely she made any attempt to penetrate the circles of the aristocracy; rather she is a *nouveau riche*.

Maresfield Gardens was part of a comparatively new development that had gradually grown up after 1876 on estates outside the central London area, which had been bought and split up into smaller properties. Not that the houses on Maresfield Gardens were that modest. Although not on the scale of the stately homes they had replaced, they were spacious and well set back from the road, they had their own carriage drives, and the grounds had been lavishly treed and landscaped. The area housed many of London's new wealthy of the turn of the century. In this setting, which was a new environment for her, Dora spent the first winter of the Great War. And many of the men who had responded to the pointing finger of Lord Kitchener, and who had survived the early battles of the war—Marne, Mons and Aisne—were settling down in new, and terrible, surroundings.

The death-toll among the aristocratic and ruling class was noticeable in the early months of the war, because their losses were appalling, and because theirs were the names that made the headlines. Four divisions of the British Expeditionary Force fought the early battles of the war alongside the French Army, and the death-toll was heavy. Two platoons of the Second Grenadier Guards were surrounded and, receiving no order to retire, fought on until every single member was either killed or wounded, the officers who led their men into battle dying with them.

On October 24, 1914, the headline in *The Times* read: "Roll of Honour. Loss of 12 officers. Lord John Cavendish killed." Victor's brother, who had served with the Lifeguards in South Africa and seen action at Spion Kop and the relief of Ladysmith, who had been mentioned in dispatches and received the DSO (the Distinguished Service Order), was killed in the First Battle of Ypres, in the early months of the war. His mother watched her son ride away from Knightsbridge Barracks in command of his squadron of the First Life Guards, and felt then she would never see him again. John Cavendish was killed on October 20, and Evie's brother, Charlie Fitzmaurice, was killed ten days later. So great would be the loss among the upper classes that, after the war, many titles passed from grandfather to grandson, and some died out altogether. In her book, *Unquiet Souls*, Angela Lambert writes:

> Their [the British ruling classes] ideology of glory, of sacrifice, inculcated at home, at school, at chapel, at university, on the playing fields, on the grouse moors and around the dinner table —had its culmination in the sacrificial deaths of their sons.

It would take a few more years of war before that idealism changed to bitterness at the waste of those young lives, and anger grew against old men like Kitchener and Field Marshall Sir John French (he of the suffragette sister), who fought the war as if they were still back in nineteenth-century South Africa. Not that Sir John French lasted long as commander-in-chief; by the end of 1915 he had been replaced—for better or worse—by Sir Douglas Haig. And not that they fought the war themselves. That was left to officers below the rank of brigadier-general. For many among the officer elite, life was much as it had been in England and Empire, as they sampled the wine cellars in the French *châteaux* they had requisitioned, or been given, for the war effort.

Devonshire House also found a new purpose in life; in August 1914 Evie and Victor handed it over to the Red Cross. Every day, where marchesas, ministers and ambassadors had danced to the music of Herr Boxhorn's orchestra, long lines of women waited patiently to offer their services to the Voluntary Aid Department, most of them hoping to serve on the front lines in France. Instead of the great formal dinners served to kings and emperors, the kitchens were cooking for the canteen run by the Red Cross and the VAD. Oatcakes and milk cost a penny, and veal and two vegetables could be had for sixpence and one rationing coupon. Chocolate mould cost threepence. *The Times* reported that the modern gas-fired equipment in the kitchen made it easy for the volunteers to prepare the meals, which were limited to one shilling and threepence for each person. A far cry indeed from *Poularde Devonshire* and *Bombe Néron*!

In Derbyshire, Chatsworth became the Red Cross Clearing House for the county, run by Evie's personal assistant, Elsie Saunders. Maud took her first aid and nursing examinations and went by bicycle every day to work at a hospital in nearby Bakewell. Before Christmas 1914, twenty-one of her ballroom partners from her coming-out year were dead.

And Eddy, the gentle little boy who had hated the whole process that prepared him for just such an eventuality as this war? He left Cambridge at the end of his first university year and joined the Derbyshire Yeomanry. With them he went to Egypt as an aide-de-camp to General Kenna, who had been awarded the Victoria Cross in South Africa. In between his official duties he would spend any spare time he had studying at the War Bureau with the officer whom the world would later know as Lawrence of Arabia.

Eddy saw action at the disastrous landing at Suvla Bay in the Dardanelles, in which General Kenna was killed, and he miraculously survived, with only his wrist-watch shot off. The action that day, August 21, is a prime example of a fiasco in a war of fiascos, the most abysmally unsuccessful of all the Gallipoli battles.

It was the Derbyshire Yeomanry's first experience of action, and they found themselves advancing across an open plain— yet still they marched in lines as if on parade, five thousand easy targets for the Turkish guns. Once they crossed the plain, no one had any clear idea of what they were then supposed to be doing, and few of the senior officers had ever seen the terrain, which was now covered in mist and raging scrub fires. By the end of the day it was clear that the attack of the Yeomanry division had accomplished nothing, and they were ordered to withdraw the way they came, to the original British front line, carrying their wounded with them. Out of a total of 14,300 men who took part in the attack, 5300 were killed, wounded or missing.

The Yeomanry then dug themselves in for the winter—a hard task, for the ground was rocky. As he dug, Eddy filled his pockets with the flower bulbs concealed in the stony soil. When the winter rains came, the trenches flooded. In November a thunderstorm with hail and heavy rain swept men and animals along the trenches, and at least a hundred men were drowned. This was followed by a two-day blizzard in which another hundred men died of exposure. In his book *First World War*, Martin Gilbert notes that "the only welcome deaths were those of the millions of flies that had gorged themselves on the corpses: when the storm passed they had disappeared."

Having survived the enemy, Eddy contracted jaundice, malaria and dysentery, and nearly died. He eventually made his way back to London, weighing less than seven stone (ninety-eight pounds,) and, although he tried many times, was never passed for active service again. Instead, he went to Paris, where he could use his excellent French, and worked in counter-espionage. Not a shabby record for the gentle man who, as a child, had always longed to be back home with his mother and his sisters. Some would argue that Ludgrove and Eton had done their job.

Bert's war is not so well documented in Dora's postcard collection. The second card is sent six months later, in April 1915:

> My dear Dora: you will see we have left Colchester. Got to Ipswich last night and left today. Am now at Woodbridge. Expect to leave here tonight. Will write tomorrow. Love Bert.

Through the years, the pictures on the postcards portray Dora's world—seaside holidays, suffragettes, courtship, the

trials and tribulations of being a servant—and now the pictures reflect that world at war. Bert's first postcard of 1915 shows a soldier with a rifle and a fixed bayonet beneath two crossed flags, alongside a photograph of the town hall in Woodbridge, in the county of Suffolk. The caption reads, "We're doing our Duty for King and Country." His second postcard of 1915, also sent in April, has the same picture:

> Dear Dora: Just a PC. Have not had a chance to write a letter yet. Arrived here last night. Boyton a little village. We are

billeted in a cowshed, but it is lovely weather so far, so we can't say anything. Will write tomorrow if I get home. Love Bert.

On May 6, Bert sends Dora a postcard with a cartoon drawing of soldiers digging trenches. The caption says, "We are getting fed up with our diggings here," and the message reads:

> My dear Dora: You will think I am never going to write but I did not have the time before. You see we have arrived at Bishop Stortford. Stayed last night at Braintree [illegible] billeted in a Salvation Army place. Hope you are [illegible] dear. Will write again tomorrow. Love Bert.

WE ARE GETTING FED UP WITH OUR DIGGINGS HERE

On May 17, on a postcard with a sepia-tinted picture of the county hospital in Hertford, Bert writes once more:

> My dear Dora: You see I have arrived here. Tomorrow morning I will write. Have [had] nearly enough monkeying [around]. Shall not be sorry to get to Salisbury Plain. Hope you are better. Love Bert.

After being moved around the country, and managing to keep in touch with Dora, Bert is at last on his way to Salisbury Plain, one of the principal training and marshalling grounds for British and colonial troops on their way to fight in Europe. He and his fellow recruits were sorely needed; the Second Battle of Ypres was costing the lives of thousands, and fresh blood was needed. If Bert wrote to Dora during the next terrible months of his life, the letters and postcards have not survived.

The only overseas card from this period is from someone called Mat, a brother or boyfriend of Alice, who herself writes to Dora on August 14, 1916, to say that "Mat is going on well." Mat himself sends Dora a postcard from a field post office on July 26. The picture on the card is a black-and-white photograph of a damaged windmill, and the caption says, "La Grande Guerre 1914–15–16. Le Moulin d'Hébuterne (Pas-de-Calais) qui fût le théâtre de furieux combats" (The Great War 1914–15–16. Hébuterne Mill (Pas-de-Calais) which was the scene of fierce fighting). The words "On Active Service" are written on the card, and there is a red censor's stamp that reads, "Passed field censor 2068." The war had now gone on long enough for some enterprising businessman to be making money on picture postcards from the front.

May 9, 1915, saw the first arrival in France of "Kitchener's Army," all those young men recruited by that accusatory pointing finger, so Bert was among the first eager volunteers to sign up for service on the Western Front. From the date on his postcard to Dora from Hertford, it seems likely he arrived in France after the Battle of Aubers Ridge, in which repeated attacks by the combined British and French forces failed to make any impact on the German lines. So acute was the shortage of shells that the battle had to be abandoned after one day, and the loss of over eleven thousand men.

Bert arrived in France at the beginning of the stalemate that would become the pattern of warfare over the next few years: raids into no man's land, shelling and sniping, with no particular gains and few clear victories for either side. On May

25, when the Second Battle of Ypres came to an end, British and Canadian forces had pushed the trenches forwards one thousand yards at the cost of sixteen thousand lives.

It is unlikely that Bert or his fellow soldiers had heard much about the full horrors of trench warfare before they left for France. Those stories had not yet come back to England with the wounded, the gassed and the dying. But the myths were beginning to return from the battlefield, phantasms and fables created by soldiers suffering from shell-shock, exhaustion and sheer terror—and by the press, who fed the British public's hunger for information, infamy, and any sign that God was on their side: a necessary assurance against an enemy with *Gott mit uns* engraved on his belt buckle.

The Angel of Mons is unquestionably the most enduring of these fables. The first major battle on the Western Front in August 1914, the Battle of Mons, had been visited by a white-clad angel on horseback, with a sword of flame, who held back the advancing Germans. The following year, on May 15, 1915, *The Times* told its readers the hideous story of the Canadian soldier found crucified—on a Belgian barn door in some accounts, on a wooden fence in others—with German bayonets piercing his arms and neck. Under the heading, "THE CRUCIFIXION OF A CANADIAN. Insensate Act Of Hate," *The Times'* special correspondent in Northern France told its readers:

> I have not heard that any of our men actually saw the crime committed. There is room for the supposition that the man was dead before he was pinned to the fence, and that the enemy in his insensate rage and hate of the English wreaked his vengeance on the lifeless body of his foe ... There is not a man in the ranks of the Canadians who fought at Ypres who is not firmly convinced that this vile thing has been done.

In the telling, the one Canadian increased to six Canadians, with further elaborations, and the myth was perpetuated after the armistice by a bronze frieze exhibited at the Royal Academy called *Canada's Golgotha*, by sculptor Derwent Wood, showing Germans smoking and throwing dice beneath the crucified man. The story was never confirmed, but the myths and rumours that filtered back from the front were reported in the press and fired the resolve of Kitchener's army and the recruits' hatred of the enemy.

But it was not only the soldier who was filled with hatred. In England, the reports of outrages against the Belgians in the early months of the war led to anti-German rioting in London and other major cities, such as Liverpool. In the early months of 1915, premises owned by Germans or Austrians were attacked and looted. Leading London clubs, such as the Athenaeum and the Lyceum, either suspended their German and Austrian members or asked them to refrain from using the premises. Many distinguished, naturalized Germans wrote to *The Times* declaring "their open condemnation of German military methods and their loyalty to the country of their adoption." Among the signatories to one such declaration was Dora's former employer, Sigismund Neumann.

German males in the working or professional classes had either got out of the country or had been interned. Some sections of popular opinion thought that women, too, should be interned—even the British wives of German nationals. German women white-collar workers, such as typists and clerks, faced the threat of internment, and certainly had no hope of finding work to support themselves. The only exception was the German woman cook who, with so few men available for the traditional male occupation of chef, still found herself in demand. According to *The Times*, one of the largest servants' agencies told them that "... though German servants were dismissed at the beginning of the war many applications were afterwards received from Englishwomen, overwhelmed by the servant difficulty, for German cooks, and these women, unless they have been dismissed as a result of the present outcry, are perhaps the only German women in British employment." When it came to matters of the table, the British hostess was not going to let a war stand between her and a good cook. British-born, Escoffier-trained Dora was going to be much in demand.

After May 1915 Dora's soldier disappears for a very long while. But Bert survives. It will be four years, though, before the silence will be broken.

In July 1916, the Duke of Devonshire was offered the post of Governor-General of Canada. His predecessor, the Duke of Connaught, had his term of office extended at the onset of the war, but was recalled in part because of his ongoing feud with Canada's Minister of Militia, Colonel (later General) Sam Hughes. Victor's eldest daughter, Maud, gives another reason in her memoirs. She says that the family's departure was put forward because the Duke of Connaught insisted on returning early to avoid having to give Max Aitken (later Lord Beaverbrook) "his decoration"—his baronetcy. That "mushroom of a man," as Sir Joseph Pope called him, was a supporter of Sam Hughes.

In what was a radical departure for the times, Prime Minister Sir Robert Borden had advocated a Canadian for the post—possibly Sir Wilfrid Laurier, an inventive way of neutralizing the Opposition leader—and was disappointed to find the choice taken out of his hands by Westminster. But at least this was not a military man, like Connaught, and he and Victor Devonshire would develop a warm friendship and working relationship.

Into this tempestuous political mix, now complicated by war, the Duke of Devonshire was asked to enter. Although he was concerned about leaving estate affairs in the hands of his agents, Victor was buoyed by the thought that he could play a useful and important role once again, after the years in the mausoleum of the House of Lords.

Once again, he met opposition from Evie. She had four daughters of marriageable age, and her duty lay in guiding them to the kind of marriage she herself had contracted. This time, there would be no easy return to England to find a suitable match, as she herself had in 1890; the seas were alive with German U-boats and submarines. Reluctantly, Victor gave up the idea. And, as had happened once before, Evie's wishes were overridden by the obligations of her class, as laid down by her father and husband.

In her memoirs, Maud describes how she and her father walked sadly over to Lansdowne House, "where he was meeting Arthur Balfour [the prime minister] and Daddy Clan [Lord Lansdowne]. They must have made him reverse his decision. Within a few minutes Granny Maud [Lady Lansdowne] interrupted my work to whisper jubilantly that he had accepted."

Lord Lansdowne loved Evie and wanted her to be happy; Victor loved Evie and wanted her to be happy. But, from the days of her courtship to her departure for Canada, her life follows the pattern approved by those patriarchal figures. The despotism is benevolent, but it is unmistakeable.

On August 26, 1916, Dora receives a postcard at Babraham Hall in Cambridge, where she is now working. The message is brief and to the point: "THE MAPLE LEAF FOR EVER."

Dora's Babraham Hall Recipe for Senna Jam as an Aperient

1/2 lb prunes
1/2 lb Demerara sugar
1 oz powdered senna (fresh)
1/2 oz ground ginger
1 wine glass of whisky or brandy to keep

Cover prunes and simmer till tender. Mix dry ingredients. Stone prunes. Pass through sieve. Mix whilst hot using prune syrup.

Servants knew a great deal about the lives of their masters and mistresses. They knew the secrets of bedroom and boudoir—and they knew who was constipated. If you never go into the kitchen yourself, and have never done so much as boil an egg—some members of the upper classes never even wound their own watches—then you would have to ask the cook or one of the servants to prepare your laxative for you. This one sounds surprisingly delicious. Of course, it is possible that Dora prepared this for herself, but she has written out the recipe and kept it so carefully in an envelope marked "B.H. [Babraham Hall] 1916," that it seems more likely it was for a master or mistress, rather than a servant.

PART FOUR

First Cook

NINE

Of Vassals and Marble Halls

An Englishman's home is his castle.
SIR EDWARD COKE, 1628

I
f a house can be a chameleon, then Rideau Hall is one of those variable beasts. Its original builder, Thomas MacKay, was a stonemason from Perth, Scotland, who had made his fortune as a contractor for the Lachine and Rideau canals, and eventually became a member of the Legislative Council of the Province of Canada. On his hundred-acre estate overlooking the Ottawa and Rideau rivers, MacKay built what the locals called "MacKay's Castle" in the style of a Regency villa, with a bow-fronted central structure that rose the height of the house, and wings on each side, complete with galleries enclosed with Doric colonnades.

An Elysian retreat. A princely mansion. A small villa suitable for the needs of a country banker. A miserable little house. Rideau Hall was many things to many people, and much depended on the new occupants' point of view and former domicile. And, if it didn't suit, then it was remodelled and refurnished and redecorated until the original Regency villa of Thomas MacKay was overlaid and embellished and surrounded by Second Empire windows, belvederes, verandas, Victorian staircases, a curling rink and a ballroom.

The interior decor changed with the tastes of the age and its chatelaines. Lady Dufferin's pink boudoir with pictures of Ireland on the walls gave way to the blue parlour of Princess

Louise, daughter of Queen Victoria and wife of the Marquess of Lorne, with old tapestries from Scotland, canaries in gilded cages, and sprigs of apple blossom, Princess Louise's own artwork, on the doors. Lord Dufferin's study with the red-upholstered furniture, green curtains and walls covered with his own sketches, acquired grey walls, a green carpet and tapestry when the Marquess of Lorne took up residence. Not surprisingly, the skeleton that Lord Dufferin kept hanging in a corner to startle visitors disappeared. Lorne's choice of *memento mori* was a relic of the Crimea: an inkstand made of the hoof of the warhorse of Major-General Lord Clyde, commander of the Highland Brigade, defender of Balaclava, queller of the Sepoy Mutiny in India, and hero of the storming of the Dilkoosha Palace and the Secunder Bagh at Lucknow.

Few changes were made to the house under the Stanleys, the Lansdownes and the Aberdeens, but the Mintos found it far too small, and added another wing to provide extra bedrooms for the children, household and servants. The Greys added a new study for the governor-general, and an elegant greenhouse.

The Devonshires' predecessors, the Connaughts, reacted with dismay at their first glimpse of their gubernatorial home— "one wonders if one has made a mistake & come up to a gymnasium flanked by a riding school with a very poor little porch connecting the two!" a disconcerted Louise confided to her diary—but ended up loving it. They added an extra cloakroom, a gallery alongside the tent room, improved the servants' quarters in the basement, and redecorated the ballroom in yellow. But the most significant change made was the addition of an imposing new front to Rideau Hall, with a lofty pediment that encompassed the royal coat of arms. Other interior modifications—the spacious reception hall, aides-de-camp's bedrooms, a smoking room, a billiard room—gave the home of Canada's governors-general the look and shape it still essentially has today.

Outside in the grounds, Thomas MacKay's cowbarn, piggery and bowling green were either added to at various times and by various incumbents, or metamorphosed into a cricket pitch, an ice house, a carriage house, a laundry, a curling hut, and a gasometer. An additional property, Rideau Cottage, which eventually acquired an extra storey, was built in the grounds for the governor-general's secretary, whose residence it has remained for many years.

Beyond the ornamental iron railings lay the capital city that had evolved from the days when its first governor-general, Lord Monck, preferred during the summer months to row up the river in a six-oared boat to attend parliament, rather than risk the potholed road between Rideau Hall and Parliament Hill. By the time the Devonshires arrived in Canada, the capital had a population of around ninety-two thousand, but in some respects it had changed little from the Ottawa described by Evie's brother, Lord Hamilton, in the 1880s as "an attractive little place ... with a note of unaffected simplicity about everything that was most engaging." Some would assert it was little changed from the town pithily described by Toronto's Sage of the Grange, Goldwin Smith, as "a sub-arctic lumber-village converted by royal mandate into a political cock-pit."

Beyond the city stretched the second largest country in the world, over four and a half thousand kilometres from the southernmost tip of Ontario to the northernmost point of Ellesmere Island in the Arctic, and more than five thousand kilometres from the Pacific to the Atlantic. Bread basket to the world, with a quarter of the planet's fresh water, if India was the jewel in the British crown, the only metaphor or image that would even remotely embody such a country would be that of the royal throne itself of that distant, sceptred isle.

The metaphor is not one that extends itself successfully to Canada. Unlike India, the North American continent was establishing an identity far different from the one the first explorers found when they crossed the great plains or navigated its rivers—an identity created by two founding peoples and the immigrants streaming in from all over Europe. For the thousands of immigrants who came to its shores, Canada was no royal throne; it was the lap of the gods.

On Sunday, March 7, 1915, when Bert was training with Kitchener's army, Dora received a letter at Mrs. Baer's house in Hampstead from 34 Cadogan Square. It read:

> Mrs Adeane will be obliged if Mrs. Dora Lee will call tomorrow at 34 Cadogan Square London S.W. before 11 o'clock & see her about a cook's place. Mrs. Adeane is leaving London at 11 o'clock tomorrow morning & would like an interview with Mrs. Lee.

All must have gone well at the interview, for a week later there is a follow-up letter from Babraham Hall, the Adeanes' country home:

> Mrs Lee: I have received a satisfactory character in the main from Mrs. Baer, also from the Countess of Albemarle, so will engage you for £45 a year, & your washing done in the laundry. I think you said you would like a holiday, so if you came to Babraham Hall on Saturday 27th or Monday 29th March that will be quite convenient. I forget when you leave Mrs. Baer. The trains go from Liverpool St. Station or St. Pancras or King's Cross to Pampisford, change at Cambridge, but the best way will be to take the 3.3 train from Liverpool St. Station to Whittlesford at 4.50 where the car will meet you. Yours faithfully, Madeline Adeane.

There is a postscript added along the side of the last page: "If you do not leave Mrs. Baer in time to have a holiday before 29th Mar, then Mon. 12th Apr will suit me." Dora may well have spent those precious few days with her soldier before he moved to Salisbury Plain.

Madeline Adeane was one of a trio of beautiful sisters, the

Wyndham sisters, who were painted at the height of their aristocratic beauty by Sargent, just as Evie had been, and the Adeane family were distinguished members of the landed gentry. At the time Dora came to work for them they had a long record of service in county circles, and have since acquired a lengthy record of service in the royal household. The family seat, Babraham Hall, came into the Adeane family when its eighteenth-century owner, an East Indian merchant, left it to his only daughter who married the local MP, General James Adeane. Dora's new place of employment was an imposing neo-Jacobean mansion fronted by a long Italianate colonnade, set amidst elegant formal gardens.

Not that those gardens were looking well-groomed any more. Weeds had begun to spring up in the flower-beds and along the unraked gravel paths, as the young and the strong answered Kitchener's call. A *Punch* cartoon of 1915 shows a lady trying to gain the services of a very unsuitable lout of a boy. "Well, Mum," says his jubilant mother, "there's bin 'alf a dozen after 'im this morning. But I shall be very 'appy to put you on the waiting list." In the grounds of Babraham Hall, four old men were left to do the work of twelve, and even the odd-job boy—a homeless orphan called Crick—had enlisted. Young Crick was destined never to return from the mud of Flanders.

But Babraham Hall desperately needed good staff, because it had become a centre of operations for part of the war effort. At the onset of war, Charles Adeane organized an emergency committee to mobilize the Cambridgeshire Territorials, and the war office established a telephone line in the house itself. Madeline Adeane was coping with more than the usual household demands, and she must have been relieved and delighted when she acquired "Mrs." Dora Lee. From one of the postcards in Dora's collection, it looks as if the exigencies of war meant that the Adeanes' new cook also functioned as a housekeeper—a common combination of titles at the level of a household such as The Ferns—because the card is from a

Mr. B. Pyle, arranging with Dora to come and sweep the chimneys "as requested" between four and five o'clock in the morning!

Given the circumstances, Madeline Adeane would not have been unduly bothered that the reference from Mrs. Baer was qualified by the phrase, "in the main." Dora, it seems, had not taken kindly to her *nouveau riche* employer after her years of service with the likes of the Guinnesses and the Neumanns. Perhaps she had been uppity with someone who did not know how to behave to the manner born; or perhaps she had been expected to take on too heavy a burden of work, and had not suffered such exploitation in silence.

Food and servant shortages affected even the privileged. At the Carlton Escoffier was working with a much-reduced staff, trying to perform miracles with venison, which was unrationed, serving it finely minced with eggs, or as a *daube Provençal*, with noodles and chestnut purée. In 1914 he organized the dispatch of Christmas puddings to the troops undergoing their first winter on the front line. Still caring personally for the members of *le métier*, he spearheaded charities to help the widows and children of those who were killed at the front.

In the first zeppelin raid on London on May 1, 1915, seven people were killed and thirty-five were injured. Certainly Dora saw zeppelins, cylindrical airships used by the Germans for reconnaisance and bombing, because in later years she recalled the fear she had felt when they passed overhead. She was much happier in the countryside, helping the war effort in her own way. As she cooked for the officers and soldiers from the Cambridge Territorials working at the hall, as she looked up at the night sky after a long day's work, with the great searchlights in the grounds raking the darkness in search of zeppelins, Bert must have been in Dora's thoughts every waking minute.

Who was he? Where had she met him? There had been many other men in her life, many chances to marry, but until she met this man, her ambition and her upward drive had kept her from giving her heart. Was he "Sardine"—or "Whisker"? Perhaps he was the Territorial in the khaki coat with whom she had flirted when she was only fifteen. Perhaps he was one of the Neumanns' glamorous footmen—the one for whom she had made a note in her almanac to drop into Charles Jaschke, the court perfumer on Regent Street, for some Ajax Hair Lotion while she was shopping at Cobbett's. However fickle or flirtatious she may have been in the past, whether it was the man himself or the uncertainty cast over all things familiar and secure by a terrible war, Dora had now fallen in love.

Among Dora's papers are two programs for church services in Babraham Church and St. Peter's Church, Babraham. As she listened to her employer, Madeline Adeane, reading and taking part in these fund-raisers and morale boosters for the war effort, Dora must have prayed as fervently as she ever had since she was received into the Anglican Church when she was Mrs. Lewin's scullery maid.

Dora stayed with the Adeanes from either March or April 1915 to September 1916, and she was clearly a valued employee. An empty envelope from that time reads, "Munsey and Co. Ltd. Goldsmiths and Watchmakers, Cambridge. Miss Lee, Babraham." Undoubtedly it once contained a special gift for services rendered—perhaps the gold bracelet that Dora habitually wore in later life. But, during that year, something happened that made it imperative for her to move again, and to move in a specific direction. To help her, she called on someone in that network of serving girls who had kept in touch all those years, and whom she herself had helped to make her way up the downstairs ladder. She called on Ada, who had found herself a position at Chatsworth, working for Mrs. Hilda Horne, Evie Devonshire's housekeeper.

The first letter from Mrs. Horne to Dora is dated August 14, 1916, and comes from Chatsworth:

Dear Mrs. Lee: Ada mentioned to me that you would like to go as a second cook to Canada at that time. Her Grace had mentioned someone. I am wondering about you, of course there would be a great deal of work to be done and I should want someone who would be prepared as I shall need someone I can leave at times responsible. I mentioned you to Her Grace this morning and told her I should write you. Have you any experience with sugar work. I should be pleased if you will let me know by return. The wages are £80 all found only I am anxious to get settled with someone. Yours faithfully, H. Horne.

The breathless style of Mrs. Horne's letter reflects the pressure she was under, getting the Devonshire staff together for the departure to Canada. Mrs. Horne's primary concern is that, whoever the new cook might be, she should be able to *cope*. Evie's priorities are different. War or no war, if she has to go to Canada, then she is going to do it in style—the style she had established over the years at Devonshire House, at Compton Place and at Chatsworth. In Dora she had what she required: a cook who had trained in Paris with one of the greatest sugar sculptors of all time.

The second letter from Mrs. Horne is dated September 5, 1916:

Dear Mrs. Lee: Many thanks for the letter of this morning. Yesterday I see Her Grace and she told me she had received a letter from Mrs. Adeane and that everything was quite satisfactory. Now I am wondering when you could come in. I told Her Grace I thought our time was the 22nd of September, but I thought you were just staying to oblige Mrs. Adeane, however, let me know. I haven't heard when we go yet, but I believe some time in October. You will want a holiday and I wanted to get away for a time but don't quite know. The man we thought about is not coming. You don't happen to know of one. It is a business. I hope we shall soon get settled with a girl, also a man.

I am not sure if they go to London, but I believe so. Hoping you are well. Yours faithfully, H. Horne.

Dora did not hang about; she immediately sent a telegram to the beset Mrs. Horne, who replied the same day—possibly Dora's telegram of acceptance crossed with the housekeeper's letter:

Dear Mrs. Lee: Received your wire, no doubt you have received my letter. Everything is most satisfactory. When do you think you could come. I am sorry everything has been delayed but now I haven't seen Her Grace for 3 days. We must arrange between ourselves. I have got a scullery maid but not a man yet. I don't suppose you know of one, let me know if you do. We are having a busy time. Hoping you are well. Yours faithfully, H. Horne.

Mrs. Horne was having to make her own arrangements, because the duke and duchess were in Windsor visiting the king and queen, and saying their final farewells. Victor records the events of those days in his diary, with his customary brevity: "Friday Sept 22.... Lovely day. Looked at the rooms & jewels [at Windsor Castle]. In the afternoon went for a walk ... saw the gardens and shorthorns. Very nice to see good cattle again. Evie Maud & I had lunch with the King and Queen." Clearly, shorthorns were much more interesting than jewels to the ducal diarist.

Hilda Horne sent Dora a brief undated note giving her an address in Birmingham where she could be reached, and another in London. She was taking a break before the departure, and planned to be away from Chatsworth until September 27, adding, "I am quite pleased to be away for a rest."

Poor Mrs. Horne's pleasure was premature. Her next letter to Dora on September 15 is from Chatsworth:

Dear Mrs. Lee: I ought to have written you yesterday but I have been so busy. Her Grace told me yesterday that some have to go on in advance, we have arranged for yourself, Ada and Jean to go which is to be the 6th of October. Amy, myself, scullery maid and scullery man to leave here on the 20th of October when Her Grace goes. I am wondering when you could come, they all start from here. Could you come here on the 3rd of October, up to the present I haven't got a [illegible] and I feel really done. I want to get my holiday but see not any chance. Let me know at once about yourself. I wasn't sure when you were leaving Mrs. Adeane and of course you want to get a holiday. Anyway write me by return when you can come down here. Hoping you are well. Yours faithfully, H. Horne.

On October 6, 1916, Dora left Liverpool with the advance party of the Chatsworth staff on the RMS *Grampian*. Her name, Dorothea Lee, appears in the ship's manifest, her profession is given as "cook," and her age as thirty. She was, in fact, only twenty-four.

It is doubtful Evie Devonshire would have cared what age her new cook was, as long as she could do "sugarwork," but Dora had added six years to her age to impress Mrs. Horne, who needed "someone I can leave at times responsible." Advertisements in the "Help Wanted" columns usually gave the preferred age for cooks as thirty, and Dora had made sure she fitted the bill. The Inspection Card she presented to the immigration officer at her port of arrival in Canada, Quebec, is still among her papers, and the Port of Quebec stamp is dated October 15, 1916.

To say that Dora Lee was upwardly mobile is to state the obvious. Since making her way to London in 1907 she had worked her way up the servant hierarchy to become one of the leading women cooks in the country. Few women had trained with Escoffier; few women were given the prime responsibility of purchasing the provisions for households such as those of the Guinnesses and the Neumanns. Even before the onset of war, by the age of twenty-four Dora had achieved more than most women of her generation in her field. Of course she would have wanted to work for one of the most prestigious aristocratic families in Britain. To cook for the Devonshires in their viceregal role in Canada was the grand culmination of eleven years of professional achievement.

This time, however, professional advancement and emotional involvement came together like something out of a novel by Dickens, that chronicler of the trials and tribulations of women like Dora and men like Bert. After his four-year disappearance, Bert will surface again in Dora's postcard collection, with two cards mailed in Canada to Dora at Government House, Ottawa. Bert was going to Canada with the Devonshires and, with Ada's help, so was Dora.

In the early days of recruitment, only the best physical specimens were taken for the battlefield, and Bert had signed up early. Many men of his class were turned down, because they were not fit enough, and thus were spared being maimed or killed. Bert was therefore taller and bigger than the average male of his class and so may well have been a footman. During the war, many men of Bert's class who returned were either taken back into the households they had left, or taken on in recognition of their service to their country. Bert the footman had survived the trenches and, since Evie planned to represent her country in style, she would need some of those ornamental creatures.

The experiences of the trenches would have changed Bert profoundly. The eager recruit who couldn't wait to get to Salisbury Plain had been left behind in the mud, the blood, the barbed wire and the artillery barrages of the Ypres salient, and the man who returned was not only physically wounded, but emotionally scarred. He may even have been patched up and sent back again to endure the lice that infested the bodies of the living and the rats that gnawed on the bodies of the dead in the trenches, and been wounded once more. Having survived against all odds, he may have decided to take a little more time kicking up his heels and shaking the chandeliers, before settling down. One thing is certain: he didn't go straight back and marry Dora.

Or he may have met someone else, in the first terrible days when he was in hospital, in pain and in shock. It happened. Some soldiers became close to the local girls who volunteered or nursed them in hospital, and found it difficult to tell the girl they had left behind them. He may even have married his new sweetheart, and kept it a secret from Dora.

On the ships' manifests that carry the names of the Devonshire household, there is no one whose name could clearly be shortened to "Bert"—possibly the manifests are incomplete. The closest is a Robert Ede, who is recorded as being married and, although the Devonshires took at least one other married couple, there is no record of Ede's wife being with him. The first Conscription Bill was introduced in the British House of Commons on January 5, 1916, by Prime Minister Asquith, and it is unlikely that Victor Devonshire would have taken an able-bodied man of twenty-five to Canada at this time, so possibly Robert Ede was a veteran.

A twenty-year-old poet, Charles Sorley, who was killed in 1915, and whose name is carved on the Loos Memorial to the Missing, wrote shortly before his death that war changed even familiar faces. He warned those back home that, even if they saw a face they had loved before, "it is a spook. None wears the face you knew."

Many of the survivors came out of the trenches with different faces. Whatever happened in those first years of the war, Dora and Bert took up their relationship where it had left off. Bert is a mystery, a spook in the background of Dora's story. Possibly Dora's Bert was in reality no longer the man she had known.

The nine days on the *Grampian* must have been tension-filled. On March 18, 1916, the Berlin Reichstag had voted for unrestricted submarine warfare, and hospital ships and unarmed liners became legitimate targets of attack. The British liner, the *Lusitania*, had already been sunk in May 1915, but now it was open season on anything and everything on the high seas. The weather was terrible, and Dora must have thought of her many stormy crossings of the Irish sea, and wished that this crossing lasted only a few hours.

On November 5, Evie and Victor left Liverpool. Maud and Blanche were with them, but the other children were to follow later, the decision having been made for Dorothy, Rachel, Anne and Charlie, in particular, not to travel with their parents. Their ship, the *Calgarian*, was one of the largest ships of the Allan Line, and it had been converted on the onset of war into an armed mercantile cruiser. They set out with a destroyer escort that, according to Maud, got no further than Belfast because it was the captain's last voyage and he had lost his nerve. In fact, the two destroyers collided with each other, which may well have had a great deal to do with the stresses of war. The weather was so bad that one of the lifeboats was washed away. Just over a year later, in March 1918, the *Calgarian* would be torpedoed and sunk off the Irish coast with the loss of forty-eight lives, in the same area as the mishap with the destroyer escort.

Before he left Britain, Victor had discussed matters Canadian with the colonial secretary, Bonar Law, himself a Canadian, and the Duke of Connaught, whom he describes in his diaries as "really obsessed with Sam Hughes," Canada's manic minister of militia. It must have given him a foretaste of difficulties to come. Evie, too, was familiarizing herself with North American culture, attending a baseball match on September 25, and getting herself photographed alongside the troublesome Sam Hughes—"rather unlucky," comments Victor in his diary.

Victor paid a brief five-day visit to the front at the end of

October, and even this minimalist diarist is overwhelmed by what he sees—the mud "indescribable," the whole sight "too strange and weird." "I wish," he writes, "everyone in England could see the desolation." It was beyond imagining and beyond words, that world in which he met the men from the Derbyshire Yeomanry whom he had known and last seen on his great estate, working the fields or beating the bushes for the amusement and sport of the men who were now their officers. In his failure to convey that desolation, Victor Devonshire is in the company of far greater writers than himself.

The new governor-general and his wife arrived in Halifax on November 12, 1916, and he was formally installed in that office in the Council Chamber of the Nova Scotia Provincial Building like only two other governors-general before him: the Marquis of Lorne and Earl Grey. Evie was back in Canada—certainly not for the first time since her teenage years, but this time in a role that must have brought reverberations of those past years: memories of her mother as chatelaine, memories of herself playing with her sister and brothers. But, however unchanged was the role her husband would play, this was not the same Evie, and Canada was not the same Canada.

Out of a nation of 8 million, 280,000 had volunteered at the beginning of the war, the majority of them being British immigrants. By the time Victor Devonshire arrived, Canada was embroiled in a fight over conscription. French Canadians were naturally reluctant to be forced to fight by the Reverend C.A. Williams, the English-speaking Methodist minister who was the glaringly inappropriate chief recruiting officer in Quebec —a man who was against French-Canadian regiments, and who expected any French Canadian to surrender both his religion and his national identity. Over the next few years, the governor-general would use one of his strongest adjectives, "tiresome," when recording his thoughts about the French-Canadian problem in his diary—particularly when audiences he was addressing in Quebec knew neither the words nor the tune of the British national anthem.

By November 1916, the Battle of the Somme had been in progress since the first day of July. Not that "progress" is an apt word for what was happening. It was, as Martin Gilbert describes it, "a daily struggle for small woods and even smaller villages." On September 16 the Canadians were sent forward into the front line, and Private John Chipman Kerr, one of fourteen Canadian volunteers from a single family, led a charge of such astonishing single-handed bravery that he was awarded the Victoria Cross. He ran along the top of the trenches firing on the Germans with such devastating fearlessness that sixty-five of the enemy surrendered to him. He handed them over and went back to the fray, without stopping to have his wound dressed—his finger had been blown off. But then, Private Kerr was an extraordinary man; he and his brother had walked fifty miles in the middle of winter from their farm near Edmonton to enlist.

After the Battle of the Somme, Canadians were given the dubious distinction of being "brought along to head the assault in one great battle after another," in Lloyd George's words. Clearly the reason was size as well as courage; the average Canadian recruit was bigger and stronger than the average Briton. In fact, Sir Robert Borden would question "the useless sacrifice" of Canadian lives in the Ypres salient which, he maintained, was being held "for purely sentimental reasons, because it comprises Belgian territory."

On September 16, 1916, forty-two Canadians died. Private Kerr's Victoria Cross was far from being the first awarded to a Canadian. On three days in succession in 1915—April 23, 24 and 25—Canadians were awarded that highest of all military honours for valour. Only one of the three survived the act of courage that gave him that honour. Across the face of Canada a distant war became a terrible reality as the wounded, the gassed and the shell-shocked gradually made their way home.

And there were thousands more who would never make that journey home again. By May 1915, less than a year after the beginning of the war, twenty thousand Canadians were dead.

The three aides-de-camp who came with the Devonshires were also marked by war, since the *sine qua non* for being an aide-de-camp during wartime was to be one of the walking wounded. Roderick Kenyon-Slaney of the Grenadier Guards had nearly died of a haemorrhage after being wounded; Vivian Bulkely-Johnston's shattered leg was two inches shorter than the other. Angus Mackintosh, who had been in Canada with the Duke of Connaught, had been shot in the lungs during the Battle of Ypres. He returned to serve the Devonshires, largely because the dry Canadian winters suited his one remaining lung.

On November 13, the governor-general and his wife arrived in Ottawa. Victor noted in his diary:

Monday Nov 13. We arrived at Ottawa punctually at eleven. Quite a number of people. They are certainly very cordial and friendly. The P.M. came up into the train & after a few minutes talk we got off. Inspected the guard of honour [his daughter Maud, in a letter home to her sister Anne, describes their faces as "bright blue" with cold] ... Got up to Govt Ho. about 12. It is certainly very comfortable & homelike. Miss Saunders & the other servants had arrived alright. Looked around the house. Had a talk with Sladen [Arthur Sladen, the duke's private secretary in Canada] before luncheon. Seems a nice man. I hope he is reliable. If not we shall be seriously lost. Managed to get out for a few minutes with Evie in the garden but it was snowy and wet ... We seem to be settling down alright. I hope we shall like the life. Wish it was a bit more countrified. Dinner went very well. At present I feel terribly shy. The staff appear to be settling down well.

The cast of characters for the next four years was now assembled in Ottawa. The lead Canadian player was Prime

Minister Sir Robert Borden, the Nova Scotian Tory leader who had visited the front lines himself, and who was hoping to persuade his opposition counterpart, the Liberal leader Sir Wilfrid Laurier, to form a coalition and avoid a bitter election fought over conscription.

At the head of the new arrivals at Rideau Hall was the Duke of Devonshire who, regardless of wartime, was accompanied by as large a supporting cast as any previous vice-regal representative. The battered and maimed condition of his courtiers would have been familiar to a medieval monarch, surrounded by his knights who had won favour fighting for their liege lord. Principally consisting of men—with the exception of Evie's secretary, Miss Saunders—this was the household, who lived upstairs. The military secretary, Colonel Harold Henderson, and his wife, Violet, lived in Rideau Cottage with their two young daughters. The Devonshires were of two minds as to whether they really approved of "Hearty" Henderson, who was fond of cocktails and doing imitations of other members of the staff.

And, just as there had been in England, there was another vast supporting cast downstairs, virtually all of them recruited in England or part of the Devonshires' original staff, down to the lowly scullery maid. Not that all of them were literally downstairs. The kitchens of Rideau Hall were in the basement, as were some of the staff quarters, but there was speculation as to where all those retainers would go. In spite of the Connaughts' improvements to the servants' quarters, and the addition of the Minto wing (which was needed for bedrooms for all the Devonshire children), space was at a premium. One of Dora's photographs gives the answer.

In the grounds of Rideau Hall there is a circular building, the gasometer, which was constructed in the 1870s during the Dufferins' time to hold gas cylinders, so that Rideau Hall would have its own gas supply. It was apparently never used for the purpose, has since served as a barracks, and currently houses the Rideau Hall archives. Dora's photograph shows a gasometer full of maidservants, leaning out and smiling or waving for the camera. Either Mrs. Horne, Miss Saunders or the duchess herself had made sure that the female staff were segregated from the men during their stay in Canada, thus hopefully reducing the risk of situations quite as explosive as any fuel the gasometer might once have contained.

A few characters in this complex cast move between the upstairs and the downstairs group: Willy Shimwell, the duke's confidential clerk; Elsie Saunders, the duchess's secretary; and Lord Richard Nevill, the comptroller, who had been with the Connaughts. In her memoirs, Maud describes him thus: "a good-looking old man, with large blue eyes and a huge moustache. He was known as Prehistoric Peep (Peep for short) as his views were quite Victorian." In his diaries Victor calls him one of the kindest men he had ever met.

For the first eighteen months of her time at Rideau Hall, Dora's trail is hard to follow. The postcards, the usual markers on the trail, are few and far between. There are many Canadian postcards, but most were purchased as keepsakes and mementoes of Toronto, Niagara Falls and Quebec, and were never written on or mailed. At this stage of her life, it is the photographs Dora kept in her hatbox and steamer trunk that give an indication of the full life Dora managed to enjoy, in spite of her responsibilities.

In photograph after photograph Dora toboggans, skates, swims, picnics. In one picture she holds a small black kitten, in others she is with her fox terrier. In another a laughing Dora wears bloomers and a wide-brimmed sombrero, and holds a small clay pipe in her hand. There are photographs of the Devonshires, photographs of Dora's fellow servants in the kitchen, outside Rideau Hall, alongside lakes. In one, a group of men in shirtsleeves sit around a table in the sunshine with their cigarettes, their whisky and their beers.

The same man appears in many of the pictures, including

one of the magnificent Devonshire footmen in their splendid livery, taken in the dining-room of Rideau Hall. There is nothing to identify him as Bert, but his recurring presence and the look he is giving the photographer in the one photograph where he is on his own suggest this may be so. But it is not only Bert who is elusive. Dora's life for the first year and a half in Canada is glimpsed through these pictures, and only a handful of cards. The pattern of those first months shadows the life of those upstairs, which is, not surprisingly, thoroughly documented.

Official business began immediately for the Devonshires: the British Ambassador to the States, Sir Cecil Spring-Rice, and his wife Florence, Victor's cousin, arrived from Washington. "Springy" seemed nervous and jumpy to Victor: "He does not inspire one with confidence," was his private observation. In fact, Springy would soon be ousted from his ambassadorial role.

Evie and Victor held their first dinner-party two days after their arrival and, from then on, the diary is full of luncheons and dinner-parties whenever they are in Ottawa. Within the first few days they meet most of Canada's leaders in the political, religious and social arena: the Bordens, the Lauriers, the finance minister Sir George Foster and his wife, Sir Joseph Pope and his wife, the bishop of Ottawa, the mayor of Ottawa —the list of luminaries goes on, and throughout the years, Victor will dutifully note them in his diary.

That first Christmas at Rideau Hall had all the traditional trappings of the season for master and servant. On December 23 Victor writes: "Distributed Xmas presents to the employees in the kitchen. Shook hands with each ... Evie rather tired & did not come down till the afternoon." Just as they would have done in England, the servants held their traditional servants' ball between Christmas and New Year's Eve, in the ballroom of Rideau Hall, and it is recorded in Victor's diaries. There is no record of it among Dora's possessions.

Victor's diary has always reflected the moods of his wife—

whether she was stressed or happy, well or "seedy" (another favourite word)—but the frequency with which he notes her tiredness in Canada is particularly striking. Charlie and Anne came over on the *Olympic*, the sister ship of the *Titanic* (which had gone down five years earlier), and arrived in Ottawa on December 8, in time for that first Canadian Christmas. The whole family came down with colds and influenza shortly thereafter, stirring up Evie's pet paranoia. "I wish we were certain about the drains here," Victor notes worriedly in his diary. Evie does not seem to have attended the New Year's Day levee, but she was at the opening of parliament on January 19, wearing a gown of green velvet, a diamond tiara and ropes of pearls. Victor notes with concern on March 1, 1917, that Evie "is hardly up to these heavy days."

Besides fulfilling her official duties as vice-reine, Evie had other family worries during those "heavy days." First, there was Charlie's education. On January 16, 1917, Victor writes, "Evie seems very tired and seedy. Charlie went off to Ashbury. Seems very low and depressed, but it would never do to have him loafing about here all the time. Dinner party."

Ashbury College, the school to which a reluctant eleven-year-old Charlie was dispatched, was founded in 1891 by an Oxford graduate and Anglican clergyman, George Penrose Woollcombe. Among its first nine pupils was the son of Sir Charles Tupper, a Father of Confederation and former prime minister of Canada. It had moved a few times since its beginnings in Victoria Chambers, opposite the Parliament buildings, and had been established since 1910 in the village of Rockcliffe, an exclusive residential area not far from Rideau Hall.

But there were more serious concerns than Charlie. Even before arriving in Canada, Maud and Dorothy had already given notice they would need careful supervision. On March 11, 1916, Victor records in his diary that a philanderer, identified only as Alwyn, had been romancing both sisters, while openly showing an interest in Maud. Victor got home from a long day at the Admiralty to be met by a distressed Evie and a bundle of letters:

> Evie was very worried as she had a long talk with little Dorothy. Alwyn has been making a thorough fool of himself & sending her a lot of very silly letters. I am afraid the little girl was quite infatuated about him. They appear to have been writing and telephoning regularly.

To Victor fell the unpleasant task of returning to Chatsworth to show the letters to Maud, only to discover that Maud too had been seeing Alwyn without their permission while she was staying with her aunt Bertie; she had gone out with him to consult a palmist. "The whole thing," writes Victor, "is very tiresome."

Who was Alwyn? After the discovery of his designs on her daughters, Evie had written to the offender telling him he should see no more of them, so presumably he had once been part of their social circle. The only clue comes much later in the diaries when Victor refers to meeting an Alwyn Fellowes after a gap of some years. There may possibly be a connection to the Fellowes who sorted out the problems with the "black-mailing letter." A likely candidate is the Honourable Ailwyn Fellowes, the second son of Baron De Ramsay (a comparatively new title dating from 1887), who at the time was thirty-two years old and unmarried. Ailwyn, the family name, is spelled differently, but in his diaries Victor is quite cavalier about the spelling of proper names. Sometimes, as in the case of the artist Philip de Laszlo, he is not even consistently incorrect. The age of the philanderer (if this indeed is the culprit) makes his behaviour with a sixteen-year-old even more reprehensible.

Evie now had a resentful Maud and a heartsick Dorothy in tow. Relationships were stormy, and tension filled the domestic air. Quite early on in his Canadian diaries, Victor records a blazing fight between Maud and her mother, sadly adding, "There seems to be no possibility of getting through the day

without a row of one sort or another." Whatever unpleasant-
ness it might cause, Evie was determined that Maud, Blanche
and Dorothy would stay firmly under the maternal wing. Did
she perhaps remember poor Willie Peel's desperate letters, all
those years ago in India—and had he in fact been given reason
to hope, until a more prestigious prospect (and gentle parental
pressure) had changed her mind?

Ethel Chadwick, the daughter of a House of Commons
clerk, whose diaries of life at Rideau Hall under the Connaughts
and the Devonshires are a useful source of information,
recorded her first impressions of the new viceregal couple:
the duke is "ugly," the duchess "rather nice." About Evie she
adds, "tall, rather slight, sharp-featured, good complexion, not
very old—about 40 I imagine [Evie was actually forty-six], dis-
tinguished-looking." She also characterizes her as "the typical long-nosed Englishwoman." In her entry for November 21,
1916, she writes:

> Lady V. [Violet Henderson, wife of the military secretary] says
> the Duchess of D. is going to have nothing to do with the young
> girls here, that they have heard all about them ... and that
> she will not allow her staff to have anything to do with them.
> What will Mackintosh do?

Angus Mackintosh, the duke's aide-de-camp, would do very
well, in spite of the best efforts of Evie Devonshire. And, whatever her reservations may have been about the wild colonial
girls of Ottawa, Evie knew it was her own girls she would have
to watch like a hawk.

It was snowing when the Devonshires arrived in Ottawa—an
early, wet snow that covered the garden beyond the windows
of Rideau Hall. As she looked through the windows onto the
snow-covered garden, Evie must surely have thought back to
those happy years when she made twill curtains for the ice
house built by her uncle, and ate Jerusalem the Golden, licking

her frozen fingers. One would think that Evie Devonshire, who cared about status, rank and ceremony, would have worn the role of governor-general's wife like a second skin. But perhaps her interpretation of that role was coloured by memories of India.

Five years before her return to Canada, Evie had gone back to India to attend the great Coronation Durbar in Delhi. George V was the first English king since Richard the Lionheart to leave Europe and, as the *Medina* passed through the Red Sea with her royal cargo, the Turco-Italian war was put on hold and the great sea beacons were lit once more. Evie entered Delhi alongside the queen-empress in an open carriage. Enthroned beneath a golden dome, their Majesties were acclaimed by 100,000 of their subjects. At the back of the great amphitheatre, three hundred women in *purdah* watched from behind cardboard screens fashioned to look like fretted stone. By the end of the ceremonies the fake stone had been pierced with extra eyeholes by hundreds of fingers.

The coverage in *The Times* was lengthy, the language of extravagance to match the extravaganza:

> The Monarchs sat alone, remote but beneficent, raised far above the multitude, but visible to all, clad in rich vestments, guarded by a glittering array of troops, the cynosure of the proudest Princes of India ... Not a soul who witnessed it, not even the poorest coolie who stood fascinated and awed upon the outskirts of the throng, can have been unresponsive to its profound significance.

With the members of the governor-general's staff, the governors of the presidencies and the provinces and the brilliantly uniformed military officers, the Mistress of the Robes watched as the maharajas and princes in their jewels and their magnificent robes, their elephants as splendidly caparisoned as their princely owners, pledged their fealty to their colonial rulers.

In India, the lines were so clearly drawn, the caste system and the class system of the British Raj meshed so perfectly, that there was no need to find a middle way. In Canada, the lines were blurred, and occasionally there seemed to be no divisions whatsoever. Remoteness was a difficult act in this dominion; there were few awed coolies to be found in Canada. For Evie, such homogeneity was confusing, and she would find it difficult to shift her ground. In India, tiaras were *de rigueur*. In India, where a maharaja recognized the caste of a duke—and vice versa—Evie Devonshire might have found her style.

But what was the style of a governor-general's wife? Where did she fit in this huge cast of characters? By her husband's side? Slightly behind him? If not hidden behind screens of fake cardboard stone, just how visible should she be? Did she take upon herself the women's causes and organizations? What, in fact, was her function? Did she have an official role and, if so, how was it defined? The role of leading political lady continues to be a tricky one to play—ask any first lady.

In his book *From Hall-Boy to House Steward*, William Lanceley, the house steward for the Connaughts, gives his view of the difficulties:

> The wife of a Governor-General, no matter how ably helped with a first-rate staff and servants, finds it a very trying time. The functions go on the whole year round like the hands of a clock. The Dominion is vast, and wherever they go entertainments are the order of the day. I really think the wife has a more arduous time than the Governor-General, whose job is no sinecure when you see it from behind the scenes.

Among the boxes of Evie's papers at Chatsworth is a notebook kept by her secretary, Elsie Saunders, during the years in Canada. Miss Saunders was with Evie for thirty years, and was much loved by Evie's staff and children. She was a meticulous and conscientious woman, and her accounts of the minutiae of being the governor-general's wife make sobering reading. On the opening page is a list headed "Register of Patronage given by her Excellency the Duchess of Devonshire to various Canadian Societies, Institutions, funds etc. November 1916."

The list that follows names seventy-one organizations, and Evie's role with them. Among them are: IODE [Imperial Order Daughters of the Empire], Hon. Pres. National Chapter; British Women's Emigration Association; NCWC [National Council of Women of Canada], Hon. Pres.; Royal Edward Institute Montreal for the Study, Prevention and Cure of T.B., Hon. Pres.; Montreal Maternity Hospital; Canadian Red Cross Society; French Red Cross Society; Ottawa Women's Canadian Club, Patroness; May Court Club of Ottawa, Patroness; Girls' Friendly Society of Canada, V.P.; Canadian Free Library for the Blind; Children's Aid Society, Patroness; Ottawa Humane Society, Patroness.

Much of this support is, of course, a symbolic endorsement of a worthy cause, but Elsie Saunders's notebook shows the kind of involvement it represented. She keeps accounts of every gift received by Evie and Victor on their tours throughout the dominion, so that she and Evie will not lose track of the dozens of thank-you letters that had to go out. On one whistle-stop alone on the 1919 western tour she notes gifts that include a flitch of bacon, a silver casket of mineral specimens, a set of mats from soldiers' wives and a "chiffon jumper."

On a Toronto visit for Armistice Day, 1919, Evie's itinerary included a visit to the Women's Institute in the morning, an Armistice Day service at St. Paul's Church, an afternoon conference with the City Nurses, and a trip to the Royal Ontario Museum, where she unpacked two gowns donated by Queen Mary and a dressing-gown and slippers that had belonged to Queen Victoria. There would, of course, have been a formal dinner in the evening. The notebook is full of sketches of seating plans for all those dinner-parties.

The names come thick and fast in Elsie Saunders's note-book, and she has noted the crowds of visitors and supplicants who board the train at every stop on every tour. On one occasion on the 1919 western tour, so many representatives of so many organizations wanted to meet Evie in Vancouver that they could not fit into the train, and she had to meet with them out on a siding. One gets the impression of a never-ending sea of faces, an endless chain of human beings, meeting, greeting, wanting to shake hands, or just staring. On what must have been a particularly tiring day in Nelson, British Columbia, Elsie Saunders has written: "Her Excellency tired and unable to do anything." The expectations of her role as chatelaine would have wearied a fit woman, let alone a "seedy" one.

But—as Dora's voice and the voices of those other women downstairs and in the Rideau Hall gasometer grow silent for a while—Evie Devonshire can speak for herself. Throughout their lives, she and her mother corresponded frequently and frankly, and fifty-six of Evie's letters have survived among the family papers at Bowood House. All but one of them are from this Canadian period—which suggests that someone, probably Lady Lansdowne or even Evie herself, destroyed their earlier correspondence.

In one of the earliest letters, dated December 10, 1916, Evie describes for her mother the changes at Rideau Hall: "The girls have got our old schoolroom as a sitting room ... My room is now a workroom, and the maid has Bertie's as her bedroom." She aims a few stylistic brickbats at the Connaughts' alterations: "Privately I think the Connaughts alterations bad. The layer built onto [a bit of the?] dining-room gets no sun, as it is overshadowed by an awful cloak room wing which might have been harmless if properly arranged ... The main part of the dining-room is now only used on big occasions and is dark and dreary by daylight."

Even the grounds do not escape Evie's critical eye: "The

Duke [of Connaught] has stripped the grounds of all the 'cedars' and has only planted a few fir trees … We are going to do a big thing in spruces and hemlock spruces for the sake of our successors."

But more important than any changes to bricks and mortar, hardwood and evergreen, is the inner Evie revealed by the letters. They reflect a woman struggling with various health problems and fighting to find a balance between her private life and her public role. The theme is not unfamiliar, and one is struck by how contemporary much of Evie's conflict sounds, if one looks beyond the tiara and the strings of pearls.

For all the remoteness, the privilege, the grandeur, Evie Devonshire was a working woman. She had had a career—or, rather, a career had been forced upon her—and she had spent much of her life away from her children as they grew up. In spite of the crucial role played by the governor-general at the time, both husband and wife were feeling cut off from the corridors of power, and in one of Evie's earliest letters she describes herself as "longing for political news."

To make matters worse, Evie was experiencing a difficult onset of menopause—not too surprising after the problems she had had as a young woman. In 1917 she describes herself as in "rather a poor way … [but] there is nothing whatever the matter except tired nerves." Later that year she writes, "The colitis is not bad but I don't digest my food properly & feel very disinclined to face functions, 'temps de la vie' [change of life] no doubt!" Painful arthritis in her right arm must have made all the hand-shaking sheer torture.

By 1920, Evie has developed a goitre, which she blames on the Ottawa water: "… isn't it tiresome—it is only a small one but it came quite suddenly & sometimes feels uncomfortable … a great number of people have them in Ottawa." That struggling thyroid will certainly have played its part in the earlier fights, the mood swings and the exhaustion recorded by her husband. Evie's hysteria, her "groundless apprehension, depression of spirits, and morbid irritability of temper," may indeed be linked to her reproductive system and her womb. Her indispositions are not purely psychosomatic—however much they may have been exacerbated by the expectations and limitations of her class and her sex.

But perhaps the most intriguing theme in the Canadian letters is the evolution of Evie's daughters, and the evolution of Evie Devonshire herself.

Along with Elsie Saunders's notebook is an album of photographs that mirror Dora's collection, a democratic reflection of the life shared by employer and employee: page after page of young women skating, performing arabesques on the ice, waltzing together holding hands, page after page of girls and young men laughing in canoes, lounging in front of tents. Pet dogs are cuddled in the girls' arms, or lie at their feet. It is a record of summer and winter in Canada, so typical that virtually every Canadian will have similar pictures—even if the skating and swimming costumes have drastically changed.

A feeling of euphoria rises from all those faded images, an impression of gaiety and lightheartedness diametrically different from the picture of Evie in Victor's diaries. Maud will step into her mother's shoes on many occasions and do her duty but, for her and for the rest of Evie's daughters, Canada is largely a round of concerts, cotillions, camping, canoeing, laughter—as it once was for a young Evie.

Evie would skate again, now and then, her slender figure elegant in her long fur coat, the skills of twenty-five years before coming back to her. She and Victor still occasionally took the long walks together they enjoyed. But only six months after their arrival, she writes to her mother, "I am very sick of this suburban life," and one is reminded of Olga and Irina in Chekhov's *The Three Sisters* longing for Moscow, or the actress Arkadina in *The Seagull*: "Ah, can there be anything more boring than this sweet country boredom?"

Evie Devonshire is certainly not Tolstoy's Anna Karenina —oh how she would have disapproved of courting public scandal to satisfy the needs of the heart! But there is something of Chekhov's older women about her, lying there in the darkness, as the young celebrate life, their optimism unquenched by war, suffering and death.

In another letter to her mother, written shortly after their arrival in 1916, she writes, "The climate seems less nice than it used to be. There is so much wind and often less snow. Today the wind is icy and all the snow has gone." The milk and honey of that happy childhood were long gone, and the Evie of twenty-five years later seems to have built yet another ice house for herself.

During the first year of his tenure the governor-general visits Toronto and Montreal and smaller centres such as Sudbury and Grand Bay, and crosses the country from the west coast to the east; Evie is not always with him. One of the pleasures Maud remembered years later was travelling "in a special train, in great luxury, with comfortable beds and real baths. There was a large Observation Car at the end of the train, with a small platform, from which my father used to talk or wave to any gathering, which usually appeared at any halt."

This was the heyday of the railway, that splendid thread that bound a vast dominion together. Seven special cars had originally been built by the Canadian government for King George and Queen Mary, when they visited Canada as the Duke and Duchess of York in 1900: the day coach, *Cornwall*; the night coach, *York*; the compartment car, *Canada*; the dining car, *Sandringham*; and the sleeping cars, *Australia*, *India*, and *South Africa*. The *Cornwall*, the *York* and the *Canada* were used by the governors-general and their staff until the 1920s.

The large observation car was the *Cornwall*, which was over seventy-eight feet long. It contained a private dining-room, bedroom suites with full-size bathrooms, and a *bijou* of a boudoir with draperies of light-blue moiré silk and divans, chairs and a table in gilt to match the trim on the wall panels. Finished throughout in mahogany, the *Sandringham* had ornate brass balconies at either end. The reception room on the train was panelled in Circassian walnut, with an upright piano to match. There was a telephone system that connected all parts of the train. In the *Canada*, there were six staterooms, including a smoking-room with a large writing-table, and comfortable sofas and chairs. It was in this car that the younger children were brought from Halifax to Ottawa to join their parents.

Ensconced in this mobile palace the governor-general and his wife traverse Canada, meeting a range of inhabitants as broad as the country itself: transplanted Britons, native peoples, Seventh-Day Adventists, Doukhobors, politicians, farmers. With his usual unshakeable aplomb, Victor will take them as he finds them, recording his reactions in his diary—reactions that are usually a variation of "quite a number of people … certainly very cordial and friendly," as though he is meeting members of some unknown tribe, and is relieved and surprised to find they are not hostile.

Only occasionally is he taken aback—once when he is taken around a prison in Guelph by a convicted murderer, complete with monocle and waxed moustache, who has had his sentence commuted—"uncanny," he calls the experience. For all his apparent easygoing nature, Victor Devonshire expected not to have to cope with any unforeseen circumstances. If he had to, then his irritation showed with such observations as "tiresome day. A lot of fussing going on."

And, in between the balls and the dinner-parties, the functions and the formalities, the journeys long and short, the leitmotif of the first two years in Canada, recorded by Victor in his diaries and Evie in her letters, is suffering and death: the death of friends, and the children of friends. Nearly every

Sunday church service is marked by an intercession for yet another member of the congregation lost on the battlefield. The same theme is echoed in Ethel Chadwick's diaries, as she waltzes on the Rideau Hall rink with old men and children.

On Monday, April 30, 1917, Ethel notes: "The Canadians distinguished themselves taking Vimy Ridge—the casualties have been awful. Gordon Heron, Jim Brown, Lance Sladen killed of boys we knew." On November 22, 1917, she writes: "Went to Madame Butterfly at the Russell ... I went first in Jan 1911 & then in March 1912. I was thinking of how many of the men who were in the theatre that night are now dead 'in Flanders Fields.' Nearly all the men who were in the Connaughts' box."

For Evie, after nearly losing her own son and the death of her brother Charles, the visits to hospitals and the decorations handed out to the mothers of dead sons were ordeals: "I had to present badges on behalf of the I.O.D.E. to almost 20 Ottawa women who had sons serving and 9 had already lost theirs. I don't know how I got through the ceremony—but the mothers were wonderful." Frequently in her letters she voices her concerns over the health of those damaged young aides-de-camp: "I am rather fussed about young Kenyon Slaney, who I find has got a patch on one lung. He says he is very well, but he has a little cough always. No doubt this place will put him right if anything will, but he is tiresome about going out without his coat and he is dreadfully thin. He is a dear boy...." In her private correspondence with her mother, Evie shows the tenderness of her nature that few others were allowed to see.

There is another recurring theme in Evie's letters to her mother: servants. Certainly it was not unique to Canada, because she and Lady Lansdowne had corresponded in the past about problems at Chatsworth with the staff there, but the servant problem was made more difficult because of the war, food restrictions and Evie's expectations of Canadian domestic help. It was further complicated by that perennial problem for the upstairs and the downstairs world: love.

OEUFS MOLLETS (DUFFENS?)

Entry in Dora's almanac: "Lunch. Oeuf Mollet Duffens." There are many recipes for *oeufs mollets*, but the puzzle here is the word "Duffens." It is clearly written in Dora's almanac, but there is nothing even remotely resembling such a word in the comparatively long list of Escoffier recipes using eggs cooked in such a way. Did Dora get the name wrong? Was it a combination she had created herself? The use of a capital letter might suggest a proper name, but no one in Dora's professional life comes to mind.

The Cooking Method for "Mollet" Eggs

Mollet is the French word for soft, light, soft-boiled, and the *oeuf mollet* is a superior version of the boiled egg. It is a perfect example of the finesse Escoffier brought to even the simplest method of preparing a humble food.

For this to work at all, the eggs must be very fresh. They are placed in a colander and plunged into boiling water just long enough to congeal the egg-white but to leave the yolks very soft. One sentence alone in the Escoffier cookbook gives an idea of just how tricky using such an egg will be: "While the egg-white is congealed enough to make the handling possible, the yolk is so soft as to make the task difficult." An egg cooked in this way would be even more difficult to handle than a softly poached egg, which is often substituted for it. Dora, however, uses the *oeuf mollet*. This is not an egg for the faint of heart!

After taking them out of the boiling water, run cold water over them and (needless to say) shell the eggs carefully. Keep them in lightly salted hot water.

The closest French cooking word to "Duffens" is *Dauphinois*, which usually involves the use of potato, and there is a delicious recipe using potatoes, but it is called *Oeufs mollets* (or *pochés*) *en berceau* (Eggs in the cradle). You bake a large potato in the oven and hollow it out so it looks like a little cradle. Then you line the cradle with finely minced chicken mixed with cream and place the egg on it coated with Aurora sauce. *Sauce Aurore* is a combination of a *velouté* or *béchamel* sauce with tomato purée, to give it the tint of a rosy dawn.

TEN

A Heavenly Place

The atmosphere of Government House was that of a large and cheerful
house-party ... In the summer there was plenty of relaxation ... There
was fishing; there was boating; there was swimming; there was flirting.
And there was also a little serious work.

HAROLD MACMILLAN, *WINDS OF CHANGE*

"The Naughty Nine," they were called— those young
ladies whom Evie Devonshire wanted nowhere near
her daughters. They had been christened by Major
General Sir Willoughby Gwatkin, the British Chief of Staff,
at a fund-raiser for the war effort held at the Chateau Laurier
in January 1916, where they had danced tangos and foxtrots
in skimpy costumes and jumped out of beribboned hatboxes
to the delight of five hundred guests.

The war was not only changing the men who came back
from the Somme, and left to fight at Vimy; it was changing the
girls they left behind them. The Naughty Nine were mad, but
not particularly bad—just rather silly—and they were certainly
not dangerous to know. They were the rather innocent fore-
runners of the flappers who would dance and drink their way
through the post-war years. "A rowdy little bunch," according
to Ethel Chadwick.

Evie wrote about them to her mother in December 1916,
concerned for two of the aides-de-camp, Rodolph Kenyon-
Slaney and Vivian Bulkeley-Johnston: "I hope that neither he
[Kenyon-Slaney] nor B.J. will get dragged into the cocktail

252

drinking fast set to which 'the naughty nine' belong. But all the rest of this society here seems very dull for young men."

The Naughty Nine come up again in a letter dated August 31, 1917, this time because Evie's eldest daughter, Maud, was engaged to be married to one of the aides-de-camp, Angus Mackintosh: "I don't want them to have a house in Ottawa … Angus knows everyone there and till we came was on *very* friendly terms with the 'naughty nine' who are very second-rate in some ways—but quite harmless."

On September 17 Evie writes to Lady Lansdowne that she is becoming more fond of Angus: "Victor has liked him very much all along … I had an idea he was rather fast, but it seems this is quite a mistake." Here perhaps is a glimpse of that other, hidden, Victor of the "blackmailing" letter—because Evie was right. Angus Mackintosh had not only flirted with the Ottawa girls, but had given "the big rush" to *both* the daughters of Lord Shaughnessy, the builder of the Canadian Pacific Railway, while in New Brunswick. Evie, wisely, took no chances, but saw to it that Angus Mackintosh was sent off to Washington as an unpaid military attaché, far away from the Naughty Nine.

Yet clearly the main problem for Evie was not mad young things like the Naughty Nine, but all those attractive young men like Angus at Rideau Hall. It was reasonably easy for her to close the door of Government House and separate the girls from the girls. It was far more difficult to disentangle them from the male members of the staff who accompanied them to the cinema to see Mary Pickford as a Scottish lassie in *The Pride of the Clan*, took them on jaunts into the Gatineau Hills, or took them on fishing trips in the Laurentians. And who lived under the same roof. Ethel Chadwick described Evie's daughters as ordinary-looking, and from the photographs none of them appear to have inherited the elegance and patrician beauty of their mother. However, Ethel Chadwick allowed that Maud, though not pretty, was "nice-looking," and had a good complexion and "a good manner too for a girl of twenty."

Faint praise perhaps, but then Ethel was a harsh judge. Ethel was missing the Connaughts, and her own youth was passing from her. At nearly thirty-seven years old and unmarried, she was presumably judged by Evie a safe companion for her daughters. Besides, she could skate wonderfully; it was like having another specialized governess to teach spirals and yorkers to the children.

Evie's letters to her mother give a good idea of their different characters. Maud had great vitality, and was excellent at public appearances—Evie does not mention the battles of will with her oldest daughter that her husband confided to his diary. Blanche was the shyest, and physically the weakest of the girls. From childhood she had suffered various ailments, and in Canada she had to see a specialist in Montreal about a grumbling appendix and a "floating" kidney. She also had an operation on her foot that left her on crutches and needing special shoes.

Perhaps because of her own problems, for all her shyness it was Blanche who served on the Red Cross committees and attended the charity meetings that her mother so disliked. She even went to sing to people in the homes for the incurables. Yet she stubbornly resisted playing the public role her mother wanted her to play: "... she has no idea of helping me in any kind of way & I can't even rely on her to do jobs I give her to do. I am sure all this comes from a kind of nervousness as she is good as gold really." Evie fretted about ever getting Blanche married off: "Blanche is getting quieter and duller if anything ... I often feel we ought to send her home if we don't want her to turn into an old maid ..."

Because of the future eminence of the man who would become her husband—and the man who would be her lover—Dorothy is the best-documented of the children. An early portrait of her by Philip de Laszlo shows an attractive and rather sensual face. She had great charm and a natural warmth of manner that made her much better than Blanche at tackling "old generals or ministers ... and [she] always has something to say," Evie wrote to Lady Lansdowne. Very much a Cavendish, Dorothy had two qualities certainly not inherited from her mother: spontaneity and the common touch.

Rachel had inherited her mother's doe eyes and her cloud of dark hair. Over the years she learned to skate beautifully, taking part in competitions with Canadian girls, and she learned to swim "like a frog," according to her mother—who also called her "a real little monkey & rather a flirt." At the end of their tenure, in 1921, Evie writes to Lady Lansdowne with undisguised relief: "... Rachel will be much better at home before the usual crisis occurs with an A.D.C."

That the "usual" crises began early on is not to be wondered at. Put a company of wounded heroes together with a nestful of nubile and nobly born young girls, and Rideau Hall becomes a hothouse of yearning and suppressed longing, its walls and corridors throbbing with the pangs of requited and unrequited love. In one of his early diary entries for 1917, Victor talks of coming back from a curling match—"strange amusement and very chilly"—to Rideau Hall, where they "found some dancing going on." When the parents were away the young were at play in the ballroom and drawing-rooms of the official residence.

While not having the makings of French farce—it is reasonably safe to say there was no opening and closing of bedroom doors, as indulged in by their married elders and betters in Edward's day—there is an atmosphere of light operetta (*Patience* meets *Die Fledermaus*, perhaps) about the events of the next few years that is strikingly incongruent with the nightmare dragging on in Europe.

Belowstairs, however, Feydeau might indeed have found material for farce—although those involved would not have found it laughable. Separate those servants as one might, inevitably they found each other out. While romances were developing upstairs during the course of 1917, the same was happening in the servants' world. On October 18, Evie writes to her mother: "The childrens' maid is leaving—she has just married Rody's servant ... We are sending Victor's valet away, as he is quite headturned and still infatuated with Stiles—so she may leave too."

The Devonshires inherited some of the Connaughts' servants, who resented change quite as much as Ethel Chadwick. Just after their arrival, in January 1917, Evie tells Lady Lansdowne that "The maid Samson is a grumbler—means well but never makes the best of things, and points out how different it all is to what *she* is accustomed to. I fancy she will dishearten the other servants but we don't like to part with her." Since Evie knows the name of Stiles and Samson, they are presumably on the upstairs staff—ladies' maids or parlour-maids.

In the same letter in which Evie talks of the grumbler Samson, she writes: "I shall have all the other girls taught domestic economy. Poor Maud doesn't know much of anything to order, & the cook has no idea either so she got scared and refused to stay, although she was doing very well."

One of the problems in both Evie's correspondence and Victor's diary is that they rarely mention the names of the downstairs staff, and it is more than likely they don't know them. It looks as if the Devonshires inherited a cook from the Connaughts, who didn't take kindly to her new employer. Evie could indeed be very scary, and she apparently failed to convey to the cook that she was "doing very well." The cook's hasty departure may well have given Dora a boost up the downstairs ladder, but Dora's papers show she did not become first cook until 1918.

Evie had not enjoyed the first few months of 1917. There were the servant problems in January, and in March she got very upset when she was expected to speak at the Women's Canadian Club. Victor writes in his diary, "We must make a rule she should not be called upon to speak." On March 25 there was a to-do when it was found that the housekeeper in Montreal had ordered over a thousand pounds' worth of goods. "It is sheer robbery," fumes Victor, and five days later he records the first of many meetings with the comptroller, Lord Richard Nevill, about the household accounts—"Afraid they are not at all satisfactory." In May, Evie refuses to go to Hamilton. Victor describes her as "very upset," and notes, "We must try to make things easier in the future." One gets a sense of just how unpleasant the row must have been when this phlegmatic diarist adds, "Spent a miserable day."

Also in May, Maud went off to Washington on a visit to the Spring-Rices and came back with an Ouija board—"It really is a great nuisance," an irritated Victor confided to his diary. One supposes that neither the palmist back in England nor the Ouija board revealed to Maud how hard the next few years would be for her.

In June the family left for the Citadel, the governor-general's official residence in Quebec City, and then were off to the Laurentians and the Gaspé for a trip on the *Lady Grey*, a yacht whose original purpose in life was as an ice-breaker. Victor had to return to Ottawa on a couple of occasions—once in July, when the Conscription Bill was carried—but the rest of the family stayed out east.

High above the St. Lawrence River, the residence of the governor-general lies inside the ancient walls of the Citadel, near the King's Bastion. In the 1870s the Dufferins fell in love with the magnificent view of the river, Ile d'Orléans, and the mountains on the north shore, and established an official residence there. Evie had stayed there before as a young girl, and in Quebec she seems to have rediscovered some of that childhood happiness—watching the ocean-going steamers that passed so close below, and walking on the Dufferin Terrace.

From the country-house comfort of the Citadel they moved on to Murray Bay (now called La Malbaie, the name originally given to it by Jacques Cartier). Murray Bay had been a summer resort since the early days of the nineteenth century and, in 1899, the Richelieu and Ontario Navigation Company built the Manoir Richelieu, a luxurious resort hotel, to attract the wealthy and powerful to the area. But on this trip the Devonshires were travelling beyond the luxury of Murray Bay. They cruised remote reaches of the Saguenay, Jacques Cartier's ancient kingdom, the wild beauty of the Iles de la Madeleine in the St. Lawrence River, and the spectacular scenery of the Gaspé. On Anticosti Island they were entertained by the chocolate millionaire, Monsieur Menier, in his splendid castle, complete with *objets d'art* and priceless tapestries.

After the towering limestone cliffs of Cap Bon-Ami, the red, yellow and grey sandstone bluffs of Ile de Cap-aux-Meubles, the villages with their charming little houses built in the traditional Madelinot style, Evie Devonshire returned to the capital to look for something natural and beautiful closer to Ottawa. She found it at Blue Sea Lake.

Among her papers, Ethel Chadwick kept the following undated newspaper clipping:

> His Excellency the Duke of Devonshire purchased this week about 100 acres of land on the west side of Blue Sea Lake, which includes a small trout lake, and intends erecting a summer home on the property in the near future. At present their Excellencies with the members of their families and the Vice-Regal staff are spending the summer there under canvas having about twelve or fourteen tents and a large marquee which is used as a dining-room.

In a letter to her father in 1917, Evie writes of the discovery of Blue Sea Lake:

> We have happened on a most heavenly place to fill in the time till Ottawa routine begins again ... a small house belonging to

an old Frenchman—official translator to the government …
on the shore of the lake, with a perfect bathing place at the
landing stage, lovely woods behind, and an excellent vegetable
garden … some of the party [there were sixteen in all] are in
tents, Miss Walton, Violet and I are in the house. The children
are having a glorious time. Last night they cooked their supper
in the wood—it looks horrible, but they said it was excellent
… they all bathe several times a day …

Many of Ottawa's elite would have been somewhat put
out by Evie's description of Blue Sea Lake as a place she
had "happened upon," as if it were unknown before it was
discovered by the Devonshires during a trek into the back-
woods of Canada. In *Tapestry of War*, Sandra Gwyn describes
it as:

… one of the loveliest and most lustrous of all the lakes in the
Gatineau country … By 1914 the shores of Blue Sea Lake
were dotted with summer places. Indeed, it shared only with
Kingsmere … the distinction of being considered a kind of
unofficial summer capital.

Matters of state would intervene, their duty would take
them on tours across the country, but that "heavenly place"
would become New Lismore, and a source of as much pleasure
as their Irish home.

With the tents spread around the little house, which Victor
described as "no more than an enlarged shack," it looked like
a real camp-site from the windows of the train that took them
to New Lismore. According to Ethel Chadwick, the duke had
to sleep in what was supposed to be the maid's bedroom, and
the children picnicked and cooked supper over open camp-
fires. But it would be a mistake to think that the Devonshires
were roughing it in the bush—far from it. Wherever they went,
the servants were with them.

By their standards the family was living simply and unpretentiously, but even on the journey to Blue Sea Lake one of the special carriages was attached to the train, and there were aides-de-camp to take care of the luggage. Evie's personal maid travelled with her, and Victor's valet, and there were governesses, and the children's maids and, of course, kitchen staff.

Dora was certainly at Blue Sea Lake, because she told her children so—for years they thought it was called "Lucy Lake." But then, even Victor got it wrong at first: he thought it was "Blue Seal Lake." On day outings to Meech Lake, Dora was with the viceregal party, preparing and serving a perfect picnic, just as she had done in Hampshire and Scotland for the shooting parties. Dora nearly drowned in Meech Lake, she told her children, but she never gave them the details.

Putting aside the possibility for allegory here, the story underlines what Dora's photographs show: in between the cooking and washing-up, the cleaning and clearing-up, there was time for swimming and sunbathing, picnicking and laughter for servant as well as master. Presumably they were sleeping under canvas, since even the duke was lodged in the servants' quarters. Dora was also at Murray Bay, because even she, who had experienced the lifestyle of the Neumanns and the Duchess of Marlborough, was impressed enough to talk about it to her family.

By this time, Maud and Angus Mackintosh were engaged, because Victor says on July 24 he received from Quebec "a telegram of a mysterious nature from Evie," which in fact was to warn him that Angus had proposed, and that she had persuaded them to wait for a month—with Maud throwing a fit of hysteria about a week later.

Maud need not have worried; her mother had accepted the inevitable. On September 13 Evie wrote to Lady Lansdowne: "Maud is *so* happy ... and Angus is a different man since they got engaged ... nothing will ever make him a very interesting person, but he is full of good qualities and is one of the kindest men I have ever met … he has never really been 'in love' so that in spite of being 32 he is like a young boy over this." The letter is typical, judgemental Evie, but maybe Angus seemed a better bet when compared to the despicable "Alwyn."

They were married in Christ Church Cathedral on November 3, 1917. Maud's sisters were her bridesmaids, dressed in pale yellow silk, with touches of skunks' fur at the neck and wrists, and the wedding feast was a simple one. Evie was trying to make everyone economize: "Rody has asked so many people to the wedding [there were a thousand guests] who need not have come … [I plan] a very simple war-time tea of whole meal and corn meal cakes." There is every possibility that her orders to the kitchen were elaborated upon, just a little.

The first of Evie's daughters was off her hands, but in a letter to her mother on November 21 she returns to the theme that would haunt her throughout their Canadian sojourn: "… it is a drawback not to mix with contemporaries of our own class. I feel it very much with our girls—but that cannot be helped." Away from the familiar structure of her own society, Evie feared the interloper within the castle walls.

In his diary, Maud's father noted that "Alwyn sent a nice umbrella to Maud." With the style of this particular diarist, it is impossible to say if Victor is being merely laconic—or allowing himself just a touch of irony.

Much had happened before that November wedding. By the beginning of September, the Blue Sea Lake summer idyll was over and, with Evie and the girls along, the governor-general toured North Bay, Cobalt, Timmins, Cochrane, Temagami and Sudbury. At the station in Sudbury they coincided with a troop train carrying a draft from Winnipeg, and Evie and the girls gave the men flowers from their bouquets.

Then it was back to Ottawa, and the frustrations of dealing

with the Colonial Office back in London: "Tiresome letter from Walter Long. They seem to know nothing about Canada at the Colonial Office," wrote a frustrated Victor, who is beginning to see things from a Canadian, rather than a British, point of view. His was a tricky role; everything passed through his office during the war, and he frequently played intermediary between the Canadian and British governments. However difficult life was with Evie, Victor was still able to discuss his political life with her, and share some of the burdens. Evie writes to her mother:

> Borden has behaved very badly to Victor on more than one occasion. Victor is wonderfully patient with him but cannot trust him to play fair in his dealings with Walter Long—and Mr. Sladen and I both think W.L. is equally untrustworthy & inclined to repeat to Borden things that Victor has written in confidence. Altogether it is sad to think that in spite of this awful lesson we have had for three years the world is still full of people who think a great deal more of party politics & big profits than of their country and their fellow creatures. Borden is I believe merely a moral coward—but some of his colleagues are just as crooked as the Liberals.

After northern Ontario, it was on again to Montreal and to Halifax. By the end of October Victor observes that "Evie [is] tired and run down. She certainly ought not to come out west." She didn't, and Victor went alone, possibly relieved to get away from the atmosphere at Rideau Hall, as described by Evie to her mother:

> The whole household is rather [illegible] at present. Rody's nerves are back and affect Mary ... Mervyn Ridley has been depressed for some time and is now in hospital [the war-wound in his arm was suppurating] ... B.J.'s leg got troublesome a few weeks ago ... 'Hearty' Henderson is well & vulgar as usual ... imitates the others & is very casual & careless.

It is not a happy scenario. That distant war continued to make itself felt in those young, damaged lives.

Based on two postcards in the collection, Dora was not on this trip. One card is from Bert himself, from Nelson, B.C. The picture is a black-and-white photograph of Kootenay Lake, and it reads: "Dear: Thanks for letters. Having a lovely time, expect will be back 2 weeks today 28th, will write later. Yours Bert." The postmark is illegible. The other card, postmarked November 23, 1917, is initialled (possibly L.T.) and is addressed to Mrs. Lee, Government House, Ottawa. The message is brief: "Am bringing him back with us." Someone on the tour is keeping an eye on Bert for her friend, Dora.

It was while Victor was on tour that Lord Lansdowne wrote his so-called "Peace Letter" to *The Times*, urging a settlement of the war through negotiation: "We are not going to lose this War; but its prolongation will spell ruin to the civilized world, and an infinite addition to the load of human suffering which already weighs upon it." The very suggestion of talking to the enemy caused an uproar, and Evie became "very excited and hysterical," according to Victor, and fired off telegrams to her father. Lord Lansdowne wrote back that he had been surprised at the number of letters from officers at the front "to say that they *welcome* the letter."

After the events of May 14 and 15 of that year, there were many in Canada who would have agreed with him. The attack of Canadian troops on Vimy Ridge had begun on April 9, in conjunction with the British attack on Arras; by the end of the day the German front lines were overrun, and the Canadians had taken four thousand prisoners. Their success had the unfortunate result of encouraging Generals Haig and Allenby to press on through the German lines in hopes of a breakthrough with troops who had been in action for three consecutive days without rest, in blizzard conditions.

On April 14, ten men of the Royal Newfoundland Regiment

held the town of Monchy-le-Preux for five hours against a German division after the death of 485 of their fellows. At Vimy Ridge itself, 4000 yards of the German line and 4000 German prisoners were gained at the cost of 3598 lives and 7000 wounded. In an unprecedented break with centuries of tradition, three British generals protested directly to Haig at the cost in human life and, on April 15, he ordered an end to the offensive.

The victory was measured in four miles of gain, and thousands of Canadian lives. On Vimy Ridge, 250 acres of land were later given by the French in perpetuity to Canada. They are now planted with native Canadian trees, and the towering memorial bears the names of 11,500 dead, their graves unknown.

By June 1917, the first American troops had landed in France. By the end of July, there was renewed fighting on the Ypres salient; in the ensuing battle of Passchendaele in October, heavy rains turned the battlefield to liquid mud and many of the injured who fell died of drowning. The battle of Passchendaele came to an end on November 10 when Canadians advanced five hundred yards into a German artillery bombardment of over five hundred guns, and continuous air attacks. Since July 31, General Haig's forces had gained four and a half miles of ground. "We have won great victories," Lloyd George trumpeted to the Supreme War Council in Paris.

Now that the casualty lists filled the newspapers, young men were no longer rushing to sign up. Around Blue Sea Lake, local French-Canadian families were hiding their sons at out-of-the-way farms to avoid conscription, and Evie writes angrily to her mother: "The French Canadians are getting exemptions everywhere—it makes me perfectly sick but it is only what we expected with FC local tribunals." It is a theme to which Evie will return, as her letters reflect a schism in the country that will reverberate for years to come.

On December 6, the war in Europe touched Canada in a

direct and terrible fashion. At nine o'clock in the morning, the city of Halifax, where the Devonshires had landed and where Victor had been sworn in as governor-general, was shattered by a devastating explosion on board a munitions ship, the *Mont Blanc*. As it backed out of the harbour it was hit by an incoming steamer and caught fire, which reached its cargo before it could be controlled.

The ensuing explosion of the munitions and the deckload of benzine the *Mont Blanc* was also carrying flattened the north end of Halifax, blew out windows across the city and hurled people from the streets, the sidewalks, the houses. Virtually every pane of glass in the city was shattered, raining from the buildings on anyone below. The initial estimates of the death-toll were staggering—two thousand in the first twenty-four hours was the report in *The Globe*—and it would continue to soar.

The injuries were appalling, and hundreds were blinded by the blast. Snow, rain and arctic temperatures would add to the misery over the next few days. Hundreds of burned, charred and unidentified bodies choked the city morgues; column after column of them, each with a number, filled the pages of *The Halifax Herald*. For some there was a scrap of material—a striped petticoat, a pair of stockings—hair colour, a ring or brooch, to identify the victim. For some even the sex could not be identified—"charred remains" became their only epitaph.

Outside the undertaker's, the snow began to cover the heaps of wooden boxes, and in *The Halifax Herald* they advertised for gravediggers. Sir Robert Borden arrived in the city on December 8 and ordered one million dollars of federal aid. Out west, Victor received an urgent telegram from Evie to say he must return. Just over a week later the Devonshires were in Halifax.

As on his visit to the front, Victor found the scene beyond description. The spare style of the diary is as adequate—or inadequate—as the wordiest newspaper account: "... pitiable

... The number of people including children who are blinded is remarkable ... impossible to imagine how terrible it must have been ..." Because of the timing of the disaster, entire school populations were wiped out. In the Protestant Orphan's Home, every single child and the matron were killed.

As Victor and Evie toured Richmond, the area most directly hit, the area the newspapers described as "a charnel house," they came across a wrecked home—one of many—with a baby cot and carriage left standing in the centre of the ruins. Someone had propped up a row of dolls beside the debris. Evie—controlled, distant, icy Evie—wept openly. In the hospitals where she gave out flowers as she had to the troops on the train at Sudbury, a five-year-old asked for an extra one for his toy frog. The story merited a headline in *The Halifax Herald*, in a time when a devastated city looked for comfort in even the most inadequate gesture. When she got back to Ottawa, Evie sent two thousand boxes of chocolates to Halifax for the children.

There were other, larger, headlines: "THRILLING STORY OF THE AWFUL DISASTER THAT THE HUNS BROUGHT TO HALIFAX AND TO ALL NOVA SCOTIA!" The kaiser was freely blamed, the likening of Halifax to distant war zones a recurring theme:

> We witnessed from our comfortable homes the rape of Belgium and the spoilation of Northern France, and sympathized as well we knew how; we read with horror of the destruction of Louvain, Ypres, Liege ... we opened our hearts and arms to those brave lads who returned maimed and mutilated from the awful chaos ... We have flattered ourselves, that here in Halifax at least, we had a fairly accurate idea of what the war was like. It has this week ... been given to us to more properly judge the actuality of the desolation that the German war lord has visited upon Northern Europe ...

In early 1918 Evie wrote of the suffering of the war survivors at Rideau Hall again to her mother: "I am very sorry for the poor A.D.C.s whose remaining brother officers & friends are probably being killed—their nerves are bad." For Rody Kenyon-Slaney, who went with them to Halifax and whose nerves had been playing up in November, the carnage and devastation must have brought back terrible memories of a war he could not put behind him.

On December 24 *The Halifax Herald* had another gigantic headline blazoned over the news of the disaster: "THE UNION GOVERNMENT ABSOLUTELY PROHIBITS THE BOOZE BUSINESS IN ALL CANADA! THANK GOD!" As part of the effort to avoid wasteful or unnecessary expenditure, Sir Robert Borden had announced the prohibition of "intoxicating liquors" into Canada. Victor agreed—one senses, with reluctance—and Rideau Hall went dry. After a dinner-party on January 16, 1918, he observed, "Quite pleasant but quiet—probably owing to our being dry. The ginger ale was not bad, but I don't think the guests approved."

Evie, on the other hand, enthusiastically stepped up her efforts to economize and conserve in kitchen and dining-room. To her mother she wrote, "We are 'dry' here now … I hear that most of the ministers are horrified at our doing it—they have filled their cellars extra full as one can't buy drinks in the clubs. Col. Henderson distributes cocktails and whisky to all comers."

Rationing had not been introduced, as it had been in England that year, but there were food shortages, and Evie was doing her best to see that Rideau Hall played its part: "We have reduced beef to once a week and cut off bacon altogether—up to now we had it twice a week and one does need fat food in the very cold weather. We have two 'meatless days' always, but as fish and chicken are allowed that is no privation. All our cakes and scones are made of Indian corn or potato flour and our bread over 50 per cent rye flour."

The wartime bread was not easy on Evie's colitis. In late

1917 she had had a "violent attack" and had been unable for a while to digest whole wheat and maize. Then she found that the servants were eating white bread—"which made me furious." One can imagine: let them eat cake, indeed.

Victor too was part of the war effort and, in his own way, was helping with the servant problem: "Victor spends all his spare time gardening. Planting seed potatoes is excellent for his figure and the FC gardeners are obliged to work hard while he is with them ... every bit of land that is fit to grow anything has been ploughed. We think of nothing but the war."

In the ducal diary, the early days of 1918 are measured out in potatoes—and stones. Day after day Victor ends his diary entry with "picked up stones," as he cleared the Rideau Hall grounds for cultivation. Victor liked planting potatoes and picking up stones, and not just for the sake of his figure. He always found physical activity soothing, and the beginning of 1918 had been particularly stressful. There were anti-conscription riots in Quebec and, as Evie wrote to her mother, "It is bad luck on him that he should not have one single man to talk freely to except Sir Joseph Pope who is old and tired & who has been away a lot." On February 14 Cecil Spring-Rice died of a heart attack while on a visit to Ottawa, and all the funeral arrangements had to be made by the Devonshires. Encountering the North American way of dealing with death was a shock for Victor: "Evie, Dick [Nevill] and I went to the cemetery. Met a dreadful man who was in charge. Talked just as if he was a real estate agent."

In April, Evie had some sort of growth removed from her eyelid (a cyst, perhaps?) and had her heart examined in Montreal, where she was given a clean bill of health. Perhaps she was experiencing palpitations, as the hormones in her body adjusted to her oncoming menopause. In spite of health problems, the show had to go on, and there was another trip to Toronto, Hamilton and Niagara Falls, where even the cards were bad: "Lady Hendrie [the wife of the lieutenant-governor of Ontario] & I had bad cards," wrote Victor, "but she never failed to throw away any chance we might have had."

Their repeated visits to the area were all to encourage the war effort. After a visit to a munitions factory and a cotton factory making canvas and webbing for the U.S. army, Evie writes to her mother: "The spirit everywhere is good and loyal. They have lost a lot of men, but will go on doing their best unless anything makes them think we could make peace if we liked—then all this work would go to bits." Doubtless Lady Lansdowne passed on this particular shaft to the writer of the Peace Letter.

On May 31 Victor writes: "Birthday. Horrible to think that one is 50." Victor always noted his birthdays with gloom, but even Evie wrote to her mother with some concern: "Victor had to wear a felt boot yesterday on account of a gouty ankle. It makes him look about 70 when he hobbles with a stick. He is 50 today but I really think he looks older than father …" In spite of his pain, Victor went on skating, snowshoeing, and resolutely planting potatoes and picking up stones.

Health, or the lack of it, was always a problem with the war-damaged aides-de-camp. During 1918 Vivian Bulkeley-Johnston was hospitalized in Montreal, and it was decided he would have to leave in August. Before his departure he gave the comptroller, Lord Richard Nevill, a gift as a joke—a book called *Lord Richard in the Pantry*. It was a light romance, written by an author called Martin Swayne, and published by Hodder and Stoughton in 1916. The dedication reads, "To the gentleman mentioned on the title page to aid him in his duties connected with the place mentioned on the title page." At some point over the next eighteen months Lord Richard gave it to Dora, and Dora kept it all her life.

Of all the memorabilia in Dora's flower-lined hatbox and steamer trunk, Lord Richard's gift is perhaps the most unexpected. It suggests a level of friendship between the comptroller of the household and a member of the kitchen staff that is, to say the least, unusual. The gift becomes even more intriguing in the light of the silver-framed photograph that Dora kept on display in her home all her life—a picture of Lord Richard Nevill. Her children remember it always being there, and the fondness with which their mother always spoke of "Lord Richard."

Lord Richard's name is also on three empty envelopes and a note, which dates from April 1919. These are not so surprising, since they contained money, and such tips were quite usual at Christmas and New Year. Not only would senior members of staff, such as Lord Richard, reward the cook, but visitors would also give gifts. The amounts were generous: one envelope passed on to Dora by Lord Richard contained a $50 Christmas gift from the duke. Dora also kept an envelope that reads, "Mrs. Lee—With the Compliments of Mr. Balfour and Admiral Browning." Arthur Balfour, the British prime minister, had visited Canada as early as 1917.

What, then, was the nature of the relationship between the lord and the cook? Certainly the fact that Lord Richard gave Dora a book about goings-on in the pantry implies that there was hanky-panky belowstairs—and that there was gossip and joking about his fondness for Dora Lee. However true that was, the presence of that silver-framed picture in Dora's sitting-room throughout her married life makes it unlikely that there was anything more than an *amitié amoureuse*—if that— between master and servant. It is a greater compliment to Dora that this charming, kindly, middle-aged nobleman shared jokes and conversation with her, relied on her and treated her in many ways as an equal, than that he abused his position of power.

The envelope from Arthur Balfour and the admiral suggests that Dora was a vital member of that downstairs staff from the beginning—probably from round about the time the senior cook took fright at what was expected by Evie and left Rideau

Hall. Certainly Dora was being financially rewarded for her skills early on in her Rideau Hall career: in her little almanac there is an entry that reads, "July 9th 1917, been in Canada nearly 9 months, saved $400 in Canadian money." A conservative estimate of the buying power of that $400 nest egg today is about $5500—certainly more than she could have earned in Great Britain during the war years. Even the very wealthy, such as the Neumanns, had pulled in their horns: there was no coming-out party for Rosa Neumann, as there had been for her sister, Sybil. And, given her wage of £80, "all found," it illustrates the size of gratuity Dora was receiving.

From about March 1918, Dora Lee comes back into the spotlight, her life in Canada highlighted by cards of a different kind: a collection of forty gilt-edged menus, crowned with the royal coat of arms in gold. The little scullery maid of thirteen has reached the glory days of her profession at the age of twenty-six, with a champion to encourage and cheer her on.

Not everyone was as enthusiastic as Lord Richard. In a letter to her mother dated May 17, 1918, Evie writes: "People are trying to save the foods that can be imported—for a long time only very few took the thing seriously. Our cook is a perfect idiot on the subject and Lord Dick simply can't understand, but I have managed to make certain rules which they can't well break." From the date of the letter, and from the coupling of cook and comptroller in the same sentence, the "idiot" cook is probably Dora. Evie's comment, of course, is not a reflection on Dora's intelligence, but on her stubbornness at refusing to compromise her standards, even in time of war—and Lord Dick is on her side.

How one wishes one could have been a fly on the wall, watching that tough survivor of the kitchen sculleries facing Evie Devonshire in her boudoir! The duchess had wanted a spinner of sugar, and that was what she had got in Dora Lee. Dora was there at Rideau Hall to create culinary magic, not to cut corners. Sparks would not have flown—Dora knew how she had to play the game—but Evie's letter suggests that there was a battle of wills between the two of them.

In the light of events later in Lord Richard's life, Evie was quite right to be concerned about his extravagance, but it is likely that Evie was expecting to have a silk purse made out of a sow's ear. Later on in the same letter, she speaks of the need for the aides-de-camp to have "lots of meat and nourishing things." Presumably the rules Evie talked about in her letter included the meatless days she had mentioned earlier to her mother, and it is interesting to look at some of the menus in the light of her edicts.

Although the menus generally give the month, only a handful give the year, so it is impossible in all cases to match a specific menu to a particular dinner or luncheon party. However, there is a simplicity about them that suggests that Dora was taking *faîtes simple*, the credo of her great teacher, to heart, and doing her best to accommodate her mistress. There are also numerous errors in the French and, since Dora had her Escoffier cookbook with her, it seems likely many of the mistakes came from the printer. It is unlikely that Dora would have written "Tournadoes" for "*Tournedos*," for instance. Only two rough drafts have survived, both for prestigious occasions, and the menus associated with them are error-free.

Occasionally Dora does use beef, but there is a greater reliance on chicken, turkey and lamb. Using her classical Escoffier training, she is particularly inventive with poultry dishes—*poulet en chaud-froid à l'Ecossaise, galantine de volaille froid, galantines de dindonneaux truffées*, for example. Lamb she tends to prepare very simply, by roasting or sautéing. As Evie said, seafood was not a problem, and Dora prepares the lobster salads she had learned with Escoffier, and of which Tum-Tum had been so fond. She cooks sole with oysters, and prepares lobster and sole Newburg. The latter appears in Dora's Escoffier cookbook, but was the invention of an American chef—a Mr. Wenburg of Delmonico's in New York, who transposed the first letters of his name to christen his method of cooking lobsters sautéed in a cream sauce.

A lunch menu dated August 16, probably from 1918, gives an example of the simple approach of those wartime years:

Oeufs froids

Canetons Rôtis
Légumes

Pâté de Poulet Froid
Salade

Glace au Cantaloupe

An appetizer of cooked, cold eggs (the style of preparation is not specified), roast duckling and vegetables, a cold chicken pâté with salad, followed by iced melon—a simple and elegant meal for the arrival of the former viceroy and his wife, the Duke and Duchess of Connaught. It bears little resemblance to the two elaborate menus that survive from the Neumann years, but Dora's strength lies in her skill and ability, not merely in her extensive repertoire of dishes. If anyone could make a silk purse out of a sow's ear, it was Dora Lee.

Dora's path follows the path of her employers through the years 1918 and 1919, and it is not only her leisure time that mirrors theirs. Ever since that beautiful black dress from Swan and Edgar, she has always loved good clothes, and her choices echo the elegance of her mistress. She is making good money and is treating herself as she never could before—in one photograph she is in a well-cut suit, a white fox fur around her neck.

The Devonshires are officially photographed with all their staff in front of Rideau Hall, and so is Dora—front and centre of that huge household. She is photographed with some of her women colleagues in the Rideau Hall kitchen, standing at a table in her chef's whites, pouring herself a glass of wine; the command in her look and her posture is unmistakeable. Those gilt-edged menus mark the golden time for Dora, when her career had reached its zenith.

The only difficulty in working out Dora's schedule arises when the duke and duchess go their separate official ways, but Dora went west on one tour, and it was probably the tour at the end of August 1918, when Evie stayed at Rideau Hall. There is a photograph showing Dora with members of the kitchen staff alongside the train, so she would certainly have used the well-appointed kitchen in the special car.

Evie stayed behind on this occasion because Maud's baby was due, and she had come back to Canada for the birth; they wanted no problems over the nationality of the child. But there had been an earlier disagreement about the demands of the official schedule on the June tour of southwestern Ontario, which Victor had noted in his diary on June 10, saying, "Afraid Evie was very tired but it is quite impossible to arrange anything which appears to suit. Makes everything very difficult." On June 16, writing from the viceregal train in Hepworth, southern Ontario, Evie pours her heart out to her mother:

> I am absolutely played out & we have got to go on till the 22nd. Victor will arrange for these long tours. Day after day we begin at 9.30 & go on all day. The so-called "off days" always get filled up with a luncheon & tea party at someone's house or an extra visit to a sanitorium or convalescent hospital. Victor has had the gout—probably from tiredness & lack of exercise. I can't get my throat & ears right & feel perfectly wretched … I merely feel a drag on Victor. He seems too easy going to settle a reasonable tour which would not knock me up & tire out the girls—& too weak to say "no" to anything he is asked to do. This is the second time he has made me quite ill by overwork & he only sulks if I say anything & it is really very difficult.

There is always something unattractive about self-pity, however justified, and it is difficult to feel too much sympathy with Evie's lengthy tale of woe, when one considers the timetable of the household and staff. Dora would have been working from first thing in the morning to last thing at night, and not only would she have worked long hours, but she would have been doing many extra tasks. Staff problems continued throughout 1918, according to Evie, with much grumbling among the servants: "The Canadian maids won't stay—they say the work is too hard & there isn't enough time off." And again, she writes, "Walter Long won't let any maids come out [from England]—it is horrid of him & very stupid, as lots of women cross every week. Canadian maids come & give notice next day—they won't work before breakfast & think the place too dull, so we shall have to shut up part of the house." There is a noticeable dichotomy here between Evie's concern over economy and her desire to keep every room in the house open.

Dora may have grumbled, but she got on with it. For years she had worked within a different tradition of service than all those lazy Canadian maids, who expected days off and reasonable hours of sleep. She did not have the luxury of withdrawing, as her mistress did on many occasions, leaving one of her daughters to fill in for her. If it had not been for her romantic tie, there was another option Dora could have taken, and that was to go to the United States. There was a considerable servant drain across the border, and British-trained servants were particularly desirable. One member of the Devonshire household actually walked away from them on the docks: twenty-six-year-old Amy Hidor hitched a ride to Halifax and then left them for a job she had presumably already arranged in the States!

One gets the strong impression that the main problem for the vice-reine is not just that she is tired, or in fragile health; she is bored, literally, to tears. "Lots of women are working splendidly, but hardly any except the English-born realizes what is going on, and the vast majority don't care," she writes to her mother. She finds the French "frankly antagonistic or else quite callous about the whole thing." One of her predecessors, Lady Aberdeen, would have waded right in to whatever fracas was underway and brought about consensus. Consensus was not Evie's forte, for she was very much a cat who walked by herself. This was not the viceregal role Evie enjoyed; this was not glamorous stuff.

Nineteen hundred and eighteen should have been a year of joy; the war was slowly drawing to a close, and the Devonshires' first grandchild was born on September 24—Arabella, whose pet name would be Arbell. Victor's recording of that birth is reminiscent of his own children's arrival into the world: "She would have liked a boy but that does not matter. Angus very happy … walked with Evie in the evening."

That September an outbreak of Spanish influenza raged through North America, as it had earlier in the year in England and Europe. In early October Angus was taken ill, and Evie left for Washington from Montreal, having wired Victor who was at the Citadel. Victor writes that, "she got there in time & that Angus knew her & asked after Maud & the baby." Angus's one remaining lung could not withstand the virus, which viciously attacked the lungs of its victims, and he died, with Evie by his side. Three years after his war was over, the First Battle of Ypres took his life prematurely, as those battles would continue to do to the men who had survived them. Widowed after less than a year of marriage, with a three-week-old baby, it must have seemed to Maud that life was over at the age of twenty-two. In her memoirs, Maud wrote of her mother's bravery in rushing to Angus's side, knowing how terrified she was of illness.

Maud's first wedding anniversary was observed with sadness on November 3. On November 9 Victor records, "Press censor sent up a message that the Emperor had abdicated. One more off his perch"—an original way for one member of the ruling class to talk about another, even if he *has* been the enemy. On November 11 Victor writes, "The Armistice was signed early this morning & so ends the fighting." On Armistice Day, Ann Peace Arabella was christened, wearing a tartan belt over her christening robes, in honour of her dead father. World events, family ritual and tragedy had come together as if they were scripted for one of those movies that the aides-de-camp and Evie's daughters so enjoyed.

On November 10, Canadian troops had entered Mons, where the first soldiers of the British Expeditionary Force had met the enemy. In a village to the east of Mons, at two minutes to eleven on November 11, a Canadian soldier, Private George Price, was shot by a German sniper. To George Price went the terrible distinction of being one of the very last casualties of a war that took the lives of 60,661 Canadians.

Within a month of the signing of the Armistice, Evie Devonshire took herself, Maud, Arbell and Dorothy back to England on the *Aquitania*, where she would stay until May 1919. Blanche was to follow in February 1919 with Miss Saunders. Rachel and Anne stayed with their father. Charlie was at Ashbury School, where he was happy—not that he would be able to stay there. Now that the war was over, he would be sent back to Eton.

Back in England, the "usual crises" continued, even though they did not involve aides-de-camp. Blanche, the daughter whom Evie feared might be an old maid, found herself wooed and engaged in just over a month to the heir to a brewing fortune: Ivan Cobbold. To use Evie's words, "A boy called Ivan Cobbold is making up very violently to Blanche ... proposing last night. Blanche won't refuse him or accept him and goodness knows what I am to do next!" He may not have had a title, but Blanche's suitor came from old money. Although the brewery was the basis of their wealth, the Cobbold family had widely diversified their interests into banking and foreign trade as far back as the beginning of the eighteenth century. Evie needn't have worried about what to do next, because "obstinate" Blanche made her own decisions—she was proposed to on March 3, and married on April 30.

Seventy-four people celebrated Blanche's wedding day at Rideau Hall on April 30, and Dora prepared a delicious cold supper for after the dancing: a clear soup, lobster salad, a galantine of cold chicken, jellied beef, salad, a variety of sandwiches, strawberries "*à la* Ritz," liqueur jellies and trifle. "A *la* Ritz" may have been a flight of Dora's own culinary imagination, since the expression does not appear in *Larousse Gastronomique*. Possibly she used champagne for this reminder of a glittering age and the man who created it with *Le Maître*, Escoffier.

Back in Canada, there was a sense of *détente* among those left at Rideau Hall that Christmas and New Year. The ending of the war contributed to the feeling and so probably did the absence of a demanding chatelaine. After the traditional celebrations were over—the handing out of turkeys to the outside staff, attending the "somewhat solemn and stately" servants' ball—Victor gathered up "the girls," Miss Saunders and Dick Nevill for a snowshoeing trip to Blue Sea Lake. Dora may have been along for the ride, because Victor comments on the "excellent lunch" in his diary. They would go again in March, making the journey by sleigh, wrapped in furs, the sound of the sleigh-bells ringing in the air with their laughter.

Like her employers, Dora took to the Canadian winter with zest—there is a photograph of her on a toboggan, smart as always in her beret and scarf. But by far the most intriguing photograph is of Dora with her hockey team. At the time of writing, no information was available about a women's hockey team that played for Rideau Hall, but this is exactly what this photograph appears to show.

Dora sits in the middle of a group of women in matching jerseys with the maple leaf on the front, skates on their feet, hockey sticks in hand. Behind them stands a row of men—presumably their coaches and sponsors—and right in the middle of the group, in pride of place, stands an impressive trophy. For Dora, this must have been a particularly thrilling moment in her life, because there is a framed twelve-by-twenty-inch enlargement of this picture among her possessions.

What scant information there is available on women's hockey teams at the time suggests that there was, of course, more opportunity for women to play and find sponsors among local businesses in Ottawa during the war years. There is a photograph in the Ottawa City Archives of a similarly dressed women's team called The Westboro "Pets," who played between 1916 and 1920, and who were "organized by Walter Turner and Art McCarthy," presumably local businessmen. There appears to have been a local league, and this picture would suggest that Dora and her team won the trophy one season—probably the winter of 1918–1919. It is quite wonderful to think of those tough English servant girls strapping skates on their feet for the first time, and taking to Canada's swift and savage national game.

Victor Devonshire had by now become an aficionado of the sport, attending games whenever his schedule permitted, and by 1918 his diary regularly notes the results of games, commenting favourably or unfavourably on the performance of his local team, the Ottawa Senators. Curling, however, would always remain a mystery to him—he found it slow and boring.

The war behind them, the spirit at the Rideau Hall parties at the beginning of 1919 was as sparkling as the champagne provided, now that Government House was no longer "dry." The military brass band played on the bandstand with vigour and *élan*, stopping only to shut themselves up now and then somewhere warm to defrost their instruments, and to defrost themselves with the mulled claret that flowed in generous quantities.

~❦~

There were two new aides-de-camp at that skating party on March 6, recruited by Evie in England. The new additions were more than welcome, because the remaining aides-de-camp were "worse than useless," and Victor had to rely heavily on Dick Nevill—"without him, life would be impossible." One of the "useless" aides-de-camp was Larry Minto, son of a former governor-general, who had inherited the title on his father's death, and had been sent out to Canada by his mother to get him away from some unsuitable women in England. Given the romance rate among aides-de-camp, this was not a smart move and, title or no title, Evie was terribly worried that he would fall for one of the girls, particularly Dorothy.

In a letter to her mother in 1918 Evie writes: "… the girls think he [Minto] is a joke, although everybody likes him. Frankly—as we are stuck indefinitely out here—I prefer to have men around who the girls could marry if they happened to want to and we would certainly feel worried if one of them took a fancy to Larry. He is not likely to cut out the very attractive M. Ridley with Dorothy which would have been a good thing." Given that this aide-de-camp was an earl, Evie's anxiety is hard to understand, but she appears confused herself: she doesn't want Minto, yet she also wants Ridley cut out of the picture.

War, and life in the dominion, has changed Evie Devonshire. Removed from the myopic constraints of her country and her class, her outlook broadens—almost in spite of herself. She now accepts that her girls should be able to marry "if they happened to want to." The warm-hearted Evie who rushed to dying Angus's side, who wept openly in Halifax, who has difficulty getting through the award ceremonies for widows and bereaved mothers, has extended that tenderness to her own daughters.

As she watches the high jinks and the flirting, that "cheerful atmosphere" of a continual house party created by those young people in spite of war and their own personal suffering, Evie may well have thought of her own youth, and her hesitation in accepting the man preferred by her father. He had wanted her to be happy, and she had accepted his definition of happiness. Evie wants her daughters to be happy in their choices of partner, and gradually she accepts their definition of happiness. "Stuck indefinitely" in Canada, her own attitudes to marriage have changed. The portrait of her own marriage through Evie's eyes and Evie's letters is coloured by affection, exasperation and resignation.

Evie was back on May 18, and there was a brief respite in that heavenly place before departing on a tour of eastern Ontario —with Evie "rather upset" about the pace, according to Victor. Actually, Evie was already upset before they set off, and Victor was none too happy. They had received news in a roundabout way of the Prince of Wales' visit to Canada in August—"Disgraceful," fumed Victor, "[that] I should not have been told. It will be an awkward time if he comes in August. But we must make the best of it."

With the depressing possibility of losing their uninterrupted summer at Blue Sea Lake, Victor took himself off in "The Canada" on a fishing trip on the Matapedia River, before a brief break at New Lismore. Then it was off to Quebec City to await the arrival of the heir to the throne.

POULET EN CHAUD-FROID À L'ECOSSAISE

This dish is taken from a Rideau Hall menu: *Dîner du 17 Mars*. It was served after the soup and the fish course— *filets de Sole aux Huîtres* (fillets of sole with oysters). Although Dora kept no notes on how she prepared this dish, both the method of cooking the chicken, and the sauce accompanying it, are from classic French cuisine, and the recipe appears in her edition of Escoffier. It was a *chaud-froid* of chicken that gave Auguste Escoffier his first career breakthrough. The description in the cookbook is brief—just over a hundred words long—but, as with the *Bombe Néron*, there is more to the recipe than meets the eye.

First, the stock is prepared. Place veal bones and chicken giblets in cold water, bring to a boil, and then simmer for about three hours, skimming off grease and scum when necessary. Then add roughly chopped leeks, carrots, onion, a small turnip, parsley and tarragon sprigs, some thyme and bay leaf and some salt, and simmer for about another hour.

Rub a chicken (roughly four lbs) with lemon and bring it to a boil in cold, salted water. Boil for two minutes only, drain, and place it in the stock for about another three-quarters of an hour to an hour—or until tender. Remove from pan, drain, and leave to cool.

Make a *roux* with four tablespoons of butter and three tablespoons of flour, leave to cool, then gradually beat in the strained stock. Cook over a low heat, add about four heaped tablespoonfuls of *crème fraîche*, and continue to cook until the sauce coats the back of a wooden spoon. Add salt and a pinch of cayenne. Remove from heat and stand pan in a bowl of ice, stir occasionally as it cools to prevent a skin forming. When it is cold, strain it by squeezing it through a cheesecloth into a bowl. This is not easy, and some recipes suggest merely working it through a fine sieve.

Cut the chicken into pieces, remove the skin and bones, leaving the wing bone and drumstick in place. Put them on a wire rack and coat them with the sauce, which may be brushed all over with melted aspic, and decorated with tarragon leaves, etc.

A *l'Ecossaise* means that Dora served the *chaud-froid* with a white sauce using the ingredients of the traditional

Scotch broth: pieces of mutton, diced vegetables and pearl barley. It is a well-planned menu, because the *Consommé Bruinoise* that opened the meal also used finely diced vegetables, and she could prepare the two together, and possibly use the same stock as a base.

The course after the chicken was sautéed lamb cutlets with vegetables, and the dessert was *Fraises Oporto*—strawberries in port.

The Parting of the Ways

The light of other days is faded,
And all their glory past.
ALFRED BUNN, *THE MAID OF ARTOIS*

“I danced with a man who danced with a girl who danced with the Prince of Wales”—so went a popular song of the day. David, as the royal family called him, was not always the desiccated exile trailing in the wake of his American duchess—which is the way many people think of him nowadays. Dashing, good-looking, blond, with a brilliant smile, he was the era's pin-up boy, and in 1919 could fairly be called the world's most eligible bachelor. Evie's secretary, Elsie Saunders, kept a picture of him arriving in Canada among her personal papers until the end of her life: in it he leans over the railing of HMS *Renown*—laughing, dazzling, gorgeous.

Like a doomed Princess of Wales over half a century later, in many ways Edward was a creation of the media, who portrayed him as a handsome, devil-may-care man-about-town, and linked his name to many women—a reincarnation of the grandfather for whom he was named. His insistence on fighting in the war had been a source of great anxiety to his commanding officers, who feared not only that he would be killed, but that he might be taken prisoner. When denied the chance to fight on the front lines, he disobeyed orders and went there anyway, causing great inconvenience and some danger to others—a lesser man would have been court-martialled. On his return, the newspapers made him into a hero, as well as a matinee idol.

But beneath that outgoing, fun-loving exterior lay the insecure child of an intellectually limited father, and a mother whose stern rigidity made Queen Victoria's personality seem warm in comparison. Noel Coward, who knew him, saw the void beneath the veneer; "He had the charm of the world," he once said of him, "with nothing whatever to back it up."

The Prince of Wales' arrival in Canada at the age of twenty-five was hailed with great excitement and certainly with none of the reluctance shown by the Devonshires. For Dora, it was the chance of her professional lifetime—to cook for the man the press called "the Prince of Golden Promise." Carême and Escoffier would have understood. Setting a dainty dish before a king (or a king-to-be), as the old rhyme goes, was the culmination of any great chef's career. But the viceregal household was desperately short-staffed, and Evie would need the organizational and creative skills of that "perfect idiot" of a cook now, as never before.

There are five menus in Dora's collection that date from the Prince of Wales' visit, and they are for celebrations at the start of his tour on August 19, when he arrived at the Citadel on H.M.S. *Renown*. The earliest is for August 21, a meal that Victor mentions in his diary: "Big dinner. Went off well. Fireworks a great success." This was what Dora and her team served up:

Dîner du 21 Août

Consommé Parisienne

Filets de sole Newburg

Suprêmes de volaille Henri IV

Légumes

Quillot de boeuf à la mode en gelée
salade

Canetons Molière
Salade d'Orange

Bombe Strogoff

It is an elaborate and demanding selection of dishes. Just to single one out for description, "Henri IV" was a name given to a meat dish (in this case poultry) garnished with potatoes *pont-neuf* with *sauce béarnaise*. The potatoes alone are a work of art: slivers of fried potatoes (cut into sticks twice as thick as matches) arranged in pairs, criss-cross fashion over the cuts of meat, which were covered with ribbons of the sauce. Sometimes artichoke hearts stuffed with *noisette* potatoes replaced the potatoes *pont-neuf*.

On August 22, Victor's diary reads: "... reception at Citadel in evening. Turned into a dance. I think it was a great success, but frequent balls would speedily bring my tenured office to a close. HRH seemed to enjoy himself." Obviously a *very* good time was had by all, with an impromptu dance breaking out spontaneously, and the supper cooked by Dora Lee topping off the evening:

Souper du 22 Aout, 1919

CHAUD

Consommé
Poussins Diablés

FROID

Consommé Niçoise Froid
Filets de Sole Alexandra
Salade de Homard Parisienne
Suprêmes de Volaille Strasbourg
Salade
Côtelettes d'Agneau Menthe

Jambon et Langue en Gelée
Salade

Sandwiches Variety
Macedoine de Fruits
Gelée aux liqueurs
Trifles
Glaces Vanille et Framboises

Here, Dora has prepared the poultry "Strasbourg" style, which means she probably served it on thin slices of foie gras coated with a sauce made by deglazing the pan juices with Madeira. Another version uses a garnish of braised sauerkraut cooked with thin strips of streaky bacon, as well as the foie gras. The sole "Alexandra" style would have been served with a white sauce garnished with asparagus tips and a slice of truffle. Domestic economy, clearly, has been thrown out the Citadel window for this visit.

The third menu is dated *"Dîner du vingt-trois aout, dix-neuf cent dix-neuf."* It is headed "Spencer Wood," the official home of the lieutenant-governor of Quebec, where the dinner was held:

Potage de queue de boeuf

Truite Vénitienne

Quenelles de volaille en aspic

Selle d'agneau
légumes

Jambon glacé Sauce Cumberland
Salade chiffonade

Sardines en Tartare
Crème framboises glacée

Fruits   Café

Victor's diary entry reads: "Sleepy after yesterday ... Dinner party at Spencerwood. House and garden illuminated ..."

The Spencer Wood of Dora's triumph no longer exists. It was destroyed by fire in 1966, but in 1919 it was a building of elegant simplicity with a long colonnade and a Doric portico that gave it the look of a white castle from the river. Close to the village of Sillery, two miles from the city walls of Quebec, there had been an official dwelling on the site since the mid–nineteenth century. Those gardens, with their majestic sweep down to the St. Lawrence, must have looked magnificent when illuminated. Certainly, even the prosaic diarist was impressed; he called the effect "great."

Again, the dishes Dora selected required many of her Escoffier-trained skills. She must have had support staff, and it looks as if there were two women in particular on whom she could rely. On an envelope dated April 4, 1919, Lord Richard tells Dora, "I am also sending presents to the two members of your staff who have been with you during this winter...." Unfortunately, he does not give their names, but the chances are that one of those women is Ada Sergeant.

The soup is the sort of classic an Englishman would love: oxtail soup. The *sauce Vénitienne* for the trout contained tarragon and tarragon vinegar, white wine, shallots, chervil and parsley, and sometimes it was combined with another classic sauce, *sauce Allemande*. This was followed by small *bouchées* of poultry cooled in aspic, and a simply cooked saddle of lamb. The Cumberland sauce for the glazed ham was a combination of ginger, cloves, dry mustard, raisins, currant jelly, orange and lemon juice and orange and lemon rind, the whole simmered in port. *Chiffonade* means that the salad ingredients were cut in thin julienne strips. There is a savoury for the gentlemen, and the dessert is one that would have met with Escoffier's approval: ice-cream made with fresh raspberries.

The band played that evening at Spencer Wood, and someone on the staff—Lord Richard, perhaps?—went back to the kitchen and gave the unseen star of the evening a copy of the official programme, which she treasured forever:

1. March Héroique   Saint Saens
2. Overture "Plymouth Hoe"   Ansell
3. Selection from "La Boheme"   Puccini
4. Valse "Destiny"   Baynes
5. Selection from "As you were"   Darewski
6. Two Parisian sketches   Fletcher
    (a) Demoiselle Chic   (b) Bal Masqué

GOD SAVE THE KING

Dora's skills were still needed when they returned to Ottawa. There was a garden party, and a big official dinner and reception which, yet again, "turned into a dance," according to Victor. "In spite of being unconventional," he added, "the evening was quite a success." Dora's menu collection includes dinner and supper on August 29, and supper on August 30. On September 1, Dora was at the Houses of Parliament to watch England's prince of golden promise lay the cornerstone for the Victory Tower. Just before the Devonshires' arrival in 1916, the Parliament Buildings had been destroyed in a terrible fire.

The first business of parliament that September day was the ratification of the Treaty of Versailles. With the war behind them, Prime Minister Robert Borden looked to the country's future: "The possibilities that the future holds of a still greater Canada will not be fulfilled," he told the dense crowd standing in the brilliant sunshine, "unless the people of Canada are animated by high ideals and just purposes."

Amid the full ceremonial panoply of horses, postillions and military escort, the Prince of Wales and the Devonshires left Rideau Hall with the fanfare and flair the British bring, *par excellence*, to such occasions. Those magnificent men hired for their size and looks came into their own on these state affairs, their gorgeous liveries and powdered hair a haunting reminder of a past age as they stood behind or rode alongside the carriage brought to Canada by the Devonshires from Hardwick Hall.

It would have been a special moment for Dora Lee as the man she had followed to Canada passed by in all the splendour of the Devonshire livery—only one of many special moments that the past few days had held for her. She had been handed many envelopes in her professional career, but the one she had just received was the most memorable of all. The words "Government House, Ottawa" were printed on the flap, and handwritten on it was the message, "Mrs. Lee with HRH the Prince of Wales compliments and thanks." Inside was a leather jewel case lined in velvet; on the velvet was an exquisite enamelled brooch in the shape of the Prince of Wales' feathers, studded with rubies, emeralds and pearls. Stamped inside the lid was the royal crown and the name of the jeweller: "Collingwood & Co. To the Royal Family. 45 Conduit St. London."

Perhaps he had given his thanks in person, flashing one of his charming smiles at her as he did so. Perhaps Dora wore the brooch on her dress when she watched the heir to the throne lay the cornerstone of the Victory Tower.

The western tour the prince then undertook was a great success. He and his staff had tried to rid themselves of any officials from the viceregal household, but had finally been persuaded to take "Hearty" Henderson along with them, to the relief of Rideau Hall. No one wanted newspaper headlines about extroverted royal behaviour at official dinners, and a relieved Evie wrote to her mother in October: "The P of W ... has done remarkably well in every way ... He had delighted the girls at each place by dancing till any hour—often with one girl a good many times—but he never sits out with them and has not done any of the things we were afraid he would do."

What those things are is not specified, but it is not too difficult to hazard a guess. Just before the prince left in November, Evie gave her mother this remarkable character assessment of the heir to the throne: "He only wants a squash court, some dancing, some noisy music to which he can contribute by thumping a drum—and a pretty little girl or two—to be perfectly happy. He speaks so well now & is much less nervous & quieter in every way than he was in August. His own staff love him which is nice."

Evie, like Dora, was given a brooch as a parting gift. In the same letter she adds wistfully: "Poor Dorothy tried hard to be nice but you can imagine that after so much talk & newspaper paragraphs she was rather stiff and stodgy."

Poor Evie! Here was the most glamorous and eligible bachelor in the world, the ideal husband for one of her girls, and—after years of romances and flirtations with lesser mortals—there had been no sparks. Rumours about the prince and Dorothy being engaged had apparently been bruited about, much to Victor's annoyance, but there was no substance to them. With the benefit of hindsight one can see that the Prince of Wales would not have been in the least attracted to Dorothy's combination of youthful inexperience and earthy sexuality. It would take fifteen more years before he found the woman for whom he would surrender a throne—and she would be about as unlike the Devonshires' third daughter as could be imagined.

Besides, Dorothy was in the process of falling for someone else—a new aide-de-camp on the Rideau Hall staff. Harold Macmillan had barely survived the wounds he had received on the Western Front, had been recruited by Evie in England, and had arrived in Ottawa in March 1919. In fact, it looks as if the two first met during the London season of 1918–1919, when Evie took Dorothy away from the attentions of Mervyn Ridley and Larry Minto. Evie wrote to her mother that "H. Macmillan got so affectionate that I had to speak to him. He was very nice & now behaves with greater decorum. We can't make out whether he has any hopes or whether ... Dorothy does not care for him in that way."

Although he liked Harold Macmillan very much, Victor had his doubts—and so, apparently, did Dorothy. She thought he was "much the nicest of all the men she had danced with in London but for a long time said he was too clever." Clever he certainly was: the crofter's grandson would one day become prime minister of Britain, with the most outstanding career of any of Evie's sons-in-law. Macmillan's devotion would triumph over Dorothy's uncertainty and they would be married in 1920 in St. Margaret's Church, Westminster, where Victor and Evie had plighted their troth in a very different world. It was a marriage that would bring Harold Macmillan great happiness and great sorrow.

The Prince of Wales' character assessment of Evie Devonshire is not as charitable as his hostess's view of him. He thought Victor "a d___d good fellow and has no side," but of Evie he said, "hopelessly pompous ... she plays the 'Queen' stunt far more than Mama would, and that doesn't go down on this side." Bearing in mind that this restless, shallow man had his own reasons for rejecting anything and anybody who reminded him of his fearsome mother and his responsibilities, he undoubtedly hit the nail on the head. This was not the Raj, where the "'Queen' stunt" worked perfectly—and would continue to do so, for just a little while longer.

In 1918 Sir Robert Borden had insisted that Canada should have separate representation at the Peace Conference, and the Canadian government had announced its intention of having its own minister in Washington. From the Peace Conference on, the dominion countries represented themselves at the League of Nations. Canada was now asking for its own voice in the affairs of the world—not the voice of a beneficent mother country speaking on its behalf. The process begun in 1918 was finally laid down in law in 1931 by the Statute of Westminster, which declares that "The Dominions are autonomous communities within the British Empire, equal in status, in no way subordinate one to another in any aspect of their domestic or internal affairs...."

~𝑒~

The newspaper clipping among Dora's papers is from a British paper, *The Evening News*. It is dated October 8, 1919, and it reads as follows:

THE DUCHESS LOSES HER COOK AND SENDS FROM OTTAWA FOR A NEW ONE. Owing to the difficulty of obtaining a suitable cook in Canada, the Duchess of Devonshire is advertising in England for a woman to fill that post at Government House, Ottawa. "Domestic servants are almost unobtainable in Canada," said the Comptroller at Devonshire House today. "Practically the whole of the Duke of Devonshire's servants are found in England. The right type does not seem to exist out there." The present cook at Government House is leaving, and the applicant for her post must be a woman of thorough experience in large households.

At the height of her achievements, Dora Lee gave in her notice at Rideau Hall somewhere around the end of September, and it was momentous enough to give her a few inches of fame in a British newspaper. Why? One thing is certain: it was her decision and no one else's. Evie Devonshire's handwritten reference makes it perfectly clear that, whatever their differences might once have been, Dora had won the admiration of a difficult taskmistress:

Mrs. Lee has been at Government House as cook for three years, first as second cook and then for eighteen months as head cook. During that time she managed very well in rather difficult circumstances, owing to the lack of skilled help at a time when the work was very heavy. She is a very good cook and is leaving entirely by her own wish. [signed] Evelyn Devonshire.

For Evie, these are warm words indeed.

Lord Richard Nevill, Dora's friend and champion, was very ill in hospital from the beginning of September for about two months. Whether this played any part in Dora's decision to leave can only be guessed at. His reference for Dora is dated November 24, 1919:

> Mrs. Lee has been in the service of the Governor General of Canada and the Duchess of Devonshire for over three years, first as Second Cook, and for the past eighteen months as Head Cook. She is leaving of her own wish, as she is anxious to return to England. I am instructed by Their Excellencies to say they regret very much she is leaving. Mrs. Lee is a first class cook, and worked very hard last winter, when there was so much entertaining and she was very short of help in the kitchen. She also did very well during the Prince of Wales' visits to Their Excellencies at Quebec and Ottawa this autumn and winter. [signed] Richard Nevill. Comptroller of the Household to H.E. the Governor General of Canada.

She could, of course, have just been exhausted. Many male chefs got out of the profession around the age of thirty, moving into areas such as catering or management, and both references make it clear that the head cook of Government House had been seriously overworked for some time. But Dora was not a quitter, and there are a few strands of evidence that suggest that it was because of Bert that Dora gave up such a prestigious position so hastily.

The strongest strand is one of the few cards from Bert.

The illustration is of a framed, cloth, needlework picture of four flags and a wreath with the words, "Christmas Greetings." The card is not dated, nor is it addressed, so presumably it was sent in an envelope after Dora had left. The pencil-written message reads: "With all good wishes for Christmas. From Bert. Try and forget. It is better for both of us." Calves before character, as the saying goes. There is something chilling about the casual juxtaposition of seasons greetings and admonition that makes one feel, all these years later, that Dora was better off without Bert, whatever the pain and heartbreak at the time.

"YOU'RE THE ONLY GIRL I EVER LOVED"

There is another card with a strange message, sent to Ada Sergeant when she was at the Citadel with the Devonshires. Although addressed, the card was not mailed, so it also was probably put in an envelope to avoid prying eyes. The message is in Dora's handwriting, "If those eyes could only speak."

Is Dora saying, as Shakespeare said, that there is no art to find the mind's construction in the face? Does she mean that everyone, including her friend Ada, had kept quiet about Bert's behaviour, or reputation, or marriage? Ada, it must be remembered, was at Chatsworth well before Dora's arrival and the departure for Canada. It is unlikely that Dora is suggesting that Ada was involved, since they are friendly enough for Dora to be given the card back for her collection. Besides, she talked with warmth of Ada later in her life—she who said so little about her brilliant career.

The strangest strand of all may not be a strand at all. It is an entry in Victor's diary for July 1, 1920, about nine months after Dora left Rideau Hall, and it involves a footman, Dick Nevill, and the house steward who was immediately responsible for the servants, and particularly for the footmen:

One of the footmen came to complain of a character Dick had given him in a letter he had written. The man is tiresome &

awkward but Dick's letter was most unfortunate & I should say libellous. I could not do anything for this man as although Dick has put himself in the wrong I could not let him down. I then got Durnford & had a disagreeable talk with him with the result that I had to tell him that I thought he had better send in his notice. I believe it is the best way out of the difficulty, but how we shall manage for the rest of my time goodness knows.

Durnford is John Durnford, the house steward, who came to Canada with his wife, Minnie, and daughter, Esme, in 1916. From the style of the entry it seems clear that the two episodes are linked, and when the governor-general is directly involved in domestic matters, things are serious indeed. It is difficult to imagine just what was so grave that a long-time employee—who, what is more, had his family with him—should be asked to leave. Victor Devonshire was not given to mistreating his staff and besides, the servant shortage was acute. On July 28, Evie writes to her mother, "Do you know of a good butler? If so please tell Dick. We want one badly."

How one wishes that Victor had given the footman's name, but he probably didn't know it. How one wishes he had been more specific about what Dick Nevill had said! Clearly, the duke is quite taken aback by his comptroller's vehement attack, which he calls "unfortunate" and "libellous"—strong words for Victor, the master of understatement. From earlier examples in the diary, the chances are it was not a problem with theft or drink, because he probably would have said so. There had been a problem at Rideau Hall with one of the menservants stealing from the bedrooms—Maud lost her watch—and Victor names the crime, though not the culprit. The chances are that this has something to do with sex, romance—and betrayal.

Whatever it was, the punishment was severe. For a servant not to be given "a character" was tantamount to professional suicide, which was why the footman in question had gone so far as to ask to see the duke himself. Lord Richard Nevill was a kind and considerate man, and he must have been out of his mind with anger to have done what he did. Maybe one of the reasons that silver-framed portrait sat in a position of honour all those years was because Lord Richard had waited in the weeds until he could avenge Dora's betrayal.

A letter dating from May 1921 among Dora's papers suggests there was acrimony among the Rideau Hall staff towards the end of the Devonshires' tenure. It comes from New Jersey, but the sender is unidentified, because Dora has not kept the last page of the letter. The incomplete sentence at the bottom of the page is intriguing: "Would you like to tell me something, don't tell me to mind my own business but I heard in New York that ..."

Presumably the letter-writer is a woman, and a former servant at Rideau Hall who has moved to the States, because she says, "... I steered clear of all G.H. lot as far as possible ... I didn't see much of Ada for which I was sorry. The others I wasn't interested in, I feel proud to think I'm not classed among them anyhow."

And that was how Dora Lee walked away from Rideau Hall, her former colleagues and Bert: proud not to be classed among them. In the gasometer that had been her home for three years—the longest she had been in any household—she packed up her Escoffier cookbook, her chef's hats and aprons, the black dress bought with that first guinea gift, the white fox fur that was the prized symbol of her financial status, the letters of reference, all the empty envelopes that had contained the substantial rewards for her talents, the Prince of Wales' brooch in its velvet-lined case, the leather-bound almanac that had been with her since she was a teenaged scullery maid— and the hundreds of postcards she had collected over her thirteen years in service. Then, with her hatbox and her steamer trunk she left on her first holiday in three years.

Dora did herself proud on that vacation. Not for her the modest boarding-house, nor a holiday under canvas, even amid the cerulean splendours of Blue Sea Lake. From Toronto she sent a postcard to her half-brother, Charles:

> My dear Charley: Just a few lines trusting you are all well. Did you receive my letter & songs I sent you. I am staying at this hotel on my holiday. The first holiday in nearly 3 years. I am now about 200 miles from Ottawa. I am going on to Niagara Falls tomorrow, 3 hours journey further on. Hope to see you all soon. Love to all: Dora.

The hotel on the card is the Queen's Hotel in Toronto, where anyone who was anyone stayed. It was built in the days when Front Street was a pleasant, tree-lined boulevard, and

there was no Union Station between hotel and lake. In winter, ice-boat parties stopped off to warm themselves in its hospitable dining-room and bar. It had welcomed under its roof great actors, such as Henry Irving, and great lords, such as the Marquis of Lorne and the Earl of Aberdeen. The Duke and Duchess of Devonshire stayed in the Royal Suite in 1899. John A. Macdonald held his so-called Red Parlour Conferences there, and is said to have outlined his plans for Confederation under its roof. When Dora went on to Niagara Falls, she may well have stayed at the Clifton Inn Hotel, where Evie and Victor had stayed on one of their tours.

When Dora turned her back on Bert, she treated herself with some of the considerable savings she had accumulated over three years and, what is more, she treated herself like a lady. Dora chose to stay where the quality stayed, and this time she was upstairs, not down. Her three years with the Devonshires had shown her that, in Canada, she would not be placed in a certain class or section of society every time she opened her mouth. All she had to do was to be able to pay the bill.

In one of Evie's letters dating from March 1918, she talks about a big women's conference, with delegates from all over Canada, that she attended: "… the socialist women were down on everything and the temperance women wanted all the whisky converted into trade alcohol for motor work." But amid the dissenters was one outstandingly able woman: "[the] Deputy from Saskatchewan was an English housemaid & only came over 8 years ago—she dropped her h's but is a born leader." In Canada, those dropped *h's* did not matter as much as the ex-housemaid's leadership qualities—even to judgemental Evie Devonshire.

Dora's return to England that winter was only temporary. By March 6, 1920, she was back in Canada on the *Mauretania*, and working as a cook at the May Court Club in Ottawa.

The May Court Club was the brainchild of Lady Aberdeen, a former vice-reine at Rideau Hall. Formed in 1889, its lady members were drawn from the higher echelons of Ottawa society, and its aims were, according to an extract from an early issue of the *May Court Magazine*, "[to accord] girls of leisure opportunities of improving their own talents and characters and of helping girls with less time at their disposal."

The club did a great deal of charity work—one of its earliest committees was formed to give aid to poor and destitute families in Ottawa—but it was also a meeting place for young women like Ethel Chadwick, where they attended concerts and debates, or heard lectures on such authors as Dostoevsky and Ibsen. The May Court Charity Ball became one of the premier events in the city's social calendar. Evie's daughter, Blanche, had been an enthusiastic supporter and member, and had taken part in activities that raised money for soldiers' families and the war effort. Dora's references from the club's patroness, Evie Devonshire, and Lord Richard Nevill would have made her an ideal candidate for employment, and in March 1920 the club hired her to run the Lunch and Tea Room. In November 1920, she gave in her notice. Sarah Sparks, convenor for the Tea Room, and a member of one of the oldest Ottawa families, gave her an excellent reference:

> Miss Lee has been cooking in a small Lunch and Tea Room for the May Court Club of Ottawa. We have found her most capable, clean—and a very good cook. She has been with us eight months and we are sorry to lose her. She has decided to return to England.

In the back of the little almanac that had been with her all those years Dora had tucked a photograph in the pocket that held a small mirror. She probably was given it on her trip back

ENGAGED.

Dear our troth has long been plighted
One has been our heart
Now dear soon we'll be united
Never more to part.

to England in 1919, and she kept it in the almanac all her life. It is of a young, dark-haired man, his cap pulled down at a jaunty angle over his eyes, leaning casually on an elegant cane. Dora went back to England in 1920 for Christmas, and came back in March 1921 as a married woman: Dorothea Mary Vince. Someone else had replaced Bert in her heart.

And what a replacement! Archibald (Archie) George Vince was seven years younger than Dora. Born and raised in Stockbridge in Hampshire, he was a gifted pianist and organist (he had been a guest organist at Romsey Abbey) and a talented soccer player. His father had served in the Royal Navy all his life and, only one day after his eighteenth birthday, Archie joined the Royal Navy and the war effort. He served on HMS *Courageous*, then joined the submarine service as a torpedoman on HMS *Dolphin*. When he met Dora Lee he was training as a carpenter and joiner, teaching piano and organ, and playing for dances and concerts. They were married on March 10, 1921, and sailed aboard the *Scandinavian* for their new life together in Canada.

Not everyone in England wished them well. Archie's sister, Olive, who played piano with her brother at all those concerts and dances, bitterly accused Dora of cradle-snatching. Olive, in fact, is a final, and important, strand in the mystery of Bert. Years later, when Dora's eldest son came back to Britain to fight in yet another terrible war, Olive told him that his mother had been jilted by a footman at Rideau Hall. Twenty years later, the bitterness was still in Olive's voice.

How to Spend a Honeymoon.

A honeymoon is the approved time for blushing, for you are about to learn how wonderful married life is.

Ladies should search their husbands' pockets to find where he keeps his secrets.

Husbands should watch their wives closely to see how much is nature and how much is art.

There's generally a lot of lace about on a honeymoon, so examine it and praise it, it leads to a better understanding between you.

Dignity is everything— even if you have confetti sticking in your hair.

Tell each other you've never been in love before— it's the only time in all your life you will be believed.

For heaven's sake don't talk in your sleep— or you'll give your past away if you've got one.

By the way if you can't afford a cradle buy an old orange box and decorate that.

Also bear in mind you're a new firm starting in business and must do your best by diligence and hard work to make a success of it.

Follow these directions and you will be quite happy.

Thirty years after that, Dora's son found the cards from Bert among his mother's papers, and remembered what Olive had said. And, if Olive knew, then clearly Dora made no secret to her husband of her former love and her betrayal. It is only what one would expect of Dora Lee.

The Devonshires' tenure at Rideau Hall was over in July 1921. Victor was disappointed; he would have liked to stay on, as the Canadian government wanted. But there were various pressures on him, one of which was his wife. In May 1921, Evie wrote to her mother:

Mr. Meighen [Arthur Meighen, the new prime minister] ...
calmly announced that he was going to let the question of the
new G.G. wait for a fortnight as it might do harm in a bye-
election which is coming. I told him that he really must get on
as the delay was causing us great inconvenience. The Canadian
govt don't really like any of the names—they expect someone
who is very well known and has had lots of political experience.
Mr. Meighen evidently fails to understand that men with all
the qualifications they expect don't always have to leave home
for five years.

If the sting in the tail of Evie's letter means that the
Devonshires had been forced to leave home for five years to
make money—as her father, Lord Lansdowne, had done—
then she was in for a rude awakening. However, the chances
are that she already knew that things were not as they should
have been. A recurring theme throughout her Canadian correspondence is the extravagance of the household, and of Lord
Richard Nevill—and her own inability to get anything done
about it:

> No-one who can look after things properly ... Victor never
> bothers much ... as usual I am the only person to question the
> cost of all we want to do. It is a bore always to seem stingy but
> I believe we shall spend something huge if I don't fuss ... Our
> household has been a source of great trouble and expense:
> Dick Nevill can't manage the servants a bit and is hopelessly
> extravagant ...

The complaints go on and on over the years, but her feelings of impotence and frustration are understandable. For all
her queenly airs and her regal presence, Evie was powerless.
Only her husband and his advisers could do anything—and
they didn't. This description of Victor, written on the governor-
general's train in 1918, sums up her husband's attitude pretty
well—at least, in her eyes:

In all the anxiety of the present times Victor is the calmest and most contented person I know. He has just enough public work to keep him occupied and does not bother about anything else. It makes him rather cross if I try to discuss plans for the future or things to do with the children, so we go on from day to day without looking forward much. His distaste for bothering about things is increasing—we all wonder what will happen when he gets home and details have to be faced.

Evie liked Dick Nevill—everyone did—but she knew that the financial affairs of the household were out of hand, and she was right. She called him "a very extravagant comptroller," and said, "... he won't let me do a thing. Victor does not attempt to check expense." When Victor did get around to doing so, it must have come as a shock.

In the reports prepared by Price Waterhouse, who audited "His Excellency the Duke of Devonshire's household accounts," the financial picture of those four years is laid out in cold, hard figures. The reports are prepared half-yearly, and from 1918 to 1921 they show the gradually increasing expenditures, and the mounting overdraft. In the second half of 1917 and the first six months of 1918, all is well; expenditure equals bank balance. But, by the beginning of 1919, the problem begins.

The bank balance on December 31, 1918, was a modest $487.70. By June 30, 1919, there is no balance, however modest, but a sizeable bank overdraft of $25,708.88. By December 31, 1920, the overdraft is an even more sizeable $115,754.38. By June 30, 1921, it has been reduced to $69,138.82, but only because the Duke of Devonshire has deposited a considerable sum of his own money: $84,912.50— roughly equivalent to over a million dollars today. So much for leaving home and becoming a viceroy to make money!

On the account sheet for the period ending June 30, 1921, there is an unusual addition to the heading "General

Household Expenditure." A bracketed entry alongside the usual items, such as provisions, fuel, light, salaries and wages, reads: "(Including advance of $1,166.62 to Lord Richard Nevill charged to salaries account)." The comptroller has obviously prevailed on the kindness of Victor Devonshire, who relied heavily on him, for an advance on his salary.

The reason for Dick Nevill's desperate need for money becomes clear in an article in *The Times*, twelve years later, on July 29, 1933. Under the heading "Lord Richard Nevill's Examination," the newspaper covers the declaration of bankruptcy by Lord Richard Plantagenet Nevill. By the time Lord Richard appeared in bankruptcy court he had assets of £447 and liabilities of £8525.

The story of Dora's ally and friend is sad, but not that uncommon: Dick Nevill had been living beyond his means for virtually all of his adult life, at the mercy of moneylenders, "from whom he had not been free for 40 years." The interest charges on his loans varied from 50 to 100 per cent, and he attributed his insolvency to this, and "to extravagance in living before 1930." He had previously been on the staff of the governor-general of Australia, but he had not worked since his time with the Devonshires in Canada.

Lord Richard was not a declared bankrupt for long; four months later he appeared again in bankruptcy court to be discharged. Certainly, he had made an effort to repay some of his debts—he always had—but the reason for the discharge is noteworthy. His age was taken into account (he was seventy), but the main thrust of the argument was that living high on the hog was a birthright of sorts: "The Registrar pointed out that the debtor attributed his insolvency to extravagance and heavy interest charges. From the circumstances of his birth and his associations it was, however, fairly obvious that considerable expenditure was necessitated."

If this was also Lord Richard's belief, it is no wonder that he ran the affairs of the governor-general with "unexampled splendour and severe indebtedness," to use David Cannadine's apt phrase about an earlier Duke of Devonshire's affairs!

Throughout Evie's letters, one has a sense of her clinging to the wreckage, trying desperately to harness forces beyond her control. One harness she would indeed be assuming once more, and that is exactly how she expresses it in a letter to her mother: "The Queen wants to put me straight back into harness ... I had hoped for a few months to settle down."

But even if she had had real power, it is unlikely she could have altered the forces at work in that post-war world. Devonshire House was gone, sold for £750,000. The gates were sold separately, to be preserved on the Piccadilly boundary of Green Park, their gilding redone "by a disabled ex-soldier trained by the Kitchener House Club." Evie was looking for a new London home—a process fraught with the usual problems: "Our Mr. Burke seems to have most extravagant ideas— as usual I am the only person to question the cost of all we want to do. It is a bore always to seem stingy but I believe we shall spend something huge if I don't fuss."

The usual problem was always money; the usual crisis in the Canada years was that her daughters would fall for the wrong person. Even Larry Minto fell victim to the usual Canadian crisis, making Marian Cook the first Canadian girl to marry an earl. Not only was she Canadian; she was a Catholic. Oswald Balfour, his best man, shadowed him for two days before the wedding to make sure he didn't sign anything that would compromise the religious beliefs of the future heir to the title. Mary Minto was very bitter about the whole affair— as well she might be. Larry's safe haven had turned out to be anything but that, and Evie's letters suggest that she had done nothing to discourage this particular aide-de-camp.

In 1920 she wrote to her mother: "It is curious to think what a difference our coming to Canada has made to our girls —it is almost certain that Maud would not have married Angus nor Dorothy Harold if we had been at home." However much she may have wanted to control her daughters, in the end she had not stopped them from following their hearts.

In one of her last letters home before they left Canada, Evie wrote: "We are just off to pay a farewell visit to Blue Sea. We have spent £5000 on the place & so far no one wants to buy it." They would never go back to New Lismore, and Lord Richard Nevill, that most extravagant comptroller, would be left in charge of trying to sell that "heavenly place."

DORA'S RECIPE FOR CHRISTMAS CAKE

30 eggs	1 1/2 lbs ground almonds
5 lbs butter	1 lb chopped cherries
5 lbs flour	4 grated lemon rinds
5 lbs sugar	black treacle and spices
1 1/2 lbs mixed peel	1/4 pint brandy
2 lbs sultanas	1/4 pint sherry or madeira
2 lbs raisins	

Mix together prepared fruits and peel. If liked, fruit may be soaked overnight in the brandy. Sieve together flour and spices. Beat butter, then cream with the sugar. Add lemon rind. Beat in each egg, gradually adding the ground almonds. Fold in the fruit and flour mixtures alternately until mixed. Add remaining sherry or madeira. A cake of this size requires long cooking for five hours or more in a slow oven (about 250–275 degrees) and needs protecting so the outside does not overcook. The pan stands on thick cardboard, and is lined with doubled brown paper, which is greased, and protected outside by layers of newspaper tied around it. The oven is too cool for any of this to catch fire. Store for at least three weeks (preferably much more) wrapped in brandy-soaked cheesecloth.

Mixing a cake of this size and texture is very hard work. Dora was a strong woman, but she had a trick of the trade: she used her hands. She told her sons it was the best way, not just the practical way, because the oils in the skin made the mixture blend more smoothly. She also made a Christmas pudding and mincemeat every Christmas, and these were kept for the *following* season.

The Duchess and Dora

... a round peg in a round hole if ever there was one

DEBORAH, DUCHESS OF DEVONSHIRE,

THE HOUSE: A PORTRAIT OF CHATSWORTH

A n alarming woman, her grandson Andrew Devonshire calls her, and that is how most people remember Evie. The years of her middle and old age would bring her many trials, and she would frequently make use of "the queen stunt" to face them and the world—the only possible front for an impossible role in the latter half of the twentieth century. In 1925 Victor suffered a stroke and, from then on, that kind and unflappable man became a morose and bad-tempered semi-invalid; only small children could penetrate Victor's silence and anger. For thirteen years there was a striking reversal of roles. It was Victor who was either distant and removed or railing hysterically against the world and those of its inhabitants who happened to be near him, Evie who carried calmly on as though nothing had changed.

It was not a bad philosophy of life in the circumstances, to control those things she could control. The preservation of Chatsworth and the Devonshire estates became the focus of Evie's life, and within that magnificent framework she continued to put on a show of *ancien régime* splendour.

In his memoirs Harold Macmillan describes the Chatsworth family Christmas, with Granny Evie receiving the family at the foot of the staircase in the great Painted Hall, the gold plate out on display in the dining-room, countless children roller-skating in the orangery under the watchful eyes of an army of nurses and nursery maids, evensong celebrated amid the Verrio paintings and Gibbon carvings of the Chatsworth chapel, the ceremony of present-giving among the Canovas in the Statue Gallery, with all the servants in attendance—"To remember them [those Christmases] now is to recall another world, almost as remote ... as the descriptions of Count Rostov's family in *War and Peace*." Unlike the Romanovs, the British monarchy and the Devonshires would survive.

Like Victor, it was only with children that Evie could let slip that alarming façade. Gone was the Evie of the 1890s, whose elderly aunts adored her, precisely because she did not have "a cutting tongue." One of the Chatsworth archivists recalls being at a formal occasion at Buxton when he was about six years old, and how kind Evie was to the children, and how happy they were. Not so the mayor, who stood close by. The small boy could hear the mayoral chains rattling in fear of his formidable patroness. But he also remembers that Evie carried a small notebook in which she kept details about people on the estate—who had a new grandchild, the name of a favourite pet dog—so that she could ask about the things that mattered in their lives.

Remoteness suited Evie very well; as she grew older she was better with things than with people. The notebooks she kept on every aspect of the maintenance of that great estate bear witness to an astonishing attention to detail. Waste not, want not, make do and mend—everything was grist to her decorating mill:

> There was some difficulty in getting old plate glass to match the other windows [in the Painted Hall]—new glass looks different from outside. Luckily for us the suffragettes broke some old windows in Bond Street. Mr. Walker bought them up & the glass when bevelled matched perfectly.

Servants would continue to be a problem:

At one time a particularly energetic head housemaid scrubbed all the statues & busts including those in plaster. There is now a strict rule that no washing should be done without permission. Soap is fatal to marble ... Not very long ago a new head housemaid rubbed all the bronzes with a cloth which must have had beeswax and turpentine on it, although she denied this. The patina of the bronzes is terribly damaged.

But Evie improved the servants' quarters, giving the kitchen maids "a decent sitting room" and seeing that the housemaids were "better lodged."

From the mildewed hangings of "the cumbrous bed" in the Red Room, to her rejection of the "obsolete and ignorant" use of old iron bedsteads to reinforce concrete, nothing escaped her eagle eye. Finally, she was mistress of her realm.

In her book *The House*, the present duchess tells a story of Evie sticking a three-halfpenny stamp on an envelope with the wrong address on it, ringing for a footman, and ordering up a kettle of boiling water from the kitchens. The footman made the long trek there and back, and Evie had the stamp steamed off the envelope. There is something about that anecdote that is quintessentially Evie.

Beyond the walls of Chatsworth and Hardwick Hall, the world went its way, careering towards another war. Lismore was pillaged during the troubles in Ireland, even though the local postmistress had phoned Michael Collins, the rebel leader, and asked him to spare the house, because the Devonshires had been good to the local people.

Evie's youngest daughter, Anne, would be left by her husband for another woman; Dorothy would carry on a very public affair with a very public figure—Robert Boothby, a charismatic Tory politician. Evie's younger son Charlie would extend even further and more exotically what had once been a tight-knit circle of interrelationships, by marrying Adele Astaire, the sister of Fred Astaire—a star in a vastly different firmament.

In holding on to past glories, Evie held them for the future —and for those who could only stand beyond the castle walls and marvel at that "unexampled splendour." As to "severe indebtedness," that has only been alleviated by turning Chatsworth into one of the most successful of Britain's palaces and great houses on view to the public. It is now run by the trustees of the Chatsworth Settlement, with even the present duke paying rent for the portion of the house he and his family use. In 1959 Hardwick Hall, its contents and surrounding farmland were handed over to the government in lieu of death duties, and it is now owned and run by the National Trust.

Victor died in 1938, writing in his diary up to about a week before his death. Evie Devonshire, the dowager duchess, took up residence in Hardwick Hall, Bess of Hardwick's great Elizabethan mansion.

Alarming women, both of them, Bess and Evie. In the deep window bay of the Low Great Chamber, Bess's dining-room, Evie worked through the years of her long widowhood repairing the superb Flemish tapestries that are among the rarest and finest of Bess's treasures. From her alcove, she could see the moorland over which another alarming woman, Cartimandua, Queen of the Brigantes, led her tribes into battle, centuries before Bess of Hardwick used ambition, intelligence and four marriages to acquire great wealth, lands and two magnificent houses: Hardwick and Chatsworth.

Lady Lansdowne was right; she had said Evie would strengthen as she grew older. In many ways, this was the most fulfilling time of Evie's life, sitting and working with patience and skill on those exquisite masterpieces. She would need the serenity the work gave her, the peace of mind she had found in India as a young woman painting the sensitive watercolour interiors of her home in the Raj, which now hang on the walls of the Mary Queen of Scots' apartments at

Chatsworth. She would outlive not only her husband, but her son, Eddy, and her grandson, William, heir to the dukedom, killed in action in 1944. Her son-in-law, Ivan Cobbold, would also be killed in the same year during an attack on London. William's younger brother, Andrew, would become the Eleventh Duke of Devonshire. If Eddy had died four months later, the heir would have been spared over two million pounds in death duties; severe indebtedness, it would seem, never ended.

Evie died in 1960 in her London home at Carlton Gardens at the age of ninety. A letter in *The Times* on April 6, 1960, from a Professor G. Potter bears witness to a rather different Evie from the one generally remembered:

> Her devotion to Hardwick Hall, her wonderful knowledge of its contents and history, her interest in the gardens, and the warmth of her welcome to many visitors, with whom she liked to take tea, were outstanding. Her own contributions to the tapestries showed her skill with the needle and her willingness to unfold her stores of information to the inquirer were aspects of her wide range and beneficent activity. She had many of the virtues of the Bess of Hardwick who built the house in which she loved to dwell without any of the less attractive features of that remarkable character.

Once, Evie was visited by an expert from the Victoria and Albert Museum who was taking a look at Bess's tapestries. When he saw Evie's handiwork, he told her she should be at the V and A herself: "You are wasted as a duchess." Of all the compliments Evelyn, Duchess of Devonshire, had in her long life, none gave her greater pleasure.

There are ghosts at Hardwick Hall, where Bess still walks the corridors of her mansion. Those who work there late at night feel her "like a sharp pain between the eyes." Evie is there too, her memory preserved in the drawing-room (My Lady's

Withdrawing Chamber), her papers still on the writing-desk with her spectacles, a photograph of a young Victor in a silver frame.

There are no ghosts at Chatsworth, they say. But when you walk down those backstage corridors with their stone walls and flagged floors, away from the dazzle of light on silver-gilt and gold, you are aware of presences: centuries of parlour-maids and scullery maids, postillions and footmen. In an alcove below a long window overlooking the courtyard sits an old rocking-horse, battered and faded, with only a few hairs left of his mane and tail. With a side-saddle on his back, his function is very clear: he is a rocking-horse for little girls.

Dora

If those eyes could only speak
DORA LEE, TO ADA SERGEANT

Indeed. The story of that thirteen-year-old's extraordinary climb up the downstairs ladder was never really told in her lifetime. Her son, Stanley, feels that if her first-born child, a girl, had survived, his mother might have told the daughter more about her life than she told her three sons. The funeral bill for two-and-a-half-year-old Nancy Mahala is still among Dora's papers, and the card from the wreath: "To our darling Nancy from her sorrowing mother and father." "She was born an invalid," Dora told her boys.

Archie and Dora began their life together in Ottawa, purchasing a confectionery store on Main Street East with some of Dora's considerable nest egg, and living in the apartment above the store. Archie may have come from a nation of shop-keepers, but he was not cut out to be one of them. The business failed, bringing them close to bankruptcy. They sold the premises, and Dora's husband enlisted in the Royal Canadian Air Force, where he found his true *métier*.

For three and a half years, the family was apart, but in 1927 Dora and her two sons went to join Archie at Camp Borden. The good times were back again, with Archie forming his own orchestra at the camp, and playing the piano for the local movie-house. Then came the war.

Men like Dora's husband come into their own in times of war. Archie Vince organized the first RCAF recruiting centre in Toronto in September 1939. By 1940 he was commissioned and quickly became a flying officer. The chief of the air staff expressed his appreciation of "the exceptional ability and zeal of Flying Officer Vince and intimated that the fullest consideration would be given to accelerated promotion of an officer with such qualifications, experience and ability...." By 1942 he was promoted to the rank of wing commander, and on April 17, 1942, Dora went back to Rideau Hall. She was there to see her husband awarded the MBE [Member of the British Empire] by the governor-general, the Earl of Athlone.

One can imagine the mixture of emotions that must have filled Dora when she went through the front gates of Government House—she, who had always taken the back entrance, walked along the driveway past the gasometer to the kitchens downstairs, watched her culinary creations carried up to the state rooms to decorate Victor's and Evie's table. Just over twenty years later, there she was once more, in those state rooms with her wing commander husband, talking to the earl and countess after the investiture, an equal among equals.

Little wonder she rarely spoke of her life belowstairs because, for all her achievements, that was how it would be perceived: as a life of servitude. "Proud not to be classed among them anyhow," Dora had put that class stigma behind her long ago, and now she was married to a man of some stature in Canadian society. But the qualities that had taken her to the top of the downstairs ladder—her remarkable perseverance, organizational skills and sheer guts—were passed on to another generation.

Following his father's example, her eldest son, Stanley, joined up as soon as he could after his eighteenth birthday, and served with both the RAF and the RCAF during the Second World War. It was his own father who pinned his wings on him when he graduated from Malton.

Dora Lee lives again in her two granddaughters: one, Brenda, has climbed the corporate ladder and is vice-president of marketing with the Royal Bank of Canada Mutual Funds Inc.; the other, Nancy, worked for Ontario Hydro's foreign service as a financial adviser in the Ethiopian hydroelectric system, and is now a manager with Nortel Philippines. Like their grandmother, both have achieved in areas previously dominated by men. Both have kept the family name, Vince.

Dora and Archie died within six months of each other: he on October 3, 1961; she on February 12, 1962. They rest side by side in Mount Pleasant Cemetery in London, Ontario.

Dora always maintained that everything British was best—often to the annoyance of her Canadian children. Thirty-six years after coming to Canada as Dora Vince, she made her first trip back to her native country. Her son, Stanley, and his wife, Beth, met her at the airport on her return. By coincidence, Prime Minister John Diefenbaker was on the same plane as Dora.

When the usual greetings were over, she looked at them both and said, firmly, "I am now a Canadian." Then she asked, "Could we stop on the way home for a glass of water—with ice cubes in it?"

They stopped in Hamilton at the Royal Connaught Hotel, named for the Duke of Connaught, the predecessor of her Rideau Hall employers, for whom she had cooked on his visit in the summer of 1919. As she sat in the bar, drinking her ice-cold water, one wonders if Dora's thoughts went back to those upper-crust stars in the British class constellation for whom she had cooked *Saumon Lucullus*, *Brochettes d'Ortolans* and *Fraises à la Ritz*, to a time when she had been as much a star herself in her own belowstairs firmament as a Guinness, a countess or a duchess, in that lost, golden world.

Menus

~ ℰ ~

Diner du 11 Juin, 1914.
——————
Cantaloup Rafaichi.
Tortue Claire.
Petites Truites au Bleu.
Poulardes à la Reine.
Selles de Chéselles.
Cailles Royales en Cocotte.
Cœurs de Laitues.
Asperges de Paris, sauce Délice.
Ananas Soufflé
aux Fraises des Bois.
Friandises.
Ramequins à l'Alsacienne.

DÎNER DU 11 JUIN, 1914

Cantaloup Rafaichi
Tortue Claire
Petites Truites au Bleu
Poulardes à la Reine
Selles de Chézelles
Cailles Royales en Cocotte
Coeurs de Laitues
Asperges de Paris, sauce Délice
Ananas Soufflé aux Fraises des Bois
Ramequins à l'Alsacienne

This is the only example among Dora's papers of a menu from her freelance days just before the outbreak of war, for an engagement party or a wedding. Many of the dishes (such as the oddly named *Selles de Chézelles*) are the same as those on the menu for the coming-out ball for Sybil Neumann, which suggests that Eugène Mangonnaux played an important role in Dora's culinary education. Among her papers are two photographs of an unidentified man and woman in Edwardian dress in a setting that, from the vegetation, could be the south of France—Chef Mangonnaux and his wife, perhaps?

DÎNER DE 16 AOÛT

Potage Nicose Froid
Saumon Grillé
Poulets Bearnaise
Légumes
Soufflé glacé au Pêche

This is the simple but elegant wartime evening meal Dora laid out for the visit of the Duke of Connaught in 1918. From the cold soup to the iced peach soufflé it is a refreshing selection of dishes for a hot summer day, and uses seasonable and easily obtainable ingredients.

SOUPER DU 6 MARS
Evening Skating Party

Consommé chaud et froid
Filets de slips Moscovite
Poulets et langues découpés
Galantines de dindonneaux truffées
Jambons froids en tranches
Sandwichs volaille
Langues
Jambon
Saumon
Bavarois chocolat
Kirsh

Café
Marasquin
Gelées curaçao
Kummet
Champagne Menthe
Glaces vanille et framboises
Gâteaux

SOUPER DE BAL

Consommé Riche chaud et froid
Poulets en Cocottes aux Primeurs
Côtelettes d'Agneau
Petits Pois
Cailles rôties
Pommes paille
Filets de Soles à la Britannia
Petits Homards à la Norvégienne
Médaillons de Canard aux Cerises
Salades à la Russe
Jambon, Langue, et Volaille à l'Aspic
Sandwich Variés
Petits Pains garnis, de Foie Gras
Macédoine de Fruits frappés au Champagne
Bavarois et Gelées
Glaces Vanille et Fraises
Pâtisseries
Rafraîchessements

There are parallels in the layout of this meal and the *Souper du Bal, 23 Mai, 1911*, from Dora's Sunderland House days: the choice of hot and cold soups, the sandwiches, the *Bavarois*, the ice-creams. Dora has omitted the salads, which would probably have frozen, and certainly would have been less welcome on a frosty Ottawa winter night. The word "slips" for the fish course is a puzzle—possibly it should read "sole." There is a similar dish, *Filets de Sole Moscovite Froid*, on the 1919 menu for Blanche's wedding. The year of this party is probably 1919, in which case the duke would have missed it, for he was away in Montreal. However, the newly arrived aides-de-camp, whom he described in his diaries as "quite charming" and "most promising," would have had a good time dancing with Rachel, as they had the previous night at Lady Kingsmill's.

Diner du 30 Avril

Consommé Quenelles
Filets de Sole Moscovite Froid
Côtelettes d'Agneau Petits Pois
Poulets Béarnaise
Légumes
Asperges, Sauce Maltaise
Bombe Marquis

SOUPER DU 30 AVRIL

Consommé Claire
Salade de Homard
Galantine de Volaille Froid
Salade
Boeuf à la Mode en Gelée
Salade
Sandwiches Variety
Fraises à la Ritz
Gelée aux Liqueurs
Trufle

These two meals were prepared by Dora in 1919 for the Rideau Hall celebration of Blanche's wedding in England to Ivan Cobbold. The duke's diary entry for the day reads: "Blanche's wedding day. Sure she will be very happy. Dinner of 74 all told for Blanche's wedding—mostly boys and girls. Danced afterwards." According to the *Ottawa Citizen* report, the dancing was to the music of the aptly named Professor L.F. Valentine's orchestra.

DINER DU 21 MAI

Consummé Bruniose
Truites Saumonée Bouilli
Côtelettes d'Agneau Petit Pois
Mousse de Volaille Veniose Légumes
Asperges, Sauce Maltaise
Biscuit Glacé Waldorf

This dinner was held in honour of Sir Robert Baden-Powell, the founder of the Boy Scouts movement, and his wife. There was a Boy Scouts Rally held at Rideau Hall, with the lads having tea in the Racquet Room and the Ball Room. Baden-Powell, hero of the defence of Mafeking during the Boer War, the man who was called "the wolf who never sleeps" by the Matabele, was dismissed by the duke in his diaries as "rather tiresome"—as was Lady Baden-Powell.

Diner du 28 Mai

Consommé Quenelles
Petit Truites Meniere
Poulet Froid Portuagaise
Salade
Filet de Boeuf Printanier
Légumes
Asperges, Sauce Maltaise
Souffle
Glacé
Jubilee

A dinner held in 1919 in honour of Sir Robert and Lady Borden which "went well," according to the duke's diary. Victor got on well with Borden, partly because he played a good game of bridge. He would later confess in his diary that he had difficulty holding on to his emotions when they said goodbye at the end of his tenure. Among the guests was Mr. Hume Cronyn, Member of Parliament, father of the actor Hume Cronyn.

SOUPER DU 30 AOÛT

Consommé Chaud
Mayonaise de Homard
Poulet et Jambon en Gelée
Caneton Molière Froid
Quillot de Boeuf en Gelée
Sandwiches Variety
Gelée aux Liqueurs
Cornets a la Crême
Framboises Chantilly
Glaces Cantaloup et Vanilla

SOUPER DU 29 AOUT

Consommé Chaud
Salade de Homard
Petit Mousses de Jambon
Salade
Patties de Poulet et Saucisses
Sandwiches Variety
Macedoine aux Fruits
Bavaroise au Chocolat et Café
Trifles
Glaces Vanilla et Orange

Two supper menus from the Prince of Wales' visit in 1919. The headline in the *Ottawa Citizen* declared "The Prince Again Dances," and described him as having "won his way into the hearts of the Canadian people by the charm of his personality and the infectiousness of his smile." Dora appears to have rung subtle changes between the two menus, which are for two successive nights; it would be interesting to know, for example, what the difference was between the two cold lobster dishes.

Note

There are errors in the French on many of the menus, but they have been reproduced just as they were originally printed.

Sources

Much of the material for this book comes from three archival sources: the private correspondence of Evelyn, Ninth Duchess of Devonshire, which is held at Chatsworth in Derbyshire, and Bowood House, Wiltshire; the diaries of Victor Devonshire, the Ninth Duke, also at Chatsworth (the diaries of the years in Canada are also on microfilm in the National Archives, Ottawa); and the collection of Dora's postcards, papers and menus held by her eldest son, Stanley G. Vince, in London, Ontario. When the memorabilia came into Stan's possession, there was little or no organization of the material, and he sorted and catalogued the postcards, papers and menus, and obtained such documents as birth certificates. He also retraced his English roots, visiting and photographing his parents' and grandparents' towns, homes and places of employment. Stan and Dora's daughter-in-law, Beth Vince, shared memories and recollections, pieces of information and insights that have added immeasurably to Dora's story.

Part One, Scullery Maid

CHAPTER ONE
HIGH AND LOWLY

The description of Evie's wedding comes from *The Times*, which gave it extensive coverage in their Court Circular, a regular feature of the newspaper, which also was used to trace the social events she attended when she returned to England in

1890 and 1891. Details of Evie's life in India, and her meeting
with Victor Cavendish, are from letters held at Chatsworth and
Bowood House. The picture of the Lansdownes' life in Canada
comes from various sources, but principally from her brother
Lord Frederic Hamilton's memoir, *The Days Before Yesterday*
(London: Hodder and Stoughton, 1920), which also describes
the Lansdownes' life in India. There are one or two possibilities for the rejected suitor, Willie Peel, but since the research
was not conclusive, it seemed best to leave well, or ill, alone.

The anecdote about Evie and "the ugly old face" was told
to me by the present duke, Andrew Devonshire, who also suggested his grandparents may have met because the two London
properties of the families adjoined each other.

The blue radzimir of Evie's going-away dress was a fine
ribbed silk produced in Britain, often dyed black and used for
mourning. Lisse was a trim of silk gauze.

CHAPTER TWO

POOR LITTLE DEVILS

The information on the early years of Dora's life comes from
the family archives, chiefly from postcards of the period. The
cards give the addresses and, in most cases, the name of Dora's
employers, but rarely do they go into more detail. In the case of
Dora's first London employer, Mrs. Lewin, very little was known.
She was traced through the London Post Office Directory for
the period, which listed her as a widow. Her husband's profession was established by tracing further back through the directories to the years before his death. Depending on the level
in society of the individual, more information about Dora's
employers over the years was found in such sources as *Debrett's*
or *Burke's* Peerage, *Who Was Who*, or the official directories of
various professions—in Mr. Lewin's case, the legal profession.

There are many books on the life and hierarchy of the servant, but the two main texts consulted were *Belowstairs in the*

Great Country Houses by Adeline Hartcup (London: Sidgwick and Jackson, 1980), and *The House, A Portrait of Chatsworth* by the Duchess of Devonshire (London: Macmillan Ltd., 1982)

For information on the aristocracy that gives both an over-all and a detailed picture of the evolution and the fortunes of the class, David Cannadine's work is invaluable. I have primarily used *The Decline and Fall of the British Aristocracy* (New Haven and London: Yale University Press, 1990), and *Aspects of Aristocracy: Grandeur and Decline in Modern Britain* (New Haven and London: Yale University Press, 1994).

Apart from the information in Evie's letters, Victor's diaries and Lord Frederic Hamilton's personal recollections, most of the material on Rideau Hall in this chapter and in Chapter Nine comes from R.H. Hubbard's *Rideau Hall: An Illustrated History of Government House, Ottawa, from Victorian Times to the Present Day* (Montreal and London: McGill-Queen's University Press, 1977).

CHAPTER THREE

An Epidemic of Smartness

Of all the books on the great Auguste Escoffier, perhaps the most complete—and certainly the most magnificently illus-trated—is Timothy Shaw's *The World of Escoffier* (New York: The Vendome Press, 1994). Any of Escoffier's recipes used in the book come from Dora's 1913 edition of his *Guide Culinaire*.

The information on Evie's reluctance to assume her sym-bolic role is from the Ninth Duke's diaries. The present Duke of Devonshire told me a story (tongue in cheek, perhaps?) about his grandmother visiting Chiswick House unannounced, after it was turned into an asylum, and walking in the grounds. When approached by staff members and asked what she was doing there, she replied, "I am the Duchess of Devonshire"—whereupon she was promptly taken inside.

Part Two, Kitchen Maid

CHAPTER FOUR
TUT TUT, DORA

Ernest Haliburton Cunard was the grandson of Sir Samuel Cunard, first baronet, co-founder of the British North American Royal Mail Steam Packet Company and founder of the Cunard Steam Ship Company. Samuel Cunard was born in Halifax, Nova Scotia, and first made his fortune operating whaling ships between Nova Scotia and the Pacific.

In 1833 he was one of the prime movers in the launch of the *Royal William*, the first steam-powered vessel to cross the Atlantic. By 1839 he had won a government contract to carry the mail between Liverpool and Halifax, and Boston and Quebec. From then on, he and his successors lived in Britain and the baronetcy was conferred upon him by Queen Victoria in 1859.

Dora's sweetheart, the "Territorial," was a member of the home defence army, which was recruited on a local basis.

The story about Edward Horner comes from Philip Ziegler's biography, *Diana Cooper* (London: Hamish Hamilton, 1981), and is also quoted in *Unquiet Souls* by Angela Lambert (New York: Harper and Row, 1984). Also from Angela Lambert's book comes the story of Lord Curzon and the disgraced maid.

Paul Levy's account of the Savoy scandal appeared in *The Observer* on May 19, 1985. The papers had been delivered to his desk two years earlier with an anonymous note, and they were photocopies of confessions from César Ritz, Auguste Escoffier and their *maître d'hôtel*. In 1985 Levy did not know the identity of his anonymous informant on what he called "the Foodgate scandal," and referred to him or her as "Deep Palate."

John Allemang kindly allowed me to quote from his *Globe and Mail* column of Aug. 23, 1997.

CHAPTER FIVE
MOUTH WIDE OPEN

Most of the background on the Pears Soap Company is from William Beable's *Romance of Great Businesses* (London: Heath, Cranton Ltd., 1926). Consuelo Vanderbilt tells her own story in her autobiography, *The Glitter and the Gold* (New York: Harper, 1952), and Canadian biographer Marian Fowler recounts the fascinating life of this beautiful activist in *In a Gilded Cage: From Heiress to Duchess* (Toronto: Random House of Canada Ltd., 1993), her book about the dollar-princesses.

Part Three, Cook

CHAPTER SIX
BEER AND BARONETS

Background on the Guinness family history came principally from two biographies: *The Guinness Legend* by Michèle Guinness (London: Hodder and Stoughton, 1989), and *The Silver Salver: The Story of the Guinness Family* (London: Granada Publishing, 1981). For all their wealth and position in society, the Guinnesses were not really part of that extraordinary class known as the Irish Ascendancy. The stories about the Irish servants come from *Life in an Irish Country House* by Mark Bence Jones (London: Constable, 1996), and the same author has a very full account of the Devonshires' life at Lismore Castle in *Twilight of the Ascendancy* (London: Constable, 1987). In fiction, author Molly Keane creates a superb picture of the class in such novels as *Loving and Giving* and *Time After Time*.

Because Dora said so little about her training with Escoffier, I have had to build up the picture from accounts of others— all men—who trained with him. The most complete picture of *Le Maître*'s methods and procedures is in Pierre Hamp's *Mes*

Métiers (Paris: Editions de la Nouvelle Revue Française, 1930). I am indebted to Cath Oberholtzer of the Cobourg and District Historical Society, who told me the story about the taboo against the presence of a menstruating woman in the kitchen —which *she* was told by a French chef in the 1980s!

CHAPTER SEVEN
BUTTERFLIES AND BIGWIGS

The story of the young Evie in this chapter is based on private correspondence—chiefly from her mother—held in the Chatsworth archives, and the early diaries of her husband. For a revealing account of nineteenth-century attitudes to women's ailments, I recommend the 1876 work of the vice-president of the Dublin Obstetrical Society, Thomas More Madden: *The Principal Health Resorts of Europe and Africa*. Apart from his views on the mental effects of such disorders, from which I have quoted, it is sobering how slowly knowledge has advanced on the understanding and treatment of endometriosis and ectopic pregnancies, for example. And, even in the twentieth century, certain spas retain a reputation for producing babies—the "spa babies" of women who return from taking the waters. This, of course, has other implications besides improved fertility that certainly do not apply in Evie's case.

The figures on Victor's parliamentary attendance are from papers at Chatsworth that were probably prepared for distribution among his constituents.

Maud Baillie's memoir, *Early Memories* (Worcester, England; Billing and Sons Ltd., 1989) has many useful personal recollections about her family in England and Canada—particularly her mother, father and older brother, Eddy. The theft of Evie's bracelet is mentioned in Victor's diaries, and the details come from reports in *The Times*. Evie herself writes about the chaos over chairs and chandeliers at Devonshire House years later in her Chatsworth notebooks.

CHAPTER EIGHT

DESPERATE ACTS

Information on the 1914–1918 war came from various sources, but I am particularly indebted to Martin Gilbert's *First World War* for information on the Great War in this chapter and Chapters Nine, Ten and Eleven. The book is a marvellous combination of straightforward chronology and evocative detail of that disastrous conflict.

Ethel Chadwick's diaries and papers are held at the National Archives in Ottawa, and have a great deal to say—from a very personal viewpoint—about the Connaughts and the Devonshires.

Part Four, First Cook

CHAPTER NINE

OF VASSALS AND MARBLE HALLS

All of Evie's letters, from which I have quoted in Chapters Nine, Ten and Eleven, are held at Bowood House, Wiltshire, the home of the Lansdowne family. The overwhelming majority of them are to her mother. All of them begin "My darling mother," and end with "Your very loving Evie." She is not only concerned about herself, but she frequently enquires after her mother's health, worrying about how rationing will affect her strength, and tries to comfort a grieving Lady Lansdowne who is having difficulty coming to terms with the death of her son Charles in the war.

An additional and illuminating source of information about the life of the governor-general's wife is the collection of photographs and papers given to Chatsworth by the family of the Ninth Duchess's secretary, Elsie Saunders, after she died. The photographs generally show the Devonshires and their entourage at play, but the papers give a far less entertaining picture of the nuts and bolts of the chatelaine's job.

CHAPTER TEN,
A HEAVENLY PLACE

Sandra Gwyn has a wonderfully entertaining picture of "The Naughty Nine" and Ethel Chadwick in *Tapestry of War* (Toronto: HarperCollins Publishers Ltd., 1992).

The story about Angus giving "the big rush" to Lord Shaughnessy's daughters is told by Maud herself in her memoirs. Her account of the family's trip to the Laurentians and the Gaspé conveys the enjoyment and pleasure the Devonshires took in those Canadian holidays, which gave the family a chance to be together.

All the enquiries and combing of newspaper columns for information about the league in which Dora's Rideau Hall hockey team played, and the trophy they won, have turned up nothing. Perhaps, hopefully, some reader may have in his or her possession another photo, or a newspaper clipping, or a program, that will throw some light on what was obviously an event of some significance.

CHAPTER ELEVEN
THE PARTING OF THE WAYS

The details of the governor-general's financial affairs are from the reports of Price Waterhouse, held in the Chatsworth archives, and *The Times* carried the story of Lord Richard Nevill's bankruptcy.

Larry Minto and his mother, Lady Mary Minto, make quite a few appearances in Evie's Bowood letters. Not only was Larry unsatisfactory, but apparently Mary Minto caused all kinds of trouble when she came over for her son's wedding by making negative remarks about the royal family! More than that, she was "most catty," complaining to the aides-de-camp about Victor and saying that the Devonshires were "out of touch." This made her sad when she thought how "intimate" she had

been with everyone when Lord Minto was governor-general—
a particularly intriguing observation, when taken in conjunction
with Chapter 21, "Minto's Folly," in Sandra Gwyn's *The Private
Capital*.

EPILOGUE

"An alarming woman," were the Duke of Devonshire's first
words to me about his grandmother. He went on to explain that
she was delightful with small children, but once you reached
the age of about six, she became over-critical, and nothing you
could do was good enough. However, when I suggested that
she never pretended to be other than she was, he said, "Yes,
she didn't dish the dirt with the rest of the girls." When I
added the previous line of the song, "She didn't go to Harlem
in ermine and pearls," he agreed. The duke told me the story
of the expert from the Victoria and Albert Museum, which also
appears in *The House*.

Tom Askey, one of the archivists at Chatsworth, experienced "the sharp pain between the eyes" when working late
one night at Hardwick Hall—a phenomenon also felt by others at night in the great house. When it happened to him, the
person he was with knew what had happened immediately and
said, "Yes, it's Bess."

Selected Bibliography

Angus, William. *The Seats of the Nobility and Gentry in Great Britain and Wales*. New York: Garland Publications, 1982.

Aslet, Clive. *The Last Country Houses*. New Haven and London: Yale University Press, 1982.

Aspinall-Oglander, Cecil Faber. *Military Operations, Gallipoli*. London: Heinemann Ltd., 1932.

Baillie, Maud. *Early Memories*. Judith Cameron (ed.). Worcester, England; Billing and Sons Ltd., 1989.

Balsan, Consuelo Vanderbilt. *The Glitter and the Gold*. New York: Harper, 1952.

Barr, Pat and Ray Desmond. *Simla: A Hill Station in British India*. New York: Scribner, 1978.

Beable, William Henry. *Romance of Great Businesses*. London: Heath, Cranton Ltd., 1926.

Bence-Jones, Mark. *Twilight of the Ascendancy*. London: Constable, 1987.

Bence-Jones, Mark. *Life in an Irish Country House*. London: Constable, 1996.

Birmingham, Stephen. *Duchess: The Story of Wallis Warfield Windsor*. Boston, Toronto: Little, Brown and Company, 1981.

Bland, John Otway Percy. *Li Hung Chang*. New York: Holt, 1917.

Bolitho, Hector. *King Edward VIII, An Intimate Biography*. New York: Literary Guild of America, 1937.

Bonham Carter, Mark and Mark Pottle, ed. *Lantern Slides. The Diaries and Letters of Violet Bonham Carter. 1904–1914*. London: Weidenfeld and Nicolson, 1996.

Borden, Robert Laird. *Memoirs*. Toronto: Macmillan, 1938.

Brown, Robert Craig. *Robert Laird Borden: A Biography. Volume II. 1914–1937*. Toronto: Macmillan, 1980.

Cannadine, David. *The Pleasures of the Past*. London: Collins, 1989.

Cannadine, David. *The Decline and Fall of the British Aristocracy*. New Haven and London: Yale University Press, 1990.

Cannadine, David. *Aspects of Aristocracy: Grandeur and Decline in Modern Britain*. New Haven and London: Yale University Press, 1994.

Candee, Helen Churchill. *Weaves and Draperies: Classic and Modern*. New York: Frederick A. Stokes and Co., 1930.

Cellier, Francois. *Gilbert, Sullivan and D'Oyly Carte*. London: Pitman, 1927.

Clemenson, Heather A. *English Country Houses and Landed Estates*. London and Canberra: Croom Helm, 1982. New York: St. Martin's Press, 1982.

Cooper, Diana. *The Rainbow Comes and Goes*. London: Rupert Hart-Davis, 1958.

Cowan, John. *Canada's Governors-General: Lord Monck to General Vanier*, Centennial Edition. Toronto: York Publishing Co. Ltd., 1967.

CPR. *His Royal Highness the Prince of Wales Tour of Canada*. CPR, 1919.

Crewe, Quentin. *The Frontiers of Privilege: A Century of Social Conflict as Reflected in the Queen*. London: Collins, 1961.

Davies, G.J.L. *The May Court Dispensary and Related Institutions*. Ottawa: Historical Society of Ottawa, 1988.

Devonshire, The Duchess of. *The House: a Portrait of Chatsworth*. London: Macmillan, 1982.

Devonshire, The Duchess of. *The Estate: a View from Chatsworth*. London: Macmillan, 1990.

Disher, M. Willson. *Music Hall Parade*. New York: Charles Scribner's Sons, 1938. London: B.T. Batsford Ltd., 1938.

Dittmar, F.J. & J.J. Colledge. *British Warships, 1914–1919*. London: Ian Allan, 1972.

Escoffier, Auguste. *The Escoffier Cook Book, A Guide to the Fine Art of Cookery*. London: William Heinemann, 1913.

Escott, Thomas Hay Sweet. *Club Makers and Club Members*. New York: Sturgis and Walton Co., 1914.

Fairchild. *Fairchild's Dictionary of Textiles*. New York: Fairchild Publications, 1967.

Fielding, Daphne. *The Duchess of Jermyn Street*. London: Eyre and Spottiswoode, 1964.

Flower, Raymond and Michael Wynn Jones. *One Hundred Years of Motoring: An RAC Social History of the Car*. Maidenhead: The Royal Automobile Club in association with McGraw Hill Book Company, 1981.

Foreman, John. *The Vanderbilts and the Gilded Age: Architectural Aspirations*. New York: St. Martin's Press, 1991.

Fowler, Marian. *In a Gilded Cage: From Heiress to Duchess*. Toronto: Random House of Canada Ltd., 1993.

Gibbon, John Murray. *Steel of Empire; The Romantic History of the Canadian Pacific*. Toronto: McClelland & Stewart, 1935.

Gilbert, Martin. *First World War*. London: Weidenfeld and Nicolson, 1994. Toronto: Stoddart Publishing Company Ltd., 1994.

Gossage, Carolyn. *A Question of Privilege: Canada's Independent Schools*. Toronto: Peter Martin Associates Ltd., 1977.

Graham, Winifred. *That Reminds Me*. London: Skeffington and Sons Ltd., 1945.

Granville, Augustus Bozzi. *The Spas of Germany*. London: H. Colburn, 1839.

Graves, Charles. *Leather Armchairs*. London: Cassell, 1963.

Guinness, Michèle. *The Guinness Legend*. London: Hodder and Stoughton, 1989.

Gwyn, Sandra. *The Private Capital: Ambition and Love in the Age of Macdonald and Laurier*. Toronto: HarperCollins, 1984.

Gwyn, Sandra. *Tapestry of War: A Private View of Canadians in the Great War*. Toronto: HarperCollins, 1992.

Hamilton, Lord Frederic. *The Vanished World of Yesterday*. London: Hodder and Stoughton, 1950.

Hamp, Pierre. *Mes Métiers*. Paris: Editions de la Nouvelle Revue Française, 1930.

Hants and Dorset Court Guide and County Blue Book, The. London: C.W. Deacon, 1897.

Hartcup, Adeline. *Belowstairs in the Great Country Houses*. London: Sidgwick and Jackson, 1980.

Hartcup, Adeline. *Children of the Great Country Houses*. London: Sidgwick and Jackson, 1982.

Hendrick, Burton J. *The Life of Andrew Carnegie*. New York: Doubleday, Doran and Company, Inc., 1932.

Herbodeau, Eugene and Paul Thalamas. *George Auguste Escoffier*.London: Practical Press, 1955.

Holbrook, Stewart H. Lewis Gannett (ed.) *The Age of the Moguls*. New York: Doubleday and Company, 1953.

Horne, Pamela. *The Rise and Fall of the Victorian Servant*. Gloucestershire, England: Alan Sutton Publishing Ltd., 1990.

Hubbard, R.H. *Rideau Hall: An Illustrated History of Government House, Ottawa, from Victorian Times to the Present Day*. Montreal and London: McGill-Queen's University Press, 1977.

Hubbard, R.H. *Ample Mansions: The Vice-Regal Residences of the Canadian Lieutenant-Governors*. Ottawa: University of Ottawa Press, 1989.

d'Hugues, Philippe and Dominique Mutler. *Gaumont, 90 ans de cinéma*. Paris: Ramsay, Cinémathique Française, 1986.

Johnson, Allen, ed. *Dictionary of American Biography*. New York: Charles Scribner's Sons, 1929.

Keppel, Sonia. *Edwardian Daughter*. London: Hamilton, 1958.

King, Robert B. *The Vanderbilt Homes*. New York: Rizzoli, 1989.

Lanceley, William. *From Hall-Boy to House Steward*. London: E. Arnold, 1925.

Legge, Edward. *Our Prince, Sailor, Soldier and Empire Ambassador*. London: E. Nash Co., 1921.

Mackenzie, Sir Compton. *The Savoy of London*. London: George G. Harrap and Co., Ltd., 1953.

Macmillan, Harold. *Winds of Change*. London: Macmillan, 1966.

Madden, Thomas More. *The Principal Health Resorts of Europe and Africa*. London: J. and A. Churchill, 1876.

Maine, Basil. *The King's First Ambassador: A Biographical Study of H.R.H. the Prince of Wales*. London: Hutchinson, 1935.

Mander, Raymond and Joe Mitchenson. *British Music Halls*. London: Gentry Books, 1974.

Mannix, William Francis. *Memoirs of Li Hung Chang*. Boston: Houghton Mifflin, 1913.

Martin, Christopher. *The Edwardians*. London: Wayland Publishers, 1974.

Masters, Brian. *The Dukes: The Origins, Ennoblement and History of 26 Families*. London: Blond & Briggs, 1981.

Masters, Brian. *Georgiana*, 2nd edition. London: Hamish Hamilton Ltd., 1981.

Mathias, Peter. *The Brewing Industry in England. 1700–1830*. Cambridge University Press, 1959.

Mitford, Nancy. *A Talent to Annoy: Essays, Journalism and Reviews. 1929–1968*. Charlotte Mosley (ed.). London: Hodder and Stoughton, 1986.

Montagne, Prosper. *Larousse Gastronomique*. London: P. Hamlyn, 1961.

Montgomery, Hugh, ed. *Burke's Guide to Country Houses*. London: Burke's Peerage, 1978.

Morris, James. *The Pax Britannica Trilogy: Heaven's Command. Pax Britannica. Farewell the Trumpets*. London: Penguin Books, 1979.

Mullally, Frederic. *The Silver Salver: The Story of the Guinness Family*. London: Granada Publishing, 1981.

Nevill, Ralph. *London Clubs, Their History and Treasures*. London: Chatto and Windus, 1911.

Newton, Thomas Wodehouse Legh, 2nd Baron. *Lord Lansdowne, A Biography*. London: Macmillan & Co., Ltd, 1929.

Nicholson, Colonel G.W.L. *Canadian Expeditionary Force: Official History of the Canadian Army in the First World War*. Ottawa: Roger Duhamel, Queen's Printer and Controller of Stationery, 1962.

Pettit, Paul. *The Country Life Picture Book of Devon and Cornwall*. London: W.W. Norton and Co., 1982.

Sanger, Marjory Bartlett. *Escoffier, Master Chef*. New York: Farrar, Straus Giroux, 1976.

Saunders, Andrew. *Exploring England's Heritage: Devon and Cornwall*. London: HMSO Publications, 1991.

Stephen, Sir Leslie and Sir Sydney Lee. *The Dictionary of National Biography*. Oxford University Press, 1963/64.

Turner, E.S. *Boys Will Be Boys: The Story of Sweeney Todd, Deadwood Dick, Sexton Blake, Billy Bunter, Dick Barton et al*. London: Michael Joseph, 1948.

Turner, E.S. *What the Butler Saw: Two Hundred and Fifty Years of the Servant Problem*. New York: St. Martin's Press, 1963.

Verney, F.E. *H.R.H*. New York: George H. Doran Co., 1926.

Williams, Basil. *Botha, Smuts and South Africa*. Hodder & Stoughton for the English University Press. 1946.

Wise, David Burgess, *et al*. *The Automobile: The First Century*. London: Greenwich House Inc., 1983.

Ziegler, Philip. *Diana Cooper*. London: Hamish Hamilton, 1981.

Ziegler, Philip. *King Edward VIII*. London: Collins, 1990.

Index